PLANNING WITHOUT GROWTH

Yvonne Rydin

P

First published in Great Britain in 2025 by

Policy Press, an imprint of
Bristol University Press
University of Bristol
1–9 Old Park Hill
Bristol
BS2 8BB
UK
t: +44 (0)117 374 6645
e: bup-info@bristol.ac.uk

Details of international sales and distribution partners are available at policy.bristoluniversitypress.co.uk

© Bristol University Press 2025

British Library Cataloguing in Publication Data
A catalogue record for this book is available from the British Library

ISBN 978-1-4473-6977-6 paperback
ISBN 978-1-4473-6978-3 ePub
ISBN 978-1-4473-6979-0 ePdf

Cover design: Qube Design
Front cover image: shutterstock/GoodStudio
Bristol University Press and Policy Press use environmentally responsible print partners.
Printed and bound in Great Britain by CPI Group (UK) Ltd, Croydon, CR0 4YY

Contents

Acknowledgements

This book has been a while in gestation and there are a number of people I wish to thank. My gratitude to all those whom I interviewed with regard to the discussions in Chapters 4, 6 and 7 about County Durham, the Western Isles and Western Ireland and Brussels; and my apologies for any misinterpretations. Thanks to the CLUES research team, including Catalina Turcu, as the work we did together underpinned some of the discussion in Chapter 8. I am particularly grateful to the groups of scholars who alerted me to the post-growth and degrowth planning literature during the COVID-19 pandemic, including me in their book and podcast projects and, thereby, helping to keep me sane during the pandemic: Christian Lamker, Federico Savini, António Ferreira and Kim Carlotta von Schönfeld. Thanks to Christian and Federico for ongoing conversations. The Bartlett School of Planning is a fantastically supportive place to work and I would like to acknowledge the role that Claudio de Magalhaes, Mike Raco and Lauren Andres have played in that. Thanks to Dan Durrant for championing post-growth planning within the School. The constructive comments from Sonia Freire Trigo, Ben Hughes and the publisher's anonymous reviewer were much appreciated. I have been blessed with amazing doctoral students to supervise in my career. For this book, the discussions with Jungha Im (who researched the social economy in South Korea) and Ruth Sepulveda Marquez (whose topic was urban gardening in Santiago, Chile) were particularly influential. As ever, George, Simon and Elli are the beating heart of our family, without which nothing is possible and with which everything is encouraged. Finally, for almost 50 years, I have had conversations with Sue that ranged from babies to gardens to teaching to economics. That conversation stopped as this book neared completion – Sue, this one is in grateful memory of you.

Chapter 4 is derived in part from an article 'Discovering the diverse economy of a "left-behind' town' by myself © 2023 Yvonne Rydin, taken from *Planning Practice and Research* 2023, © Informa UK Limited, trading as Taylor & Francis Group 2023, available online: DOI 10.1080/02697459.2023.2231711, reprinted by permission of Taylor & Francis Ltd.

1

Planning and the pro-growth agenda

Introduction

The Monday morning edition of the *Financial Times*, a global financial newspaper, lands on the doormat. On the Opinion page are three articles (Sharma, 2022; Lewis, 2022; Muellbauer, 2022). The first debates whether the US is on the brink of a recession or not. In line with the precepts of the 'dismal science', various economists consider that a recession is coming and financial markets concur. Sharma argues that many of the economic signals point a different way but, either way, it is taken for granted that a recession is a 'bad thing'. Economic activity should grow and public policy should encourage it to grow.

This is not just a general public sector imperative but implies a very particular perspective on planning systems and what they should be doing. Under the headline 'Growth friendly reforms for the UK's broken planning system', a second *Financial Times* article by Muellbauer (an Oxford economist) extols the virtues of land value capture. Using this policy tool, the uplift in land value consequent upon the grant of planning consent for a new land use or development could be split more equally than currently between the landowner and national or local government, enabling the latter to meet the infrastructure and/or housing needs arising from urban change. He further argues for using public debt to finance more public land acquisition on the basis that 'planning consent would soon enhance land values'. Here the planning system is seen as beneficially involved in the endless onward drive of growth as represented by the demand for urban development and rising land prices. The argument that Muellbauer sets out is a classic example of growth-dependent planning – the planning system can deliver affordable housing, infrastructure and other public benefits, but only by facilitating urban development and taking a share of the development gains, particularly the uplift in land values.

However, the third article suggests the scope for an alternative perspective and a potential debate with the proponents of economic growth. Lewis reviews a new book about Japan. In this Kohei Saito (2023) writes about the social and environmental perils of economic growth, but Lewis's interest is in how this is garnering a wide audience. Japan is a country that has experienced two decades of stagnation around the turn of the millennium, with stationary wages, zero interest rates and an absence of growth. While Saito's book is couched as a Marxist take on sustainability and climate change, Lewis acknowledges that his views have much in common with the wider degrowth philosophy. He is drawing attention to the debate that could be had on the value of growth.

What would be the implications of such a debate for planning systems, their policies and practices? In 2013, I argued in *The Future of Planning: Beyond growth-dependence* that planning systems were increasingly reliant on market-led urban development and urban growth in order to fulfil their wider public interest goals. While this produced impressive new developments in many locations, it also created significant problems in terms of the ability to meet social equity concerns and respect ecological limits. But I particularly pointed to the way this rendered planning largely ineffective in areas with low growth pressures. I was concerned at the implications of this for the planning project as a whole. In other language, one might say that planning had become captured by the neoliberal project and moved away from its original visionary and ethical potential. In that book, I put forward some rather tentative proposals for how to capitalise on urban growth pressures when these were present and how to develop some alternative form of planning in areas where these pressures were absent. Now, over a decade later, I come back to these ideas and seek to develop them more fully.

One of the great challenges in discussing the relationship of the planning system to growth is that the prevailing discourses go largely unquestioned. Growth is seen as self-evidently a 'good thing' and a desirable goal of planning. Planning becomes framed as managing and encouraging growth. And it is assumed that we know what growth is. In this chapter, the debates about planning and growth are set out and unpicked. The chapter starts by considering more fully the arguments for fostering growth, and specifically for using it to support planning action, before outlining the key critiques and opening the way for the discussion in the rest of the book.

Pursuing economic growth

There is a very strong orthodoxy that economic growth should be a public policy goal. Growth, as measured by indicators such as gross domestic product (GDP), means an increase in the total value of goods and services exchanged through the marketplace, that is, bought and sold for money. These may be physical goods, in-person services, rentals of premises or equipment or loans of money itself. Wages, salaries, profits, rent and interest paid all make up the national income. As such, economic growth represents an aggregate expansion in the total monetary value of the work of businesses in a country and the total monetary income of that country's residents. It is seen as increasing wealth generation, income levels and standards of living. Potentially this ensures that everyone in a society has their basic needs met. For lower-income countries, economic growth and increases in aggregate national income are a way of pulling households out of poverty. But, beyond that, higher national income means that people can satisfy their wants and desires and not just live at the basic level of sufficiency.

But what about the distribution of income and life chances? Potentially, increased income can spread to the majority of the population, but that is not assured (Piketty, 2022). The evidence from the past suggests that many people are 'left behind' when national income expands and that the distribution of income and wealth across society may even become more unequal as total income and wealth increase. However, even if the overall distribution of income is not rendered more equal by growth, many people may still receive more income than before, be purchasing more goods and services and thereby experiencing (in these terms) a better quality of life as compared to the past. This is the lure of economic growth.

Increased economic income does not just enable increased exchanges of goods and services in the marketplace. This is because the public sector is largely financed by taxation of income earned in the market – either levied directly on the income of firms and households or through taxes on consumption bought by that income – alongside fees for services rendered in a market (another form of consumption) and sales of debt to organisations that have funds to buy them. Therefore, increased economic income enables increased expenditure by the public sector. Not only does this provide certain universally available goods and services but it also can protect the most vulnerable from not having enough personal income to meet their core needs. In this way, health services, education, public transport – where these are provided at least partially through public finance – are dependent on economic growth for their expansion and improvement.

The scope for improvement is more generally important here. Increased levels of economic activity potentially enable resources to be released for investment, from either increased household savings or greater corporate profits. Such investment allows for innovation in the provision of goods and services so that we can enjoy new goods and services or more of them arising from efficiencies in their provision. This investment may occur in the public or private sectors or, often, in a combination (Mazzucato, 2018). Furthermore, economic theory suggests that economic growth itself is dependent on levels of investment and the innovation that this can promote. Thus, the argument runs that growth can feed itself over time in an apparently virtuous cycle, with increased economic activity leading to investment leading to further increases in economic activity, all to societal benefit.

While some of the improvements associated with growth may be considered trivial by some – better graphics in online games, say – there will be others that may be thought fundamentally important, as with uses of gene therapy or AI in medicine or ways of enabling a transition to a zero-carbon economy or expanding our knowledge of the origins and future of the cosmos. While talk of emphasising sufficiency (Coyle, 2011) suggests it is easy to separate out unnecessary over-consumption from more fundamental improvements in our lives, in practice these are difficult judgements to make. People have very different views on what is significant, and these are shaped by their material circumstances as well as their values and desires. The prospect of expanded space travel or improvements in electric vehicles may seem unimportant to those struggling with mouldy homes that they cannot afford to heat.

For all these reasons, from a political perspective, economic growth is seen as attractive. Contemporary culture, particularly as reflected in the mass media, suggests that growth in consumption of goods and services is desired by the general public and therefore governments will succeed electorally if they promote growth. This also increases the tax base and opens up the opportunity for governments to invest in public services and infrastructure. It offers the scope for policies to benefit certain groups without requiring other groups to feel the pain of loss of income to finance this. Rather than outright redistribution, a larger share of the growth in national income can be directed to specific sectors of the population. Growth can also help with public finances, as the increased tax-take can potentially be used to finance interest payments on public debt or buy back some of that debt, reducing the total amount.

The discussion of growth so far has been at the aggregate scale of the national economy, but national economic activity is the sum of such activity occurring at regional and local levels. Thus, the understanding of how such activity is fostered at these scales is relevant, particularly given that most planning action is also focused on these scales. Local economic development theory provides an understanding of how growth occurs in specific localities that has proved widely influential (Pike et al, 2006). It has driven not only academic research but also policy approaches at national, regional and local levels.

This theory emphasises the importance of spillovers or positive externalities arising from businesses co-locating in a specific place. In particular, it highlights the way that clustering firms together leads to a chain of beneficial effects such as economies of scale in the supporting infrastructure, increased demand along the supply chain and more retail expenditure in the locality by workers. However, it is the role of information and knowledge that has received the most attention, in a context where the cutting edge of economic activity is identified as residing in the post-industrial sectors. Clustering is seen as enabling the transfer of key information and knowledge between companies to allow them to expand activities, innovate, increase productivity and reap greater profits. Key knowledge actors such as high technology and research and development (R&D) companies, consultancies and universities are often central to such clusters. Such business activity can then finance increased consumer activity through household salaries and wages. This is often supplemented by household credit, itself guaranteed by notions of future growth. More retail, leisure and hospitality land uses represent a consumer-led boom, and they have their own multiplier effects as the wages of employees in these sectors are also spent on goods and services.

Such an understanding has informed local economic strategy and been deployed to respond to the considerable inequality at the regional scale and between rural and urban areas that typify almost all countries. Economic activity is not evenly spread across space. Where that activity is dependent on natural resources such as minerals, coal, oil, even water, then this fixes economic activity to certain locations or area where those resources can be readily transported. However, most middle and higher-income countries have passed through the phase when natural resources were the dominant factor in economic growth. Now other factors shape the spatial pattern of economic activity including the age profile of the local population, migration patterns, the skill-set of the labour force, past investment in infrastructure and in places, and the distribution of public finance expenditure and investment. These vary across space and the resulting inequality in economic outcomes such as employment, wage levels and investment in the built environment is usually apparent as one moves around a country.

This has led to regional and local economic development approaches that seek to foster knowledge-based clusters across the countries to spread economic activity and growth, with implications for local planning as discussed later (Martin and Sunley, 2003; Porter, 2000). However, not all locations have proved equally attractive to the knowledge-based sector or able to create clusters through attracting inward investment. Cities, particularly the larger ones, have come to be identified as key nodes where knowledge industries will cluster and this has directly influenced planning policy for urban areas. It has, further, encouraged the accommodation of urban development in such locations to create and intensify clusters, enabling them to act as 'engines of growth', to use a common phrase. Here the retail, leisure and hospitality developments of the consumer boom are also encouraged. But many other areas have remained beyond the impact of such urban development; current terminology often describes them as 'left behind' (Pike et al, 2024; Tierney et al, 2024), but the truth is that there is little prospect of knowledge-led and consequent consumer-fuelled economic development spreading evenly across a country.

The role of planning in relation to growth

As Barry says: 'we do have to recognise that growth occupies not only a central but one could say "constitutive" position within planning' (Barry, 2019: 123). There is a powerful discourse that aligns planning with economic growth in three ways. First, a primary *raison d'être* of planning is to ensure that economic growth is not restricted through limited or poorly planned urban development because, as already discussed, such growth is of wider societal benefit. Second, planning should actively promote economic growth through the ways in which it contributes to the design of urban development and plans infrastructure. Third, planning needs growth because this increases the gains from urban development that are available to finance a variety of social and environmental benefits for local communities and wider public benefit. But before exploring these different aspects of growth-oriented planning, it is worthwhile clarifying terminology, as there tends to be an elision in planning debates between different applications of the word 'growth'.

Growth is defined by economists and picked up by media and in common parlance as an increase in the value of traded goods and services within a geographically bounded area, usually a nation-state. It is measured by change in the metrics of GDP or GNP (gross national product) or GNI (gross national income), although there are also measures such as GVA (gross value added) used at regional scales. The critique of these measures will be covered later, but for now it is sufficient to understand that these metrics assess the amount of goods and services traded in the market, adjusted in various ways for imports and exports or taxes and subsidies.

Furthermore, growth rates are just that – the rate of change in a given metric. It is not the same thing as the scale or level of economic activity, which is measured by the absolute level of GDP, GNP, GNI or GVA. The absolute level is an indicator of the size and (in market prices) the value of the traded economy and can be used to distinguish higher- from lower-income countries. It is also used as an indicator of the material standard of living. However, growth is often talked about as an indicator of economic welfare, whereas it should be remembered that it is a rate of change, not an absolute indicator of consumption, production, income and so on.

Planning, through its attention to the physical environment, new urban development and the spatial organisation of activities has a largely indirect relationship to the level and rate of change of economic activity. It can help shape the context for economic activity and thus potentially enable or discourage growth in that activity. It has been more directly concerned with urban growth, and its growth-management strategies are oriented towards controlling and shaping urbanisation. Often, such urban growth is seen as synonymous with economic growth, and, indeed, that has been the experience of countries historically and currently. Urban growth enables economic growth, and economic growth drives urban growth. But this is not an automatic relationship; rather, it is one that can be questioned. Therefore, it is important to distinguish economic and urban growth and to be clear which is being addressed. It is also worth noting that urban growth can take different forms, from spatial expansion of settlements to densification of existing patterns of urban development to transformation of formerly rural areas into urban settlements.

That said, the development sector – the construction industry and its suppliers and subcontractors, property developers, architects and other professional services – is an important element of the economy, and its marketed goods and services constitute a significant part of GDP (or related metric). Thus, urban development in aggregate is directly related to economic activity and its growth in monetary terms. This means that the most obvious role that planning can play within a pro-growth agenda is to permit and encourage development, both because the development sector is an important part of the overall economy and because expanding businesses need the bigger and better premises provided by such new development. This would suggest a planning system that enables development by reducing the application and stringency of regulation and that, further, identifies and rapidly consents land for development. This can be supported by fiscal measures (tax breaks and subsidies) to encourage construction and, potentially, transfers of sites for development at low cost from public inventories.

The rise of neoliberal ideology as a society-wide discourse has influenced planning debates in many parts of the world. Neoliberalism here means the extension of the market and market-akin forms of governance, rule and control to increasing areas of life (Boland, 2014). It has been a core argument of neoliberalism that planning policies and practices have been inhibiting economic growth and the planning system should, therefore, be reformed and relaxed in order to stimulate such growth. That planning systems entail excessive regulation has been a key part of such a discourse. In addition, relaxing regulation and increasing the supply of property overall through new development is seen as a way to resolve problems of property affordability by reducing prices (or at least limiting price increases) (Cheshire et al, 2018). This relies on a fairly simplistic application of neo-classical economic theory that limited supply in conditions of demand will drive prices up. Hence a relaxed planning system is presented as both pro-growth and pro-affordability. The key point from a neoliberal perspective is that planning practice needs to be flexible and responsive to market actors; the planning system needs to act as an enabler rather than to control or direct, both of which are seen as placing obstacles in the way of urban development, competition and growth. The influence of this perspective was apparent, for example, in Boland's study of Belfast: it 'was clear during interviews that competitiveness was *the* unquestioned policy lever' (Boland, 2014: 778, original emphasis), and this is a repeated theme in much planning research.

However, a pro-growth approach to planning does not have to imply the roll-back of planning activity and associated deregulation. There are arguments put forward that planning can play a positive role in promoting economic activity and growth. These are often propounded by the planning profession itself in response to the neoliberal call for deregulation. The key arguments relate to the ability of planning systems to minimise the negative consequences of unregulated urban development and, further, to actively shape that new development, in relation to the existing built form, in ways that are more productive for economic activity. Advocates for planning argue that it has the potential to foster spatial patterns of development and to create urban places that are more beneficial to society than market-led urban change, because a planned environment is more likely to generate growth. It can also use the power of compulsory purchase or eminent domain to assemble sites for development in better locations than would come forward through market processes.

A long-held rationale for the very existence of planning systems is that unregulated market-led development generates negative externalities and an undesirable pattern of urban development from the perspective of society as whole (Reade, 1987). Such negative impacts of development can include, *inter alia*, pollution, public health risks, traffic congestion, disorderly land use patterns, segregation of social groups and loss of cherished landscapes and heritage assets. It can also leave key infrastructure and development needs unmet, including public utilities, public transport and housing for lower-income groups. If these problems are left unaddressed, it is argued, the undesirable consequences of unregulated growth will eventually act as a break on economic activity. Furthermore, the planning of urban areas and infrastructure can make places more economically attractive, for example by better servicing with transport links, information and communications technology and utilities and creating more attractive locales. In this way, planning action can be generative rather than restrictive of economic activity.

This is where planning policy can link into prevailing ideas about local economic development and how to foster economic growth at the regional, metropolitan or local levels. As indicated earlier, contemporary thinking on local economic development points to the importance of planning for clusters of economic activities so as to garner the benefits of spillovers or positive externalities, particularly around knowledge exchange. This suggests planning policies to foster new commercial centres or sub centres oriented towards the knowledge industries and spin-off consumer activities. But, more than this, it is argued that the labour needs of such industries are quite specific and planning should seek to create urban environments that will attract such workers (Grant, 2018). This implies the need to plan attractive residential areas providing the facilities that workers for knowledge industries and related activities will expect; it is often assumed that such workers will be younger, more highly educated, better paid and demanding of a certain cosmopolitan lifestyle.

So, in addition to planning for commercial clusters, this suggests a planning approach creating new, high-quality residential environments with a mix of leisure and retail land uses and a quality environment in terms of design and green/ blue space provision. This plays into common planning templates for desirable urban developments, such as waterfront complexes of mixed uses. Since this orients housing provision towards more highly paid workers, it can actively justify gentrification of urban areas. There are assumed to be spillover effects for lower-income groups through employment opportunities arising from servicing these commercial and residential areas and along the supply chain of firms, although the efficacy of this can be questioned. These social consequences are discussed further later.

In less economically buoyant areas, this thinking is often framed as a planning strategy of property-led urban regeneration. The aim is to promote greater levels of urban development, often at increased urban densities and, thereby, generate higher land values. Adams et al (2017) have documented the growth of property-led urban regeneration since the 1980s, seeing it as a potential form of market-making. A key feature is the use of low-value land or land that has no current market value for new development and facilitating such development through investment in environmental measures such as decontamination and flood protection, and in connecting infrastructure. The involvement of market actors in the development sector is encouraged by heavily subsidised land transfers, boosting the profitability of new projects.

The close association of planning for new urban development with the signals of the market-led development industry not only supports economic growth directly but is further seen as offering the opportunity for redirecting some of the financial gains of such development to meet wider planning goals. This could include green space provision for the wider local community (not just incoming new residents), affordable housing or critical infrastructure needs. The more profitable the development and the greater the quantum of development that is permitted, the greater the potential for financing such benefits. This is commonly referred to as planning gain, and in the UK is captured through Section 106 agreements or a Community Infrastructure Levy. The assumption that granting planning consent creates value which can be captured also underpins both land value capture and tax increment funding approaches (Purcell and Ward, 2023). In the former, part of the increase in land value can be used to fund a variety of community benefits, with the land value increment being extracted by means such as public landownership and taxation, as well as planning gain. In the latter, it is assumed that the increased value will give rise to increased tax revenue over time, and this will both fund community benefits in the future and offer the potential for borrowing against these tax increments to fund them in the present.

The argument that market-led urban development can produce social and environmental benefits is an important justification for neoliberal forms of planning, although it can be married with a more proactive approach by local planning authorities in terms of providing land, investing in infrastructure, protecting heritage and natural assets and ensuring high-quality urban designs. There are situations where this marriage has been effective in both facilitating and directing new urban development in ways that are of wide social benefit. But the difficulty is that this use of market-led development to deliver on broader planning goals and potentially benefit more sectors of society can readily tilt into growth-dependence.

Growth-dependent planning is about planning becoming reliant on new urban development and associated urban growth and losing its effectiveness to deliver benefits without that development and growth. If economic growth tends towards zero, then the amount of such urban development and associated urban growth will be limited to a fixed quantum per annum. This cannot increase, and so this limits the aspirations of planning authorities and planning systems. It depends on that fixed quantum of development, its profitability and the ability of planning systems to take part of the resulting profit. Reducing the level of economic activity implies a reduction in the level of urban development per annum and, then, a declining ability of planning to deliver on its broader goals. As a result, there is pressure to increase the rate of urban development to release more social and other benefits.

This has been linked to a broader shift in how local governments operate, termed 'municipal entrepreneurialism' (Harvey, 1989). In their study of London and North East England, Ferm and Raco (2020) show how planning has become dominated by concerns with development viability and locked into the search for land value capture. They situate this within the shifts in local government finance, arguing this has intensified since the 2008 financial crisis which initiated public sector budget cuts and propelled local authorities into searching for new sources of finance; English local authorities' budgets were cut by 49 per cent in real terms over 2011–18. However, the shift towards municipal entrepreneurialism has longer roots, particularly in the US, where growth coalitions and urban regimes involving local authorities with private sector actors pioneered this approach (Harvey, 1989). More recently, this has taken a new form with the growing influence of financialisation under which tradeable paper assets based on the built environment circulate globally, reshaping financial markets and national economies; financialisation is discussed further later on and in following chapters. In the London context, Beswick and Penny (2018) have shown how financialised municipal entrepreneurialism is pushing local authorities into the role of property speculator, with all the attendant risks, in an effort to provide local housing and generate an income stream. Zhang and Wu (2022) have shown how municipal entrepreneurialism and financialisation have shaped the pursuit of new urban development in China.

Thus, prevailing discourses and practices see planning and growth (both economic and urban) as intrinsically linked. While neoliberalism champions this and many see this as inevitable, there are a range of cogent critiques of this reliance on growth.

Critiques

There are three main critiques of this pro-growth agenda and the resulting growth-dependent nature of planning, focusing on economic, environmental and social implications.

Firstly, the prevailing discourse around economic growth sees it as an upward trend that can and should be maintained. This belies the reality of how economic activity changes over time, indeed how it fluctuates. The period over 5–12 years is often referred to as the business cycle, a pattern of increasing and decreasing economic activity in the economy as a whole that seems endemic to how capitalist economies work. Upturns describe the years of expansion in GDP, and downturns or recessions the years of contraction. This is the cycle that leads to unemployment and falling incomes in downturns and the opposite in upturns. Indeed, the upturns can pose the threat of inflation as demand pressures from rising incomes exceed the capacity of the economy to meet those demands. Sometimes downturns coincide with inflation arising from other causes, a situation termed stagflation. Traditionally, fiscal (taxes and subsidies) and monetary (interest rates and sales of government bonds) policy has been used to try to manage these upturns and downturns of the business cycle, following the precepts of Keynsianism and, later, monetarism. However, it has not proved possible to eliminate or even regulate these swings.

The hope of sustained economic growth is that this business cycle will happen around a long-term upward trend in economic activity, so that each downturn and upturn in the business cycle is at a higher level than the previous one. The key to this is assumed to be investment in R&D and infrastructure generally and, more specifically, in those sectors showing evidence of innovation and an ability to generate new products and services. Such investment and innovation are linked to the search for greater labour productivity, whereby each worker generates more economic value through the goods and services they produce. Increases in labour productivity are generally associated with greater deployment of capital per worker. Analyses of the assumed problem of low long-term growth frequently focus on these two imperatives: increasing investment and improving labour productivity, both linked with innovation and technological change.

However, increases in economic activity may take a quite different form, that is, as a speculative bubble driven by increased consumption, either in the retail or property sectors. Retail sector bubbles relate to consumer-led growth, which can be fuelled by rising household incomes or payments from savings, but also often by increased household debt. Property sector bubbles refer to increased flows of money into domestic and commercial property purchases, including new urban development. Property-led growth is inevitably associated with increased debt, given the large scale of the purchases involved and the general inability to finance this through household or corporate income. This debt comes from a variety of financial institutions (and some high-net-worth individuals) and is thus linked to the flow of financial assets through the economy.

In speculative bubbles, debt drives up demand from both the household and corporate sectors and this pushes up asset prices. New urban development will expand supply in response to such prices rises, but increases in debt-fuelled demand can continue to outstrip this. The issue of this debt is premised on future increases in asset values, that is, property prices, as much as on the ability of households and firms to repay the debt and cover interest charges. However, any faltering in the ability to repay (or perception of such faltering being likely) can bring the house of cards crashing down. When debt is recognised as 'bad loans', then asset prices fall, producing a property market crash.

The growing significance of financialisation (see earlier for a definition) within global and national economies has raised the prospect of speculative booms and crashes becoming more common. It also threatens contagion when crashes occur, as the debt funding development and property purchases in one country is traded globally and impacts on debt-holders far away when property values fall. In 2008, the eventual acknowledgement of bad debts based on the sub-prime property market in the US led to some banks and financial institutions in Europe coming under existential threat; they had bought such debt, often in forms that had repackaged bundles of debt several times into new financialised, easily tradeable paper assets (Krugman, 2008). This debt was supposed to be an asset on the banks' and institutions' balance sheets but fell in value as the properties in the US also lost value and even became worthless, with frequent abandonment of buildings in both commercial and residential sectors. Currently, the travails of massive Chinese property developers similarly threaten financial instability, with properties remaining empty or half-built.

Taken together, these aspects of economic growth mean that there are substantial question marks over the economic and financial stability of a pro-growth approach. These problems can be compounded by two other aspects. First, there is the underlying association of economic growth with demographic change. Broadly, economic growth is linked to the number of economically active people in a society. Countries with ageing populations will face a problem in that the number in employment will fall at the same time as the care requirements of the older groups rise. Deferred childbearing, smaller families and choices not to have children have reduced birth rates in several countries to the point where overall population decline is likely. International migration would help resolve these problems, but populist politics is driving a campaign of vitriolic opposition to this.

Second, there is the question of public debt. Such debt is not in itself a problem but, rather, a way of delivering public goods and dealing with economic downturns (Esteves et al, 2021). However, it becomes a problem when governments only issue debt (that is, borrow) and never repay it. This has become more common and, again, fits with an increasingly financialised world where government debt circulates as a financial asset, often in repackaged formats (see Chapter 3). As with debt in the built environment, issued government debt can also become less valuable if repayment prospects are undermined. This, in turn, affects the ability of governments to issue more debt, debt which might be essential to maintaining public services or other functions of the state. This heralds political as well as economic instability and further throws doubt on the idea of growth as an economically sustainable option. Rather than the solution to economic problems, it seems that the pursuit of growth has its own in-built economic problems.

Turning to the environmental and social critiques, a starting point is the recognition that the metrics by which growth is measured are fundamentally flawed (Dietz and O'Neill, 2013; Mazzucato, 2018; Pilling, 2018). GDP in particular has been subjected to detailed criticism, emphasising that it was created for a very specific purpose, and its creator, Simon Kuznets, himself decried the wider use of the metric as a policy goal. It counts only goods and services that have been traded in the marketplace and values them at their traded price. This clearly ignores many issues. It means that childcare provided by a private company does count within the metric, while such care provided by family or charities does not. More broadly, much of the care that people require to function within society is excluded from the growth metric; it should be noted that this care is predominantly performed by women.

In addition, the treatment of environmental aspects is problematic. Since many aspects of the environment take the form of externalities and public goods, these are not priced into market transactions. The impact of pollution generated by an industrial process does not feature in the accounts of the industrial company and, therefore, is excluded from growth metrics. However, if a company makes a profit from engaging in clean-up technology and services rendered necessary by the level of environmental pollution, this does count within GDP. This implies that if GDP (and other related metrics) are used to guide policy and planning, then the environmental impacts of growth will be under-emphasised. Thus, Pilling (2018) argues that GDP should be reconfigured to exclude polluting activities, along with crime, missiles, long commutes and long working hours. It should, however, include green space and sustainability, alongside good jobs and decent healthcare.

Expanding on the social critique, many point to the stream of evidence that inequality is not reduced under conditions of growth but, in many countries, has actually increased (Piketty, 2022). This may be related to the relationship between employment and growth. While the promotion of growth often assumes that increased levels of economic activity will lead to more employment, there is the possibility of jobless growth, where the value of economic activity increases but the number of people employed do not. There is also the question of the levels of remuneration for those that are employed. Growth in economic activity may produce low-wage jobs (Standing, 2011). The idea of the precariat also suggests that these may be insecure jobs. This clearly has social consequences, as an increasing proportion of the economic value created by growth goes to those lucky enough to be employed at higher wages and/or to owners of capital that has been invested to achieve that growth. The latter category includes owners of landed property increasingly able to extract rents from occupiers under conditions of growth.

A similar story can be told at the local level, where the impact of planning oriented towards promoting urban development and local economic growth is concerned. New urban development has often been associated with gentrification which has not been balanced by sufficient planning gain. In addition to direct displacement of people and businesses in low-value properties by new construction, there is often indirect displacement as rising property values put premises beyond the financial reach of existing residents and firms. Lack of political will and/or weak regulatory powers can limit the extent of the planning gain that is extracted from the development profits and, indeed, such planning gain may not be used to benefit displaced groups. It cannot therefore be assumed that new private sector housebuilding will benefit those in housing need, for example. The market price of new homes may be above what local households could afford and the planning gain extracted may not produce an adequate supply of affordable housing.

Looking at property-led urban regeneration, for example, there is a wealth of evidence that a property-led planning approach is not always effective and, indeed, may have significant adverse consequences (Bernt, 2009: 189; Dillon and Fanning, 2015: 761). In Ireland, where there has been a strong orientation towards property-led growth measures, the Urban, Town and Rural Renewal Schemes of the 1990s onwards were found to have perverse benefits. In urban areas, physical redevelopment did take place but there was no growth in population. The increase in employment was largely due to the in-migration of new residents, not the creation of new jobs, with out-migration by existing residents (Norris et al, 2014). In rural areas there was no noticeable increase in population or employment but, rather, an oversupply of housing, displacement of investment in manufacturing towards the construction sector and limited additionality, in that the development would probably have occurred anyway (Gkartzios and Norris, 2011). McInvoy concludes that 'trickle-down' and 'trickle-out' from areas of urban change does not work (McInroy, 2018: 2).

Adams et al's (2017) review of this approach finds problems of inefficiency and ineffectiveness. In particular, they see a tendency to take for granted the property market conditions required for such a strategy to work; as a result, land in many areas remains vacant. This points to a grave problem with a pro-growth approach; that is, it renders planning largely ineffective where market demand is weak or non-existent. Given that economic activity is unequally distributed over space, not only will the impact of growth-oriented planning be uneven across space, reinforcing existing disparities between areas, but it also means that the purpose of planning activity is radically different in places where market demand potentially offers the scope for planning gain, as compared to places where this remains a forlorn hope.

Turning to the environment critique of the growth paradigm, this raises further fundamental issues. It highlights how the growth paradigm implies an endless capacity of our planetary system to deliver required resources and to cope with resultant emissions and waste (including carbon emissions and other greenhouse gases). A wide range of analysts and commentators argue that this is a fundamental mistake (Jackson, 2009; Dietz and O'Neill, 2013; Raworth, 2017; Pilling, 2018). Proponents of growth have responded by arguing that the pursuit of growth produces wealth which can be used to either tackle these environmental problems and/or steer economic activity into pathways that are less environmentally burdensome. For example, the shift from producing goods to providing personal services is seen as a way to permit growth to continue as economies shift from primary (resource-based) and secondary (manufacturing) economies to tertiary (service-based) and quaternary (knowledge-based) economies. However, the resources required by service- and knowledge-based industries are not negligible, and it cannot be assumed that these shifts actually reduce environmental costs (Haskel and Westlake, 2018).

What is at issue here is the failure to decouple economic growth effectively from resource use and waste generation. Such decoupling can be absolute or relative. Absolute decoupling is where economic growth continues to be achievable with declining resource use and waste per unit of economic activity. Relative decoupling is where growth occurs at a faster rate than the growth in resource use and waste. In this situation, the environmental impacts per unit of economic activity are on a downward trend, but the overall impacts may increase with the continuance of economic growth. As Chapter 2 will detail, absolute decoupling has not been achievable. As a result, this critique has led detailed examination of the claims for 'green growth' and calls by some for a halt to growth or even degrowth.

For example, in an analysis of urban development policy in Copenhagen, a city which is explicitly adopting pro-environmental forms of planning, Krähmer (2021) shows how sustainable urban development breaches the constraints of ecological sustainability in three ways. First, the claim to climate neutrality was based on externalising most carbon emissions, counting only those that were locally produced and ignoring the impacts of consumption by households and the purchase of intermediate goods by firms. Second, Copenhagen's policies focused on the efficiency of activities in the city rather than their overall impact, laying claims to sustainability open to the critique of the rebound effect or Jevons' Paradox, whereby total consumption may rise when resource efficiencies are achieved. And, third, the city's approach fell within the idea of a 'green fix' or 'sustainability fix', whereby sustainability measures are used to increase local competitiveness and actually promote economic growth in the city.

The increasing recognition of the environmental crisis that we face is a key driver in this questioning of growth-dependent planning, but it is allied to long-standing concerns that this kind of planning cannot deliver livelihoods and well-being for all sectors of society; rather, growth-based planning is deeply implicated in the inequalities within society. This sets the context for the analysis provided by this book.

The rest of the book

The aim of this text is to understand the relationship of planning systems, policies and practices to economic growth without simply assuming that this should be a matter of growth promotion and management. Following on from this discussion of the relationship of planning systems to economic and urban growth and the argument that planning systems have become increasingly dependent on market-led growth dynamics, Chapter 2 explores some of the emerging alternative perspectives on growth and planning, looking at the prospects for delivering 'good' growth or 'green' growth and the idea of degrowth. The limitations of these alternative growth paradigms are unpacked and the chapter ends by pointing towards the potential of a post-growth perspective. Chapter 3 provides a pragmatic account of a post-growth perspective, arguing that this requires a reconceptualisation of economic activity and not just of the relationship of planning to the economy as currently conceived. It looks at the ideas of the foundational economy and diverse economies, including the social economy, bringing out the importance of market-based and non-market-based activities, of monetised and non-monetised exchanges.

This establishes the rationale for the various initiatives that are examined in the rest of the book, initiatives that operate across the borders of the market and civil society. The key argument of the book is that these kinds of initiative have the potential to deliver goods and services that communities need without being embroiled in the pressures for growth that have proved so problematic in economic, social and environmental terms. It is further argued that these initiatives offer a new direction for planning systems, one that enables them to operate effectively and positively in low-growth contexts. The discussion is analytic, fully aware of the limitations of these approaches and of the prerequisites that need to be put in place to make them work, as well as to deliver social equity and environmental protection.

Chapter 4 looks at local economic development and the role of smaller businesses. It includes a focused discussion of planning for local businesses in County Durham, England, specifically in the town of Shildon. In Chapter 5 the potential of the social economy, and particularly cooperatives, is explored, with a focus on the cooperative movement in Sweden. The issue of providing housing is examined in Chapter 6, looking at the potential of community land trusts (CLTs), with a focus on one such CLT in Brussels, Belgium. Chapter 7 considers the role of social enterprises in operating community assets and providing community services and facilities. Three such social enterprises in the Western Isles of Scotland and on the western coast of Ireland are explored. Chapter 8 looks at community-owned infrastructure, with a focus on community energy in France. Finally, Chapter 9 opens out the discussion to consider the claims made for urban commoning, with a specific focus on urban greening and the role of community gardens, orchards and similar spaces.

The points of focused discussion are based on literature review, document analysis from internet searches, a selection of informative interviews and site visits. They are not intended as in-depth case studies but, rather, provide examples which elaborate some key themes from each chapter. They not only range across a selection of different countries but also look at national programmes (cooperatives in Sweden, community energy in France) as well as the urban and regional level (urban greening in Liverpool and local economic development in County Durham) and specific organisations (social enterprises in the Western Isles of Scotland and western Ireland, a CLT in Brussels). These chapters provide the basis for a final chapter, which brings together the analysis and the key insights to be drawn from the discussion in Chapters 4–9. It considers the limitations of such approaches, the framework that is needed to support them and the safeguards that should be put in place to ensure that social and environmental policy goals are met. It concludes by outlining the implications for planning at both national and local scales.

On this basis, I argue that post-growth thinking has great potential to retool planning systems for the challenges of a world where growth is more and more difficult to achieve, where the demographic, political and economic preconditions for such growth are increasingly absent and where we recognise the need to avoid growth if planetary health is to be ensured. This is not without its challenges, and throughout the discussion in this book the limitations of the initiatives examined are highlighted as well as their potential. This offers a more nuanced conclusion on how to plan without growth.

2

Alternative perspectives on planning and growth

Introduction

The previous chapter highlighted the centrality of the pursuit of growth both to broader political and policy discourses and to the specific case of planning, suggesting that planning policy and practices are not only linked to the pursuit of economic growth as a goal but have become dependent on the promotion of such growth through new urban development in order to achieve their goals. However, the chapter also outlined a range of problems with the pursuit of growth through planning. These included inherent economic instability, inequitable outcomes, the adoption of inappropriate measures of progress, failure to take account of important social and environmental issues and an inability to operate effectively in areas where pressures for growth and new development were weak. The widespread acknowledgement of these problems has opened up new debates about growth generally and planning and growth specifically, although these have yet to challenge successfully the hegemony of a pro-growth agenda. This chapter reviews these new debates, looking first at alternative ways of defining growth to deliver 'good growth', before going on to consider varieties of 'green growth' that seek to marry pro-environmental goals with increasing economic activity and, finally, turning to the recently (re)emergent arguments for degrowth. As will be seen, each of these positions has its own limitations and challenges.

Good growth

As the previous chapter discussed, gross domestic product (GDP) as a measure of progress has long been criticised, leading to a distinction being made between growth and development. Development is seen as a way of measuring increases in people's quality of life, and not just the exchange of goods and services in the market. A variety of alternative metrics have been used to try to capture this idea of development. For example, the Human Development Index is a United Nations (UN) sponsored metric which combines three elements: health, education and standard of living (United Nations, nd*a*). The last of these uses the conventional economic growth measure of gross national income or GNI, presenting it in per capita terms. However, the logarithm of income is adopted to give more weight to increases at lower income levels. The health dimension is captured by life expectancy at birth, and the educational dimension by the mean years of schooling for adults aged 25 years or above plus the expected years of schooling for children about to enter school. This has been used at the national level to compare countries, but it does lack an environmental dimension.

The concept of sustainable development is intended to be more comprehensive, covering economic, social and environmental aspects, and suggesting the potential for an alternative agenda to the pursuit of conventional economic growth. Indeed, the UN's Brundtland Commission in its 1987 report *Our Common Future* (WCED, 1987) made a clarion call for a new era of growth, under the banner of sustainable development. Their analysis established that conventional growth was inadequate either to meet the needs of current generations or to safeguard the position of future generations. The UN has since led the way in developing new policy goals based on the idea of sustainable development to guide policy in a different direction. These are currently termed Sustainable Development Goals (SDGs) and there are 17 such goals, including No 11 calling for Sustainable Cities and Communities, which is particularly relevant to planning United Nations, nd*b*). The result is a suite of targets and indicators that recognise the need to do more than maximise GDP and maintain its rate of increase. While these are rather high-level goals, there is an ongoing effort to localise them for use in policy settings at different scales (United Nations nd*c*). But the problem with such suites of indicators is that there is always scope for trading off the different dimensions and sub-dimensions of sustainable development against each other. And yet the overall concept remains quite abstract, vague or difficult to pin down. As a result, the outcome of adopting a suite of sustainability indicators to guide policy and planning often remains uncertain (Rydin et al, 2003).

A similar critique is made of the idea of 'inclusive growth', which had a vogue in the early 2010s, particularly in the UK. The general idea was that increases in economic activity ought to deliver benefits for all sectors of society rather than just for niche groups or the most well-off. Waite and Roy (2022) looked at how it was applied in four areas in Scotland. In Edinburgh it was used to shape how the benefits of strong conventional economic growth could be shared more equally, while in Aberdeen and Glasgow – given the pressures arising from the running-down of the oil industry and de-industrialisation, respectively – it framed new economic pathways for growth. Only in North Ayrshire was a more radical alternative to conventional economic growth considered; here there was more emphasis on building a bottom-up economy through local value and sustainable employment. Not surprisingly, Waite and Roy concluded that inclusive growth is a 'fuzzy' concept and not a helpful guide to good growth.

A framework that has proved more attractive to many policy makers is the doughnut economics model developed by Kate Raworth (2017) as an explicitly polemical way of getting across the limits that ecosystems place upon our activities. She references the Great Acceleration of 1950–2010, when population, GDP and resource use increased enormously; GDP rose by seven times in real terms during this period. The image of a ring doughnut is central to this framework. The outer boundary of the doughnut represents the limit beyond which the economy cannot be allowed to grow without irreversible damage to ecosystems, notably through climate change, loss of cultivatable soil and biodiversity collapse. It identifies certain ecological 'guardrails' that should not be breached. But doughnut economics also includes an argument for growth. Following the central account of the Brundtland Report (WCED, 1987), doughnut economics recognises that we live in a world where not everyone has their basic needs met and that therefore some economic growth is required to meet these needs. This is represented by the inner boundary of the doughnut. If we are situated within the 'hole' in the doughnut, then we don't have enough growth. Therefore, we need to find the quantum of economic growth that places us on the ring of the doughnut, between the inner and outer boundaries.

While Kate Raworth's doughnut economics model has proved influential (not least because of the imaginative use of the image and metaphor of a ring doughnut), like the SDGs, the model is rather high level. It operates with seven broad principles, including the need to adopt a systems perspective and understand complexity. It sees the economy as embedded in social and ecological systems and human beings as adaptable. It is agnostic with regard to GDP growth, but recommends an economy that is distributive and regenerative by design. Here there are elements that overlap with the circular economy (discussed later), but it is less precise about the specifics of how economic activities work, and hence the pathway to change. It is also clear that doughnut economics is as much an argument about the distribution of economic wealth and income as it is about growth per se (as the Brundtland Report was before it). We are currently in a situation whereby certain groups in society are living lifestyles that, if adopted by everyone, would greatly exceed the ability of the planet to sustain life; yet, other groups live greatly impoverished lives, and for much shorter periods of time. This implies the need to redistribute the benefits of economic activity from high-consuming social groups to those in basic need. In Fell and Mattsson's (2021) use of doughnut economics to review the literature on public-private partnerships, this justice dimension of the framework comes out clearly.

As with the SDGs and the hopes of inclusive growth, doughnut economics sets a normative model for what the outcomes of economic activity should be but does not explore how this could come about, other than through a shift in the political agenda and effective public policy. These approaches to good growth largely posit an alternative policy goal or set of policy goals, using indicator sets or groups of principles. These perform a political function in seeking to persuade that a goal other than conventional economic growth is desirable. And, because the policy goal that they propose is a hybrid one, comprising different elements (often social as well as environmental), there is the need to consider which of these different elements should be prioritised and where trade-offs should be allowed. The broad range of issues that is encompassed by the SDGs and implied by doughnut economics raises questions of how priorities are to be established and how the result will be that different from current policy agendas and practices. After all, in the planning domain, planners already claim to be adopting a holistic approach to the range of impacts associated with urban development and thus can see themselves as pursuing sustainable development.

There are, however, approaches that seek to find commercial benefit in pursuing new pathways to growth, marrying government policy with market-led economic drivers. Many of these come under the banner of green growth, and are discussed next.

Green growth

The idea of using the economy to deliver environmental protection fits within the conceptual framework of ecological modernisation (Gouldson and Murphy, 2000). Ecological modernisation argues for the central role of technological innovation in devising new modes of economic activity that combine benefits to the environment with profitable outcomes. It looks for the sweet spot of synergistic advantage to the economy and the environment. Politically this is, of course, highly attractive. Key business stakeholders can buy into the idea of a policy that does not aim to restrict growth but, rather, supports – often financially – transitions to new commercial opportunities. These might involve investment in renewable energy infrastructure, developing businesses in energy efficiency and energy demand management or generating new ways of monetising the services that nature provides.

The monetising of nature links back to a tradition of valuation established partially within cost-benefit analysis practices but expanded under the banner of environmental valuation, particularly during the 1990s (Pearce et al, 2002). This branch of economics provides techniques for giving a monetary value to how nature is currently used (use value), may be used in the future (insurance value), is used by other social groups (vicarious value) and is desired regardless of any human use (existence value). While this was primarily intended to lead to new ways of assessing public sector projects, it embedded the idea that the protection of nature could be given a monetary value. It linked with frameworks that describe nature in terms of capital, distinguishing critical natural capital – which cannot not be substituted with man-made capital – from other forms of natural capital – which can be so substituted. The widely adopted Ecosystem Services Framework is another template that lends itself to identifying environmental services so that a value can be put upon them (Maasakkers, 2016).

But the key link to economic growth occurs when the services and assets provided by nature or ecosystems are not just factored into evaluation of public sector projects but also form the basis for commercial opportunities. If an environmental service or asset can be valued and monetised, then there may be scope for creating new market opportunities to capture that value and thereby generate profit. Commercial companies within urban development and tourism, in particular, are looking to incorporate nature within their business plans in this way. Within urban development, nature-based solutions are seen as a way to improve urban design, not only to reduce environmental burdens but also to generate higher property values and/or greater profits. For example, sustainable urban drainage systems and landscaping that promotes local biodiversity can reap the environmental benefits of reducing flooding risk and enhancing nature conservation while also creating urban environments that are more attractive and hence command higher prices.

More broadly, green growth argues that it can be profitable to adopt environmentally sustainable options and the economy should, therefore, be reoriented towards these options. Steering the economy towards a new kind of green growth requires the adoption of innovative technologies and a rethinking of production processes, including their use of resources and generation of waste. This implies a role for regulation by government and, while planning systems have limited leverage over many production processes, they do regulate urban development. Planning can, therefore, influence the nature of new developments and, by implication, processes of construction and urban development more generally. There are, by now, a wide range of ideas and indeed practices that show how buildings, developments and construction processes can be made more environmentally friendly (Garcia et al, 2021).

Planning regulation can encourage more resource-efficient buildings through revised designs, including lean design, which reduces the quantum of resources used, and 'passiv' designs, which radically reduce the energy required when occupying the building to potentially at or below a zero energy bill. Use of Life Cycle Assessment can calculate the amount of carbon embodied in the materials used, alongside their transportation and assembly, to be added to the carbon involved in occupying a building over, say, 60 or 75 years. This assessment can support alterations to the development design to incorporate long-lived components and reduce the frequency of their replacement during periodic maintenance. Taking all these aspects into account, there are accepted and increasingly effective ways to reduce resource use (including energy use and carbon emissions) in the construction and occupation of urban developments. With knowledge of how to achieve this, planning regulation can act as a spur to lower-impact urban development.

Planning can also reduce environmental impacts and enhance nature conservation through incorporating a concern with habitats and multi-functional green spaces into developments. This can range from bee-friendly planting and insect 'hotels' to using sustainable urban drainage systems to 'make space for water' and avoid urban flooding. The design concept of the sponge city has been particularly influential with regard to flood risks, increasing the quantum of absorptive surfaces in urban areas (Chan et al, 2018). This focus also implies conservation of important aspects of existing nature and ensuring that there is not a net loss of green spaces upon development. Going beyond this, the idea of biodiversity net gain has been introduced to require a net increase in natural features as a result of development (Simmonds et al, 2022).

While such planning regulation can deliver new kinds of urban development, they only indirectly influence wider economic processes. Advocates of the circular economy see this as a model for a more broadly impactful version of ecological modernisation, and also a model that implies a new planning approach. The circular economy has been defined as: 'a regenerative system in which resource input and waste, emission, and energy leakage are minimised by slowing, closing and narrowing material and energy loops through to long-lasting design, maintenance, repair, reuse, remanufacturing, refurbishing, and recycling' (Geissdoerfer et al, 2017: 759). The key aim is to replace a linear model of production and consumption with a circular one. In the linear model, there is a chain from resource exploitation through production (usually broken down into multiple stages) and then on to consumption, before final generation and disposal of residual waste. While improvements in resource efficiency may seek to limit inputs and waste outputs, increases in the levels of production and consumption can readily outstrip these efficiencies. Therefore, the circular economy proponents suggest a model in which the focus is not only on reducing inputs and waste but also on making use of remaining waste products as inputs into new rounds of production. It seeks to close the loop that is stretched out as a linear thread in current modes of economic activity. Given that both the sourcing of resources and waste disposal are costs to businesses, this should have financial benefits which can spur the shift towards circularity.

The implementation of the circular economy implies changed design of products and production cycles, and altered waste management practices (Ellen Macarthur Foundation, nd). Products should require fewer inputs, last longer and be more capable of repair and maintenance, as well as dismantlable for reuse and recycling of component elements. Demand for new products could also be reduced by allowing for more sharing of products and assets (including building space) thus increasing the intensity of use of individual items and, by implication, the resources that went into them. Such a new approach to economic activity sees growth as compatible with ecological integrity, provided that recirculation of waste-as-resources keeps pace with the scale of economic activity and there is no leakage of waste out of the circle.

Planning regulation can spur the move towards a more circular economy through setting requirements on reused materials, on waste generation and on the longevity of buildings. The circular economy highlights the importance of the materials that embody the built environment and the resources, including centrally the carbon involved in the energy used to manufacture these materials, transport them and combine them in a constructed building. It prompts the property sector to reduce the amount of new materials that are used in construction and to reuse materials wherever possible but also suggests the reduction of demolition prior to redevelopment, pursuing instead refurbishment that reuses as much of the existing building as possible. The concrete and masonry cores of buildings are particularly important to conserve and repurpose. One possibility to explore is the potential of deconstruction of the built environment as opposed to demolition, where buildings and developments are designed for dismantling. Lynch (2022) studies this use of the 'velvet crowbar' in Vancouver, highlighting the need to move deconstruction beyond a niche market of recyclable materials. But he also details how this implies financial and time costs. Site inspections and material audits are needed and a functional materials hub in a central location is important, ideally working with industry-wide standards. At present, however, there is a shortage of relevant knowledge, skills and expertise and the concept is being appropriated by the waste management industry.

Many aspects of the circular economy require action within the economy itself. It suggests the need for expansion of the repair and maintenance sector and investment in research and development within this sector. This would enable buildings to be occupied beneficially for longer before full or partial demolition. Materials from (partially) demolished buildings may be saved for recycling, either on-site as with the use of some demolition waste for hard-core or off-site as where valuable metals in, say, wiring, can be recovered and sold. This also points to the importance of secondary markets for recycled building materials that facilitate the transfer of recovered materials to a new user, alongside innovative virtual platforms informing about supply and demand for such materials (Williams, 2021). A final aspect that the circular economy model suggests is the possibility of sharing equipment, premises and perhaps even labour. This may be particularly relevant to the small and medium enterprise sector, which will be more likely to be budget-constrained in access to such resources; but it could also be relevant to larger firms where they have equipment that is idle for periods of time or have spare capacity in their accommodation that could be shared.

Williams (2020 and 2021) has identified four roles for spatial planning in relation to transitioning to circular urban development. First, planning should intervene in markets to provide space for the low-value activities needed within the circular economy, spaces which might otherwise be built upon and replaced. This includes spaces for recycling and repurposing, typically low-value activities. Second, planning should enable the localised looping of resources within the city-region. Rosado and Kalmykova (2019) have detailed one such attempt to apply the industrial symbiosis approach usually used for eco-parks to part of the city of Gothenburg. This involves developing clusters incorporating symbiotic links between multiple products' supply chains. In Gothenburg, an urban food production cluster was generated linking supply and waste chains for the production of lamb and beef, chicken and fruit and vegetables.

The third of Williams's suggestions is support for the roll-out of infrastructure for circular activities at urban, regional and national scales. Such infrastructure – while necessarily implying considerable resource use in construction – does set the context for resource use more broadly within society. Therefore, the expansion of public transport networks and cycle-path routes, of renewable energy at all scales (from micro-hydro to off-shore wind), and the roll-out of efficient (rather than old, leaky) water supply systems all contribute to lower resource use into the future. To these could be added the importance of green and blue infrastructure networks as opposed to isolated green and blue spaces and the creation of a waste management infrastructure that encourages carbon-efficient means such as recycling, biogas generation and energy recovery from incineration at the most efficient scale (Tunesi et al, 2016). Finally, there is the need to generate demand for circular activities and products through conditions placed on new developments at the planning regulation stage.

While this suggests a new green growth agenda, circularity can be rife with ambiguities in use. Corvellec et al (2022) found over 100 definitions inventoried, and this is also reflected in planning practice. Fratini et al (2019) reviewed the use of the concept in Amsterdam, Paris and London. Amsterdam is often cited as the exemplar of local planning for circularity. Here the concept is allied with those of the smart city and the sharing economy. It forms part of a Green Deal (a typical form of ecological modernisation) with an emphasis on resource flows, job creation, sectoral transition and innovation through strategic niche management. Meanwhile in Paris, the circular economy is used as a unifying vision for improving social cohesion, framing policies for localisation of production, low-income family support, education and learning, and movement to a social and solidarity economy. Finally, London provides a case where the circular economy remains closely tied to production activities, with a focus on renewable inputs, recovering end-of-life value, prolonging product life and developing the sharing economy. Here the transformation of socio-technological regimes, particularly for waste and energy, is also emphasised.

But, at the core – and stressed in most accounts – is the idea of technology driving industrial change. Thus, in their study of Brussels, Keblowski et al (2020) found that the circular economy frame went with existing long-standing urban development agendas. There was little evidence of a stable growth coalition of corporate and political elites in favour of this combination of urban development and circularity, but there was evidence of the circular economy provide an urban 'sustainability fix' whereby ecological goals were selectively incorporated into urban governance strategies, essentially to justify the latter.

While, the normative models of good growth do not offer an understanding of the dynamics by which they may be delivered – other than relying on the policy tools and powers of the state – the frameworks offered by the ecological modernisation and circular economy frameworks are rather different. They see commercial incentives as potentially aligned with pursing technological innovation, new market niches, new product designs and new production methods for delivering an environmentally less burdensome economy. This is fundamentally challenged by Bauwens's (2021) work. He identifies a number of new business models implied by the circular economy: narrowing or increasing resource efficiency; slowing or extending the use phase of goods; closing or recycling; dematerialising or replacing physical products with services and software solutions; and intensifying material loops or sharing. He argues that moving to most of these models would involve businesses in additional costs, at least in the early stages. Narrowing is identified as the model most likely to go with profitability. However, the business opportunities that arise are also likely to be niche and/or high-end in terms of market value (see also Corvellec et al, 2022). Bauwens concluded that 'a circular economy is likely to remain a mere pipe dream as long as the growth imperative drives the economy' (Bauwens, 2021: 2).

The main concern with the models of ecological modernisation and the circular economy, however, is not profitability but whether they are capable of living up to the promises they make to respect ecological limits. These approaches may enhance the resource efficiency of commercial activity and incorporate more mitigation measures – say, against climate change or biodiversity loss or pollution generally – but they do not necessarily reduce or even contain the overall level of resource use and environmental degradation. They are clearly intended to maintain growth in economic activity, and commercial profitability remains the signal for such activity. The concern, therefore, is that growth in economic activity will continue to outstrip resource efficiency and waste management improvements, due to the ongoing expansion of consumption within and across social groups.

The difficulty is that, without absolute decoupling, continuing trends in expanding economic activity will outrun the beneficial environmental impacts of models of ecological modernisation or the circular economy and, as a result, ecological limits will continue to come under pressure. Critics have particularly targeted the idea of the circular economy, arguing that it ignores the laws of thermodynamics and entropy (Corvellec et al, 2022). From this perspective, Raworth has stated that 'a truly circular economy belongs with the fantasy of perpetual motion machines' (Raworth, 2017: 222). In addition, it can be argued that the circular economy model involves a simplistic view of waste streams and waste management. Corvellec et al (2022) identified a number of aspects of this. Dissipation and contamination are largely ignored, as is erosion of materials. The complexity of existing waste streams and the emergence of new ones are downplayed. Recycling markets can be unpredictable and toxic waste, in any case, cannot be recycled. There are practical difficulties in connecting waste streams of potential intermediate goods to producers and these may imply considerable transportation, with its own energy costs. Finally, the existing substantial stores of materials and artefacts are underestimated, particularly in relation to material flows within production processes.

Current research on the extent of absolute decoupling is not encouraging for green growth proponents. An analysis of 116 countries undertaken by Hubacek et al (2021) found that 32 had achieved absolute decoupling between GDP and production-based greenhouse gas (GHG) emissions over 2015–18 and 23 had achieved such decoupling if consumption-based emissions are assessed. Only 14 had achieved both, and even countries in the decoupling category were still adding emissions to the atmosphere. Haberl and colleagues also point to the often temporary nature of decoupling, so that countries can move in and out of this category. In a major systematic review of 835 peer-reviewed articles, Haberl et al (2020) found that examples of absolute decoupling were rare and that 'large rapid absolute reductions of resource use and GHG emissions cannot be achieved through observed decoupling rates' (p 1). Vogel and Hickel (2023) looked at the carbon emissions of 11 high-income countries which had recorded declining consumption-based carbon emissions while their GDP figures grew (that is, absolute decoupling) over 2013–19. These 11 were selected from 36 countries for which data was available; that is, the other 25 countries were not absolutely decoupling. But even for the selected 11 countries, their analysis showed that the resulting emissions fell far short of rates that would be compliant with the 2015 Paris Agreement: 'At the achieved rates, these countries would on average take more than 220 years to reduce their emissions by 95 per cent, emitting 27 times their remaining 1.5°C fair-shares in the process' (Vogel and Hickel, 2023: 759).

Looking at the Nordic countries, which have claimed to achieve 'genuine green growth', Tilsted et al (2021) argue that this is based on very specific assumptions built in to the carbon accounting approaches that they adopt, at both national level and in relation to global carbon budgets. They describe their conceptualisation of green growth as 'partial and potentially misleading' (p 1).

Tim Jackson addressed the 'myth of decoupling', as he terms it: 'Despite declining energy and carbon intensities, carbon dioxide emissions from fossil fuels have increased by 80 per cent since 1970' (Jackson, 2009: 71). He extended this argument to material throughput more generally, concluding: 'The efficiency with which the global economy uses fossil resources and generates carbon dioxide emissions is improving in some places. But overall we are making faltering progress at best' (p 71). Instead, he called for 'flourishing within limits' rather than the pursuit of growth; this fits within the third approach, that of degrowth.

Degrowth

We have seen that there are arguments both for conventionally measured economic growth and for a form of growth that is differently formulated. However, both routes raise severe doubts in terms of their ability to remain within ecological limits and to deliver equitably on social goals. Some 50 years ago the problem of economic growth breaching ecological limits was already recognised, leading to calls for a more radical approach. A key reference point in the environmental movement's questioning of the pursuit of growth was *The Limits to Growth* published by the Club of Rome (Meadows et al, 1974). In this, a collective of experts pointed to the implications for natural resources running out if growth patterns were to continue on the pathways that had been set by post-war economies. Assumptions about the resource efficiency of economic activity were built in to the analysis that proved to be somewhat pessimistic, although an updated analysis repeated the fundamental conclusion (Meadows et al, 2005). The book set the template for arguments that growth could not continue unchecked indefinitely, even allowing for periodic increases in the efficiency with which resources were used and other technological innovations (Jackson, 2009; Dietz and O'Neill, 2013).

This line of thinking has given rise to the degrowth approach. This is highly relevant to a global perspective, actively addressing the different positions of higher- and lower-income countries. The starting point is the argument that higher-income countries have already taken a disproportionate share of the earth's resources and its capacity to absorb waste (such as carbon emissions). Given that lower-income countries require a degree of growth to improve livelihoods and quality of life, this means that higher-income countries need to reduce their environmental burden through lower levels of economic activity. Thus, it is not enough to aim for a steady-state economy, starting from current levels, but, rather, higher-income countries need to develop paths that involve lower levels of production and consumption.

Globally, this implies redistribution of economic activity from higher-income countries to lower-income ones. This is a point repeatedly made at international meetings to discuss climate change. Higher-income countries have benefited from economic growth based on the exploitation of fossil fuels and thus have disproportionately contributed to ongoing global warming and consequent climate change. Lower-income countries have therefore argued that the restrictions on economic activity needed to control the extent of global warming should impact more heavily on these higher-income countries. This is both just in terms of responsibility for GHG emissions and also essential if lower-income countries are to achieve a sufficient level of economic growth to meet the basic needs of their populations. The resistance of higher-income countries to this argument has led to the watering-down of proposals at many meetings of the CoP (Conference of the Parties) seeking to agree a new climate change protocol, most recently in Egypt in November 2022 and Dubai, UAE in November 2023.

The degrowth approach looks for alternative models of economic activity. One example of this is the work by Tim Jackson (2021) following on from Herman Daly and his formulation of 'steady-state economics' (Daly, 1992). This set out the idea of moving towards a steady-state economy defined as a stable level of resource consumption and a stable population. The population control measures turned out to be somewhat controversial, but the point about stable resource use remains a key environmentalist aspiration. Jackson has not only presented highly effective popular polemics against reinforcing the growth agenda (2021) but has also demonstrated through economic modelling that the economy can continue to function without increases in gross national product year on year. Together with Victor, he showed that a capitalist economy can sustain a stationary or non-growing state with the inclusion of debt finance (Jackson and Victor, 2015). The model included credit creation by banks, private equity and a balanced foreign trade account. They found that neither credit creation nor charging interest on debt creates a growth imperative in and of itself. They argued that it was, therefore, possible to move from a growth path to a stationary state without crashing the economy or dismantling the system (as some degrowth theorists advocate – see later). This finding was replicated in a study of the Canadian economy (Jackson and Victor, 2020).

In 2018, Jackson and Victor considered Picketty's hypothesis that declining growth would necessarily lead to rising inequality. While finding that in some circumstances this might be true, they also argued that there were other conditions in which inequality could be significantly reduced even as growth declined. They modelled inequality as dependent on three related structural features: the ease of substitution between labour and capital; the importance of capital investment to output levels; and the behaviour of savers. Given these, they found that a combined policy package of a graduated income tax, a tax on capital and a universal basic income (UBI) could eliminate inequality even without growth, but only such a combined package would be able to overcome the negative impact on equality of replacing labour with capital.

Intriguing as these analyses are, they only go partway for some degrowth advocates. They suggest that current levels of economic activity could be stabilised, a radical enough rejection of the current commitments to growth. Degrowth proponents would seek to go beyond this (Buch-Hansen and Koch, 2019), to actively reduce levels of economic activity in some countries so as to make space for increases in global locations that still need this. This implies action within the realms of international diplomacy, foreign aid and international market structures to address inequalities between countries. But these high-level debates have also sparked a degrowth movement within urban planning, both inside and outside academe. This seeks to put into action a definition of degrowth as the 'equitable down-scaling of production and consumption that increases human well-being and enhances ecological conditions' (Schneider et al, 2010: 512).

The shifts in spatial patterns of economic activity consequent upon financial crises (such as in the post-2008 period), major political changes (such as the reunification of East and West Germany) and demographic change (such as the ageing population of South Korea) have created cities which are actively shrinking in terms of population and economic activity and where new planning approaches are demanded. There are close parallels here with the ideas of degrowth, and this has given rise to discussion of planning approaches to urban shrinkage which are akin to degrowth planning (Bernt, 2009).

Wiechmann and Pallagst (2012) provide a four-way typology of different forms of shrinkage, drawing on research in Germany and the US. They distinguish, on the one hand, demographic shrinkage from demographic growth and, on the other, economic growth from economic decline. They note that population and economic growth going together produces the classic policy of creating urban growth poles or clusters, discussed in Chapter 1. Where there is economic decline with population growth, there is an emphasis on inward investment to 'urban gravitation centres'. Economic growth coinciding with population decline is relatively rare, although there are examples in the former East Germany. In other research, Bernt (2009) found a shift in such East German cities from entrepreneurial growth strategies to coping with decline, an approach that was very dependent on central government funding and resulted in grant coalitions emerging, rather than the classic growth coalitions of much urban politics.

The exemplar of shrinking cities, however, is where population and economic decline coincide, and here a policy of active downgrading of urban space is often promoted (Wiechmann and Pallagst, 2012). The aim is a form of planned or smart shrinkage that manages the decline in need for urban infrastructure and engages in selected demolition of unused buildings both to provide land for other uses and to stabilise property markets. Detroit, US often features as a key example with its proliferation of community gardens and low-value urban activities in the years after 2008. The Detroit Future City framework has provided a narrative about improving quality of life for residents in the face of irreversible degrowth. The use of landscape infrastructure and physical greening of the city has loomed large in this story, which has been situated within an attempt to reject austerity urbanism and trying 'to neoliberalise the city out of crisis' (Schindler, 2016: 831).

However, the city also provides a cautionary tale, since the devalued property in parts of the city has underpinned a new cycle of urban redevelopment, including selective gentrification. This has been termed degrowth machine politics (Berglund, 2020; Schindler, 2016). Berglund has shown how elites in Detroit proposed a variety of development scenarios as a way of triaging investment opportunities in the city and thereby channelling the diminished amount of funds available. Philanthropic foundations have played a leading role in the coalitions for development that have resulted. As a result, land use intensification has been occurring in Greater Downtown Detroit, leaving other areas of the city, which are considered high-risk locations, undeveloped and – it might be argued – unplanned. As Schindler (2016: 823) states: 'needless to say, politicians do not win elections on platforms of scaling back consumption and shrinking the economy'. It therefore seems that much planning for urban shrinkage is still embedded in the idea of stimulating growth, after downsizing.

For these reasons, those looking for a degrowth planning approach have moved beyond the concern with shrinkage. Savini (2021) set out a comprehensive critique of urban planning from a degrowth perspective, with recommendations for change. He identified functional polycentrism, which Rydin (2022) found to be embedded in many local and regional plans, as the spatial paradigm that structures competition and enables urban growth, acting as an engine for wider economic growth. This competition is then further perpetuated through the creation of conditions of land scarcity, using urban planning, which both maintains land prices and makes public goods dependent on land development and the profits that it generates. Zoning policies are central to maintaining competition through the contest between property rights owners for sites to develop. Lang and Marsden (2018) similarly saw growth-oriented competition as inherent to contemporary planning practice.

As a counter proposition to this current situation, Savini posits three transitions necessary for movement towards urban degrowth (Savini, 2021). The first is a new regional imaginary of polycentric autonomism, perhaps linked to the earlier bioregionalism of the environmental movement. The second embeds the paradigm of finity in development. Xue (2022) has considered what this might mean practically in planning policy, suggesting the following: urban development that is dense and close to the city, limiting land take per capita; housing which has maximum and minimum space standards as well as high energy efficiency; mobility that is environmentally friendly with reduced car ownership and use; and more localisation of activities. Savini's third transition involves care for habitability as a principle of spatial organisation. He argues that this would enable a shift towards an economy based on care and reciprocity, with disinvestment from activities based on finance, rent and fossil fuel. Such an economy would de-commodify housing and enable a revaluation of domestic work, with expanded non-work time; this could be supported by a UBI scheme. The initiatives that arise from these transitions would include cohousing, self-sufficient housing, a focus on slow mobility, urban gardens and farmers' markets, and non-commercial sharing. There would also be a new regenerative relationship between cities and their hinterlands. This version of degrowth implies de-commodified practices of eco-living, a symbiosis between the urban and the rural, and democratic autonomy in cities.

In a more recent intervention, Savini (2024) makes it clear that he envisages new social movements promoting new social goals, with the principle of satiation taking centre stage. Planning can then play a role in supporting a variety of initiatives promoted by such social movements, but this is radical spatial planning that is engaged with radical voices and resists capitalist values in all their forms. It is an interesting ideal, but one that is politically far removed from current agendas and which might prove difficult to get political support for. In relation to this point, Savini hopes for processes of legitimation for radical spatial planning and degrowth social movements arising from prefiguration (or practising the future), popularisation and political pressure.

The degrowth agenda is currently a radical position and could be considered a utopian one. Not only does it present itself in opposition to prevailing pro-growth positions, but it also tends to promote a clear divide between market-led economic activity – which is seen as intrinsically growth oriented – and actions based in the commons, civil society or collective action (see also Bärnthaler, 2024). While examples of such actions can be drawn upon to illustrate alternative futures, they are generally lauded within the degrowth literature for their opposition to market-based capitalism and for prefiguring a comprehensive alternative. The examples studied tend to be examined from a sociological or political perspective and pay little attention to the economic dynamics involved or the role that economic actors could play in an emergent future. While there is growing interest in degrowth ideas, they can be accused of not being political feasible, and residing in oppositional politics rather than suggesting pathways for planning policy and practice.

Towards post-growth thinking

This chapter has considered alternative debates on growth and planning. In discussing good growth approaches, including sustainable development, inclusive growth and doughnut economics, it was apparent that these seek to deliver increases in economic activity that would benefit a wider range of people, particularly those at the lower end of the income spectrum, and – to varying extents – also consider the need to limit the environmental impacts of that growth. However, they are characterised by considerable inherent ambiguity about how to define good growth. Further, they often include – again to varying extents – scope for trade-offs between different aspects of economic activity and their impacts. This further contributes to the ambiguity over what might be expected as outcomes. It is also not clear how they would be implemented, the common assumption being that public policy will be able to steer growth in these desired directions. They remain more of a wish list and a contribution to changing political debates than a detailed analysis of how change could be achieved.

In terms of green growth, these perspectives are highly attractive, as they offer the prospect of market-based economic activity being the vehicle for delivering a transition to a greener economy through identifying win–win options that are both profitable and less environmentally damaging. Public policy is often identified as needing just to pump-prime or steer businesses towards these options, through mixes of subsidy, regulation and indicative planning. However, the major concern here is whether these new directions for economic activity do enough to delink the continued pressures for economic growth from resource use, pollution and other environmental impacts. There remains concern that the emphasis on growth within this approach may undermine its positive potential. It also has little to say about social aspects of economic activity and the distribution of its benefits.

These limitations of existing frameworks for considering the desired direction for economic growth have led to a degrowth movement that questions the very fundamentals of increasing economic activity, pointing to the incompatibility of our finite and bounded planet with ever increasing resource take and use of pollution and waste sinks. The requirements for the healthy functioning of ecosystems and the rule of the law of entropy limit the ability of the planet's systems to cope with increasing economic activity and its waste products. Climate change, desertification, depletion of potable water, land contamination, biodiversity loss and possible shifts in marine systems such as the Gulf Stream are the outcomes of this incompatibility. Convincing as the degrowth arguments are, they pose considerable problems of implementation, particularly given current political systems. They are heavily addressed towards a global arena, since they centrally concern relationships between nation-states and how living standards in some can be balanced by reducing economic activity in others. Locally, they tend to espouse an oppositional stance to capitalism and market-based approaches.

This book is centrally concerned with how planning, focused on the built and natural environments through interventions at the local, urban and regional scale, can engage with the implications of these debates in an effective way. It takes a pragmatic approach, looking for options that could be implemented through the agency of planning systems as operated by local governments. By doing so, it hopes to move beyond the paradigm of growth-dependent planning, outlined in Chapter 1, with its intrinsic reliance on economic growth to drive urban development through market mechanisms. The search is for a new approach to planning that is less reliant on the drivers for growth – both economic and urban development drivers – and that could revitalise planning efforts in areas that are experiencing low market demand and, hence, limited economic activity. Without the ability to leverage growth pressures, planners have often found themselves trapped into growth-dependency discourses and yet unable to effect much in the way of change to improve lives and livelihoods for local communities. It is hoped that this post-growth approach could provide a template for a form of planning that would deliver social and economic benefits from reshaping urban and rural environments without the adverse environmental consequences of conventional economic growth and the adverse social consequences of much conventional urban development. It might therefore have broader resonance for degrowth debates also.

With the focus on pragmatic implementation, it is important to understand the dynamics by which goods and services can be delivered without a reliance on growth dynamics. Rather than positing a vision in opposition to contemporary economic processes, the analysis looks for ways already existing within current modes of producing and distributing goods and services that are less linked to the imperative for growth and could, therefore, form the kernel of new alternatives. The emphasis is on the pragmatics of economic dynamics rather than utopian vision. For this it is necessary to reconsider how the idea of the economy and economic activity itself is conceived, and this is the task of Chapter 3.

3

A post-growth framework for exploring planning without growth

Introduction

The discussion in the previous chapters surveyed the debates about growth, including looking at arguments for good growth, green growth and degrowth and highlighting some key issues. From the debates reviewed in Chapter 2, several key lessons emerge. First, it is necessary find ways of delivering the goods and services that people need and want without recourse to the dynamics that fuel high rates of economic growth. This is not the same as avoiding all market-led economic activity, but it requires a careful interrogation of the means by which goods and services are produced and distributed, particularly in societies that are no longer subsistence economies. Economic activity, including market-based economic activity, is an essential feature of how societies work. The key problematic is to understand economic activity in a way that enables an effective form of planning to operate and yet that is not reliant on standard growth-oriented agendas and conventional market-based suggestions. This requires an economic focus for planning, but also a new way of thinking about the economy, a rethinking of what economic activity is. To be clear, this is not a normative programme for how society might be reorganised. Rather, it is a call for a better way of understanding the way that economic aspects of society currently work. On this basis, it will be possible to think about how planning can be more widely effective and relevant.

Second, the implications of means of delivering goods and services in social and environmental terms need assessment. There are baseline concerns here over resource use, pollution and waste that are integral to environmental sustainability, and over social impacts and the position of more marginal households and communities that are integral to social sustainability. In one sense this is just to reiterate the idea of planning as a synthetic activity that seeks to take into account all aspects of an area or a development proposal. However, just as indicated in the discussion of good growth, this can lead to implicit prioritisation and downgrading of different elements of the overall policy goal. The pro-growth agenda tends to the assumption that specific social or environmental goals are less important than the pursuit of increased economic activity. The debates around growth impress that consideration of how economic activity relates to these social and environmental aspects is essential and should not be downgraded in importance. This requires a fresh and detailed examination of how economic activities relate to social and environmental outcomes.

Finally, given that the focus here is on planning systems and their practices, the framework needs to be relevant to this work. It needs to recognise that planning systems have specific foci and work with a limited range of tools. So, there will be emphasis here on how local planning systems specifically can fit with a perspective that does not emphasise growth. This is not to say that action at national and international scales and within policy domains other than planning are unimportant; they may well be more significant. But that is not the subject of this book; here an attempt is being made to explore how planning can occur either in the established absence of growth and/or without focusing on the attraction of growth.

This analysis is presented as a form of post-growth thinking, but in presenting this analysis there is an explicit redefinition of what 'post-growth' and, in particular, 'post-growth planning' means. This term is widely used in differing ways and a consensus has not yet grown up around it. For example, Savini (2021) frames post-growth thinking in opposition to the green growth model, while it can be seen as more of an umbrella term for the many different ways of thinking about growth. Indeed, this could be argued to be one of its strengths, as it allows for a widespread debate around the role of economic growth and how to move beyond an obsession with growth as a goal. The ambiguity of the term reflects considerable dynamism within these debates, rather as with sustainable development in the immediate aftermath of the publication of the Brundtland Report in 1987 (WCED, 1987) and the 1992 Rio Earth Summit. An apparent consensus here has gone along with a dilution of the term 'sustainable development' and a reduction in its usefulness, particularly in driving action on climate change and environmental protection.

In seeking to avoid this fate for post-growth planning and maintain a critical edge within current debates, the term post-growth planning is here defined as a form of planning that seeks to delink from the pursuit of economic growth as conventionally measured. It does not, however, seek to delink from economic activity as it currently occurs under the prevailing mix of direction from market incentives and public sector policy. Here, a post-growth approach does not necessarily imply an anti-capitalist approach; and while in Chapter 9 the commoning movement is discussed, post-growth is not aligned exclusively with practices that occur outside of market processes. Instead, the post-growth framing adopted here seeks to rethink the nature of economic activity and how markets, the public sector and civil society interact. From a fuller understanding of these processes, it is argued, a relevant post-growth approach can be built. This would allow points for leveraging new directions for local planning to be identified.

The starting point for this is to re-examine the essence of the economy and economic activity. Two directions are taken in this re-examination. First, the way that analyses of market processes tend to emphasise high-value activities and the importance of global trade and financial flows is identified. To counter this, the foundational economy approach is discussed, with its counter-emphasis on the under-valued economy. Second, it is argued that it is not helpful to draw a hard distinction between market and non-market, capitalist and non-capitalist activities. Rather, using a reading of Gibson-Graham's (2006) work, an approach that recognises the essential diversity of means of providing and distributing goods and services is adopted. This leads to a discussion of the social economy and the role that it might play. As explained at the end of this chapter, this shapes a different agenda for thinking about planning without growth and for taking forward post-growth debates. The chapter ends with a description of the remaining chapters in the book and the ways they explore different paths for post-growth planning.

Recovering the value of the overlooked economy

The conventional view of the economy is that it exists to provide goods and services to households, firms and the public sector and that it does so by responding to demand manifested through market signals. It is supported in these activities by investment and loans from the financial sector through a variety of instruments and mechanisms – equity shares, bonds, loans and so on. Market mechanisms match supply and demand through interconnections between different sectors: finance, production, distribution and retail. So why should these processes of providing goods and services imply growth? Why do they result in the drive towards increased production and consumption, with its associated resource use, waste and pollution? What are the dynamics that push the scale of economic activity to be increased? Why should it not be the case that businesses remain at a relatively stable level of activity so that – allowing for some growing and some declining firms also – the economy as a whole remains at a 'steady state' rather than growing? Turning the question the other way around, why is the prospect of growth needed for firms to engage in economic activity? Why is a certain level of return, perhaps relatively modest, not sufficient to support such activity?

One answer is that businesses seek to expand market share as a primary organisational goal. But this rather begs the question: why? Economic theory tells us that firms seek to maximise profits, but it also identifies equilibrium points at which such profit maximisation occurs. Therefore, the assumption of profit maximisation does not in itself suggest a push for an ever-increasing scale of operations. Furthermore, profit maximisation may not be the dominant motive within firms and businesses. Some suggest that satisficing may commonly operate (Artinger et al, 2022), whereby the scale and nature of business activity is enough to generate desired returns and there is not further impetus to expand those activities. The idea of an inevitable search for opportunities to expand a business seems to rely in a questionable psychological model of the entrepreneur as always restlessly looking for new avenues for risk taking and for undertaking new ventures.

Another line of inquiry is to look at the influence of the finance sector on the businesses producing goods and services. Almost all businesses require start-up capital, which may be small or large scale depending on the activity, the amount of capital equipment and assets required and the extent to which a period of research and development has to precede business trading. The economic activity of a business needs to reach a sufficient scale and associated profitability in order to pay back this capital, whether this is in the form of a loan or direct investment in the business. If a loan, then there is little incentive to further grow a business once the loan has been repaid. If there is an equity investment in the business of some kind, then there may be pressure from the investor to provide a growing stream of returns. The finance sector itself may be subject to different sets of motivation than business entrepreneurs and managers. But this is unknown; some investors may be satisfied with a steady return of, say, 5 per cent rather than looking for ongoing growth in shareholder value. Such low-return patient capital investment has operated historically and in different countries.

One concern that many commentators have is that the long rise of the significance of finance capital within the overall economy and the shift towards financialisation may have fundamentally changed the nature of capitalism. As outlined in Chapter 1, financialisation is a process by which more and more tradeable financial assets are created out of stakes in productive enterprises, ownership of physical assets, rights within contractual arrangements and indeed other financial assets themselves (as with the bundling up and then splitting of debts to create a new paper asset that can be bought and sold). The trend towards financialisation has accelerated in the 21st century, with a global reach. The Foundational Economy Collective (2018; see also later) identify a significant shift that occurred in the 1980s with the growth of high-yield bonds and of assets allocated to private equity in the expectations of high returns. This was supplemented in the 1990s by the mantra of shareholder value, which made it an institutional requirement for the value of equity on the stock market to be protected, leading to an emphasis on the generation of a surplus over payments to debt holders.

Financialisation shifts the focus towards making gains in the trading of these various assets, essentially a form of speculation. The decision to purchase a financialised asset is many steps away from the decision to invest in a productive enterprise, and yet those enterprises can be fundamentally affected by the pressures arising in the financial sector to maximise returns on traded financial assets. The sources of the pressures for growth today may not be found entirely in the sector concerned with providing goods and services but, rather, with the machinations of financial organisations alongside the many brokers and intermediaries in that sector. The built environment has been particularly affected. Property, as the word itself connotes, inherently involves relations of ownership alongside demarcation of a physical part of the environment, that is, land and buildings. Property has long been held for its ability to appreciate in capital value as well as generate an income stream (monetary or imputed, in the case of owner-occupation). But, since the 1970s, the upward trend in property values has been stronger and there has been a proliferation of debt-based paper assets (bonds, mortgages, equities) that are owned and traded in the expectation of value appreciation (for example, Raco and Brill, 2022). This means that investments in the built environment are often influenced by the trends, fluctuations and crises in the markets for paper assets, again with global reach.

Turning to the specific implications for local planning, Conte and Anselmi (2022) detail how the greater importance of financial actors in urban development has affected the governance, and hence planning, of the city of Milan, Italy. They point to the mutual dependence of the local state and capital investors as an evolution of previous growth coalitions. Urban governments are now more formally dependent on finance capital and land is treated primarily as a financial asset (see also Beswich and Penny, 2018, for a UK discussion). This drives the privatisation of urban space and means that the local government mobilises land use in an instrumental way in order to cover the risks of financial investment and meet investors' expectations. Purcell and Ward (2023) see planning implicated in the process by which '[u]nder the financialised urban process, investors actively seek out rent extraction opportunities' (p 7). Rent extraction is supported by increased demand fuelled by mortgages and debt, and scarcity of supply induced by competition between developers. Land value capture (as discussed in Chapter 1) leaves local planning authorities dependent on these rentier logics.

The foregoing account would suggest that the economic sectors most prone to growth pressures are, firstly, those companies where the organisational culture is oriented to expanding market share and, secondly, those companies that are very subject to the pressures from the financial sector for increasing the value of the business, including the property sector. These are likely to be larger firms, to be publicly quoted on stock exchanges and probably more international in their focus. The problem for planning systems is that these growth-oriented firms are precisely those that are targeted by strategies for attracting inward investment and creating agglomeration clusters. These larger firms are more likely to underpin plans for major urban development and regeneration that generate community benefit only through extracting planning gain.

This reinforces the need to look beyond these strategies in the search for how to plan without growth. It suggests the importance of fostering local and smaller businesses precisely because they are less implicated in the growth dynamics of the wider financialised economy. Raworth (2017) argues that such small firms have been underemphasised to date. Over 1998–2008, only 13 per cent of credit went to small businesses, while some 75 per cent went to buying stocks or housing (p 182). And yet, small and medium enterprises (SMEs) account for 90 per cent of all firms worldwide and, in the UK, for over 99 per cent of private sector businesses. There are over 16 million workers employed in this sector in the UK, that is, 60 per cent of the private sector workforce (Baranova et al, 2020).

The foundational economy model provides a new way of thinking about processes of provisioning goods and services that fits with this emphasis on often undervalued aspects of the economy. The foundational economy is defined in terms of the goods and services which are the social and material infrastructure of civilised life because they provide the daily essentials of that life (Foundational Economy Collective, 2018). The approach emphasises the heterogeneous nature of economic activity. It argues against the prevalent emphasis on the high-value, large-scale commercial activities that much economics, local economic development policy and growth-oriented planning focuses on (Russell et al, 2022). In the words of the Foundational Economy Collective (2018), 'mundane activities have vanished from view' (p 12). This is a strong critique of growth-dependent planning, with its pursuit of knowledge clusters as a way to promote local economic development. The Foundational Economy Collective (2018) pointed out that in the EU28 (at the time), high-tech manufacturing and knowledge-intensive services employed just 4 per cent of the workforce (ranging from 2.2 to 7.4 per cent across the 28 countries). By contrast, they calculated that the foundational economy employed 40 per cent, with health and care on its own amounting to almost 11 per cent.

Instead, the Foundational Economy Collective (2018) provide a new taxonomy of economic activity, distinguishing foundational, providential and overlooked aspects of the economy. The foundational or material element comprises those aspects that support the essentials needed for a good quality of life, including much public infrastructure. This covers water, energy, retail banking and the food sector. Providential activities encompass those elements of the welfare state that support us in case of life's difficulties, such as health services and incomes transfers, but also education. The model argues stringently against the idea that public sector services are surplus consuming, seeing them as making a vital contribution to the overall economy. Finally, the overlooked part of the economy covers the many businesses – often small scale and local – that meet the needs of local communities and enhance quality of life.

This new perspective on economic activity also implies a stringent critique of financialisation, which the Foundational Economy Collective view as 'the process by which businesses are driven by the logics of maximising shareholder returns and by financial engineering in the new world of finance for its own sake seeking high returns regardless of foundational activity characteristics' (Foundational Economy Collective, 2018: 81). Instead, they favour the generation of modest long-term streams of value from business activities. They also see a preoccupation with increasing worker productivity as less relevant to the foundational economy model. Many of the key sectors within a foundational economy have limited potential for increasing productivity; the replacement of labour with capital is inimical to their purpose. Furthermore, there is little in the way of a productivity gap across regions in these sectors. 'In sum, the aim of higher productivity in many foundational economy sectors is not necessarily meaningful' (Froud et al, 2020: 14). Productivity and altering the capital–labour ratio are not the assured way to increase wages in these sectors; rather, training and reorganisation of functions will be a better path to higher incomes for employees.

Russell et al (2022) distinguish the foundational economy approach according to three characteristics. First, they consider it to take a zonal perspective. By this they mean that there is not 'one economy' but, rather, different zones within it. This links the model closely to the broader analysis of Gibson–Graham (2006) and the diverse economies framework discussed next. Second, Russell et al see the foundational economy as promoting maximal social innovation. Rather than seeing innovation purely in terms of the application of new technologies to the development of goods and services in the market place, it becomes possible to open up innovation to changes beyond bringing new things to the market (De Saille et al, 2020). De Saille et al see potential here for delinking innovation from growth and, rather, using it to build well-being within a secular stagnation. Third, Russell et al see the foundational economy as involving a reconstitution of citizenship. However, this sees citizenship as purely in the domain of civil society and points to a 'blind spot' when it comes to unwaged work, an aspect that the diverse economies model directly addresses.

The foundational economy is also a reaction to the neoliberal shifts in governing which have led to public sector outsourcing, privatisation of public assets and austerity politics driving down key areas of public sector expenditure. By distinguishing different parts of the economy, the aim of the foundational economy model is to expand and protect those parts of the economy delivering overlooked activities, which often fall to the remit of SMEs. In their study of planning for low-growth areas in Turku, Finland, Kosunen et al (2020) argue that resisting growth-dependent planning requires a shift from demanding certainty to being more open to different kinds of change and that could imply an approach that nurtures 'supportive structures for everyday life in urban neighbourhoods' (p 565). This is a statement of support for the foundational economy.

In line with the preceding discussion of the market economy, the foundational economy perspective argues for the importance of SMEs (Foundational Economy Collective, 2018: 139). It argues that such SMEs should be mapped locally and a deep understanding of their capabilities developed. This also involves understanding their sources of precarity and recurrent problems, such as retirement of or early sales by founders. This, in turn, suggests initiatives such as promoting small contracts, requiring prompt payments to SMEs, supporting managerial capacity and drawing on the resources of other local firms through urban networking. The relevance of links to broader economic networks is recognised, so that a foundational economy approach does not necessarily imply radical localisation or the ensuing autarky.

But the foundation economy model also argues for the importance of access to social infrastructure for all, including to adequate affordable housing and the protection of lower-valued urban environments that play a part in the overlooked everyday economy. Social infrastructure is central to this perspective, but it takes time to build this up and it can be rapidly destroyed, as Tomaney et al (2023) show. It requires committed long-term local action and is the result of 'radical hope', which is itself the result of a sense of belonging and deep attachment to place. While there is often a need for some central government finance, it cannot be legislated for from above. Foundational liveability thus depends on income, mobility infrastructure, social infrastructure (libraries, parks, high street, community centres) and grounded local services (health, housing, utilities, education, care). Planning systems can support all of these. This suggests a reorientation of local planning away from marketing for a mobile elite and towards living in ordinary places. That said, the detail of what such planning would look like is still largely missing, as well as consideration of how such planning would relate to the grassroots initiatives of the foundational economy. The following chapters hope to address this.

The importance of a diverse economies approach

If our concern is with how goods and services are provided rather than with private sector market dynamics per se, then we also need to look beyond the conventional economic focus on private sector firms driven by profit incentives or, indeed, the recourse to the public sector as the only alternative. Here the diverse economies framework of Gibson-Graham (2006) provides a conceptualisation of the economy that goes beyond the private sector and includes a variety of civil society and hybrid activities, including the social economy. Gibson-Graham's project is about reimagining economic possibilities through a new economic language. They aim for a process of deconstructing current notions of 'the economy' and instead tracing the contours of a radically heterogeneous economy. They accept that capitalism is not just a signifier that can be displaced; 'it is where the libidinal investment is' (p xxxv). But they argue that the situation by which the economy is seen as hegemonic, real and non-negotiable has gone with a shift to a situation where the economy governs the state and society rather than seeing the other way around as being a possibility (p 53). They term this capitalocentrism.

Gibson-Graham (2006) look for the 'unmapped possibilities that are present in every situation' (p xxxvii). Arguing against the idea that projects of non-capitalist construction are naive, utopian, already co-opted, off-target, too small and weak, they see the prefigurative potential of new ways of providing goods and services. They argue against indulging in 'pure strong theory', in favour of experimentation; but resist the idea that this is necessarily only local experimentation: 'we also need to work on the moralistic stance that clings to a singular conception of power and blocks experimentation with power in its many forms' (Gibson-Graham, 2006: 6). They similarly resist the idea that a community economy is necessarily other to the 'real economy' (p 86). Rather, they look for heterogeneity within the economy or for diverse economies. This would include unpaid and informal forms of economic activity, such as work by women and within the household, and also emphasise the interdependencies between different forms of such activity (see also p 95). Raworth (2017: 80) also considers that mainstream economics has overlooked how much the paid economy depends on this core economy within the household.

In the attempt to create a new language, Gibson-Graham (2006) devise a series of typologies for transactions, labour and enterprise (pp 71 and 75). While transactions within conventional economic models may privilege exchange within markets for money, there are also transactions that occur within alternative markets such as local trading systems, ethical and fair-trade markets and those using alternative currencies, and well as exchange by barter or through cooperation and other informal means. In addition, there are various non-market forms of exchange, such as those occurring within a household or involving gifting, or based on foraging, hunting and gleaning. Indigenous communities may have alternative modes of exchange as does the state also, giving as of right but also expropriating. In terms of labour, capitalism prioritises wage labour where work is given in exchange for a wage or salary. However, there are alternative forms of labour including self-employment or employment/ownership within a cooperative. Less attractive forms of alternative labour include indentures or work-for-welfare schemes. Unpaid labour also is readily apparent in society through housework, family care and private gardening. But this unpaid labour can also be collective, as in neighbourhood care activities or volunteering. Again, the dark side exists, as with slavery, including modern-day slavery. Finally, there are different forms of enterprise to the 'ideal type' of capitalist risk taking in return for profits. Alternative forms of capitalist enterprise include state enterprise (including municipal enterprise), green capitalism where environmental values dominate the search for profits, socially responsible firms and non-profit organisations. And outside the category of capitalism completely one can find communal activities (communes and commoning) as well as feudal and slavery systems.

Interestingly, if transactions, labour and enterprise are to be diversified in this way, then the idea of generating a surplus also changes. In conventional economics, a surplus is purely financial and takes the form of profits or returns on an investment. Gibson-Graham (2006) instead see surplus as essentially diverse, 'an imaginary, unquantifiable social surplus made up of all these surpluses combined' (p 91), that is, from all different forms of activity: 'In a diverse community economy, it is the capacity to produce social surplus in a variety of forms, and not just surplus value, that is of interest, as it is this surplus that can be used to replenish and expand the commons and the productive base' (Gibson-Graham, 2006: 95). Taken together, this provides a radical new way of understanding the processes by which goods and services are produced and distributed and, hence, of economic activity and of the economy itself. Such an analysis breaks down the divisions between the private sector and civil society. This has two implications.

First, it suggests close attention to the informal economy. Sheikh and Bhaduri (2020) make an important point with regard to the informal economy, that the importance of this part of the economy is often underestimated because it is not seen as generating exchange value. Yet the informal economy is substantial. Sheikh and Bhaduri cite the Organisation for Economic Co-operation and Development estimate that two-thirds of the world's population depend on the informal economy. More significantly, they argue that grassroots innovation in the informal economy can have a number of benefits, including community relations, individual self-esteem, enhanced competitiveness and entrepreneurship. More widely, recognising the informal economy can broaden discourses of the economy and economic relationships.

Second, it suggests that the social economy should be considered an integral part of economic processes and not a distinct and somehow subordinate economic sphere. The social economy describes the collectivity of organisations that combine commercial values with broader public or community interest goals. They are characterised by being collectively organised, profit seeking but using at least part of the surplus so generated for social and/or environmental purposes. Fasenfest et al (1997) distinguish the social economy from the market paradigm in terms of having a different scope (consumption and use value as opposed to subjective utility) and involving different measures when it comes to considering standards of living: labour hours, participation quotients, social power measures and measures of inclusion and exclusion, as opposed to money prices. When reflecting on the data needed to understand the contribution of the social economy, they highlight: the proportion of prices and unpriced use values produced and consumed; the gender division of labour in paid and unpaid work; and the distribution of unpaid services by gender and race.

Social economy organisations can take a variety of forms, partly due to the varying institutional and legal framework in place in each national context. Murtagh (2019) lists cooperatives, mutuals, associations and foundations as possible forms, but across these he identifies four distinct models. Type A is a non-profit model that operates on grants and contracts from public sector bodies and other third sector organisations. Profit and asset transfer is constrained unless to other non-profit organisations. Type B is a corporate social responsibility model and covers environmental, ethical or Fair Trade business, as well as for-profit employee-owned ventures and public-private partnerships with social aims. For Type C, Murtagh describes a more-than-profit model in which social enterprises marry a commercial motivation with links to some other organisation, such as a charity trading arm, that generates surpluses and uses these for social investment. Finally, Type D is a multi-stakeholder model and covers a variety of social enterprises such as cooperatives, charities, voluntary organisations and co-owned businesses that seek to deliver social and economic benefits using direct and representative democracy within the organisation and paying attention to equity of distribution.

Defourny and Nyssens (2013) see social enterprises within the social economy as straddling various key divides: between for-profit and not-for-profit, and between public and private. They see the economic and entrepreneurial dimensions of a social enterprise as covering the production of goods and/or services while carrying a significant level of economic risk and undertaking a minimum amount of paid work, often alongside volunteering. To this can be added a social dimension which includes an explicit aim to benefit the community, roots in citizen or civil society initiative and a limitation on the distribution of profits. Participatory governance is central to all social enterprises with a commitment to a high level of autonomy from outside control by the state or private sector organisations, a form of decision making that is not based on the ownership of capital (compared to, say, public companies that are answerable to shareholders) and a participatory culture throughout the organisation.

In addition to interrogating the different forms of social enterprise, there is a debate on how significant a difference they can make. In this regard, Spicer and Casper-Futterman (2020) identify three different types. One is close to growth-dependence, one fits with neo-endogenous development, but one is termed 'transformative', marking a shift towards a more democratic economy through opposing both neoliberal tendencies and also wider globalisation trends. The UN Agenda 2030, in recognising that the social economy can play an important role in delivering the Sustainable Development Goals, also sees this as a source of transformative change (Chaves-Avila and Gallego-Bono, 2020).

Dufays et al (2020) see the importance of social economy organisations as challenging the strict division between the lifeworld and the system, to use Habermas's framework (1987). The lifeworld is the domain of family, friends, non-governmental organisations and civil society. In Habermas's theory of communicative action, this is the realm that is governed by communication and deliberation, oriented towards mutual understanding and meaning-making. This contrasts with the system found within the state and the economy, where strategic action dominates. The social economy exists at the interface of these two realms. This creates the threat that social economy organisations may lose their distinctive character and become entirely captured by the system, become merely capitalist entities, tools of the state or dominated by managerialism. However, it also opens up new opportunities for delivering goods and services and, further, for resisting the wider colonisation of the lifeworld by the logics of the system. The social economy, for those that are involved, enables individuals to build new and stronger resources to maintain the distinctiveness of the social economy. Further, it allows them the possibility of participating in a redefinition of the priorities associated with the institutional arrangements within the system.

For Curry (2022), the social economy holds the potential to address the failures of the growth-oriented economy. He looks at rural food hubs run by communities, and specifically at Community Interest Companies. These are distinct from producer food hubs, which bring together commercial agricultural interests to better serve the local market. These community food hubs are able to address community cohesion, food waste, food poverty and local people's health. They are based in local volunteering, the local environment and local identity. However, Curry found that while such food hubs found a place within the local economic development strategies of some rural areas, they were limited precisely because those strategy documents still espoused growth orientation.

Social enterprises can also play a key role in developing and shaping the development of the sharing economy. Schor and Fitzmaurice (2015) provide a typology of the sharing economy distinguishing non-profit from profit subsectors. While the profit subsector includes AirBnB, Zipcar and similar commercial enterprises, the non-profit subsector includes community-based food swaps, time banks and even non-commercial sharing between businesses or with businesses.

Thus, there seems to be transformational potential in terms of provision of goods and services associated with the expansion of the social economy, although the Foundational Economy Collective see the scope for transforming local economies with regard to formal employment and expenditure as more limited (Foundational Economy Collective, 2018: 141). But it is possible to see the benefits of social enterprise in more local terms, more suited to areas that stand outside – for political or economic reasons – prevailing growth dynamics. It is this more pragmatic approach that is taken here. The social economy is viewed as an alternative to purely market-based economics and to provide a way of delivering desired and needed goods and services, alongside broader community interest goals. Thus, several of the following chapters explore social economy organisations in delivering various goods and services. They also explore the difficulties involved. As Diprose (2016) shows with regard to a Wellington Timebank in Aotearoa New Zealand, the 'process of building a community economy is fraught' (p 1412); it involves building an ethos of radical equality and diversity, requires the negotiation of everyday anxieties and is an example of enacting 'being in common'.

Exploring planning without growth in practice

This rethinking of economic processes has guided the structure and content of the following chapters. In these, the undervalued economy of small, locally embedded firms (Chapter 4) are studied alongside different examples of the social economy, including cooperatives (Chapter 5), community land trusts (Chapter 6), community assets owned and managed by social enterprises (Chapter 7) and community infrastructure projects (Chapter 8). Finally, commoning is explored in Chapter 9. A wide range of international research literature is drawn upon in these chapters, but each one has a more extended focus on a specific initiative or location. In Chapter 4, the local economic development approach in County Durham, England is examined, honing in on the experience of a small town, Shildon, which has experienced a decline in local economic activity. Chapter 5 considers different types of cooperatives, across the productive sector, housing and retailing. The specific focus or more extended discussion is on the experience of Sweden, where the cooperative movement has a long history. Turning to the role of community land trusts (CLTs) in Chapter 6, a case study is provided of CLT-Brussels looking at the role it has played in housing provision for lower-income and marginalised groups in the Belgian city. The discussion of community assets in Chapter 7 draws on local rural examples in the Western Isles of Scotland and the western coast of Ireland, where a variety of services are provided and activities supported. Chapter 8 considers community infrastructure, but with a particular emphasis on community-owned energy, looking in more depth at French examples of this sector. Finally, Chapter 9 considers a wide variety of examples of commoning and pays attention to urban gardens of different kinds that are initiated through commoning practices.

As these chapters will highlight, in all these cases there is a blurred line between the categories of the market and civil society. Hybridity seems to be at the core of ways in which goods and services can be provided to people, along with employment (paid and otherwise) and thus must be central to post-growth thinking. Also highly relevant are the capacities that exist within local civil societies and local business communities. As Chapter 10 will draw together, this provides important lessons for planning without growth about the capacities of local civil society and business communities, the importance of social capital in creating connections, the detailed ways in which contractual arrangements bind together the different sectors and the importance of landownership institutions in establishing the (literal) ground rules for their interaction and engagement.

4

Economic development and small local firms

Introduction

Having reviewed the debates on planning and growth in Chapter 2, Chapter 3 provided a new way of thinking about economic activity, drawing on the literature on diverse economies and the foundational economy. A key conclusion to be taken away from this discussion is that monetary valuations should not be taken as the main or only arbiter of the value of economic activity to society. This chapter addresses this argument by looking at how commercial enterprises – firms – can be involved in improving livelihoods and quality of life in a locality without necessarily becoming implicated in the drive for economic growth in any substantial way. The focus is on the smaller and locally embedded firms, rather than the larger companies – including those that may be branches of multinational corporations. These larger firms are more likely to be driven by pressures for growth, increasingly so in a financialised world where corporate equity and debt are owned by investors worldwide, looking for an abstract financial return and with little interest in the on-the-ground activities in any specific locality.

Smaller firms are more likely to be embedded in a place, to rely on a localised labour force and to utilise (at least in part) local or regional supply chains and means of distribution. They have concerns about viability and continued existence rather than necessarily being driven to grow as a primary motive. Some will, of course, grow bigger, but there are also many firm deaths in this sector, so that the overall pressure is not towards endless expansion. The value of their enterprise is often relatively modest in monetary terms, but this should not lead to their economic contribution being dismissed. As North (2020) emphasises, 99 per cent of enterprises worldwide are independent or fall in the small- to medium-sized category and, further, 'Advocates of small local businesses argue that, as they are embedded in their local communities, they will stay through good times and bad' (p 102).

The chapter begins with an account of the neo-endogenous theory of local economic development, a theory that recognises the importance of locality. It considers the research that explores the relationship of social capital in the locality to such business activity. It goes on to look at the experiences with various policies that have espoused neo-endogenous theory, before concluding with consideration of the specific role that local planning can play in the light of this discussion. Along the way, a focused discussion of local economic development in Shildon, County Durham, England is provided.

The neo-endogenous theory of local economic development

As was outlined in Chapter 2, many – from the United Nations to non governmental organisations (NGOs), governmental bodies and academics – draw a distinction between growth and development. While growth is the increase in metrics such as gross domestic product, based on the monetary value of goods and services being traded, development is used to denote a shift towards a better way of living and an improvement in quality of life. That said, theories of economic development build on those of economic growth. As such, they start from seeing growth in output as a function of growth in three factors: the capital stock in an area; the labour force; and technological innovation. Each of these three factors can grow endogenously (that is, within the local area as a result of local dynamics) or through imports, that is exogenous influences from outside the locality. Labour and capital can also flow out of an area, affecting the skills profile and investment potential.

Looking specifically at local economic development, Pike et al (2006) start from the premise that economic activity is rooted in the relationships between: local firms, skills in the local labour market, the available infrastructure and inward investment. Three of these four factors are aspects of the locality. Thus, endogenous local economic development theory sees human capital, technology and externalities (side-effects of economic activity) as partly shaped by the local economy and not just inputs to that economy. This does not mean that they are necessarily internal to the local economy, in that they may be found outside the immediate locality also. Nevertheless, this approach suggests a focus on the role of skills, networks and capital at the local or regional scales. It suggests the value of localised agglomeration economies, such as cost savings resulting from labour market pooling and the availability of specialist suppliers, as well as technical knowledge spillovers within the area.

The focus on the locality also points to the importance of local networks of trust and of cooperation as well as competition. This emphasises the value of local social capital embedded in the civil society of the area, as well as market-based factors such as wage labour, supply chains or firm-to-firm knowledge exchanges. Indeed, it blurs the distinction between local civil society and the local economy. It sees localities as demonstrating a capacity to promote social learning, adaptation, innovation and entrepreneurship. Formal and informal local institutions are vital in generating this local social capital, and also a quality termed 'institutional thickness'. Positive path dependencies in the local area can be identified and built upon, creating virtuous cycles.

Pike et al (2006: 158) refer to this as working with the grain of the local economy and reaping the benefits of a smaller scale and incremental development. Local and regional knowledge of needs and context is important alongside the relationships between actors, the durability of ongoing support and experiences of mutual learning and cooperation. Pascoe-Deslacriers (2020) also argues for focusing on the distinctive micro and meso features of local economies. He sees this as offering the potential for better economic activity, not just more activity. This refers to the types and quality of jobs, not just the number, as well as the nature of employment relations and the role of employees. A good-quality job here covers pay, self-validation, self-development, well-being, participation, as well as contractual stability and income predictability.

This implies quite a different approach to one arising from an emphasis on factors external to the locality. Exogenous local economic development theory, by contrast, seeks the pursuit of growth through attracting inward investment. The principle mechanism for this attraction is the existence of economies of scale both within individual firms and within the locality as a whole. The exogenous approach thus favours larger urban areas and the clustering of enterprises as outlined in Chapter 1. It sees clusters of enterprises as having access to specialised inputs, labour, information and knowledge as well as institutional and public goods, localised complementarities and incentives. This is understood to foster innovation through a better understanding of buyers' needs and to promote learning. As a result, new businesses form alongside innovation partnerships benefiting from low barriers to entry, increasing returns and spillover effects.

Exogenous local economic development (LED) theory suggests planning policy oriented towards research, science or business parks where specialist clusters of firms and research and development organisations can co-locate. It also suggests a bias towards particular types of economic activity. Lavoratori and Castellani (2021) argue that younger, more productive firms benefit from these urban externalities operating at a larger scale, where the knowledge externalities involved seem to be more diverse. The adoption of exogenous LED theory thus favours a growth-oriented approach that supports concentration of firms in urban areas and investment in new, growing sectors, often with an emphasis on creative or new technology sectors. It is a theory that aligns with growth-dependent planning and, indeed, provides a basis for promoting high-value concentrations of new development to attract investment from outside the area, that is, mobile capital. Potential mobile labour is also targeted, and this requires new urban development to house and service such labour, promoting urban growth alongside economic growth (as outlined in Chapter 1).

By contrast, a more endogenous approach implies assisting, growing and sustaining existing businesses, alongside establishing some new businesses and upgrading labour skills. Lavoratori and Castellani's (2021) work suggests that older and less productive firms benefit from specialisation externalities operating at a narrow geographical scale – the locality – reducing costs for established firms which are not looking to expand into new types of business. It is important here that the type and form of new businesses align with the local culture. Other infrastructural support can include affordable childcare, recycling opportunities and internet-based services, as well as ensuring an available supply chain through component subcontracting and a range of service provision. There is also a role for a property-based approach through planning, providing sites and premises and ensuring connectivity to key infrastructure such as information technology and transport. Business incubators can help with start-up firms, provided they are affordable, suggesting scope for subsidised and shared accommodation. This type of local planning will be explored further later.

It has been argued that endogenous LED can be limited by the scope of local capacities, the existence of local power differentials and the potential for elite capture (Goodwin-Hawkins et al, 2022). Therefore, neo-endogenous LED theory includes elements of both endogenous and exogenous theory. It is place based and participatory and seeks to leverage the local qualities of place. However, it also recognises the importance of multilevel networks and multiscale linkages, connecting the locality to the wider milieu. Using Ward et al (2005) and Marango et al (2020), Table 4.1 characterises the three different approaches to LED.

The key difference in neo-endogenous development is the mobilisation of resources through networks that operate within and beyond the locality. The marriage of local knowledge and capacities with the benefits of wider networks is the central dynamic. In a Danish rural context, Fisker et al (2022) found that local actors had access to knowledge and networks that public authorities did not. Similarly, Ward et al (2005) considered neo-endogenous development in northern England and found intangible intellectual assets being mobilised through learning, innovation and enhancement of human and social capital in the localities. The result in this case was the diversification of businesses, the promotion and development of small and micro businesses and encouragement of community enterprise (see later chapters).

Innovation is a feature of all forms of LED but its definition within neo-endogenous theory is wide, including not just technological change but a variety of new ways of operating within the local economy and local civil society. This affects the relationship to growth, as innovation and economic growth are often

Table 4.1: Exogenous, endogenous and neo-endogenous LED

Exogenous development	Endogenous development	Neo-endogenous development
Creates and leverages economies of scale and concentration	Harnesses local resources	Seeks to maximise the value of local resources
Promotes urban clusters of economic activities	Promotes local initiative and entrepreneurship	While keeping a local-scale focus, extra-local resources used to benefit local development
Often focuses on newly emerging sectors, such as creative industries and ICT	Seeks to diversify the local economy, particularly in the service sectors	Participation of all actors in the locality needed
Low productivity and peripherality seen as a problem	Limited capacity to participate seen as a problem	Mobilising local and non-local resources through networks can be a problem
Industries need to modernise through capital application	Local economies need to build capacity	Innovation – widely understood – needed

seen as going hand in hand, with innovation acting as the driver for economic growth. However, increasingly, it is being recognised that innovation does not have to be seen in this light. Innovation can be defined in broader terms than just the application of new technology to the creation and sale of goods and services. It can be seen as having a role in improving quality of life and livelihoods, quite separate from increasing levels of monetised sales of goods and services.

In their exploration of the 'associational economy', Cooke and Morgan (1998) develop a view of innovation as a form of creativity, something that can break everyday routines. They particularly consider it in relation to firms, stressing the associative capacity of the firm, that is, the capacity for forging cooperation within the firm, along the supply chain and at the interfaces between the firm, its locality and the wider milieu. This involves recognising, assimilating and exploiting new forms of knowledge. But the same point can be made with regard to social routines within civil society and across civil society and the local economy. Bock (2016), focusing on rural development, considers how social innovation can combat rural marginalisation. Such rural social innovation is seen as distinctive in that it depends on civic self-reliance and self-organisation, but this also emphasises that innovation is not unique to cities, being found in smaller settlements and rural areas also. The embeddedness of firms and institutions in the locality is important, as this links the economic and the social. That said, too much embeddedness can hinder innovation and the potential for disruptive change. The problem remains that smaller firms are often under-capitalised and lack internal planning capacity, both of which can limit the take-up of innovations (Eisenschitz and Gough, 1993).

An important finding here is the emphasis on hybridity across the local economy and local civil society within endogenous and neo-endogenous LED approaches. This leads to an emphasis on the importance of social capital in a locality. This is not a one-way relationship; rather, social capital in a locality is seen as supporting LED and, in turn, LED that uses and relies on social capital is effective in building further social capital. A virtuous cycle can emerge, involving both LED and social capital creation and maintenance. Research into LED in a variety of settings reinforces this point.

In a Chinese context, Ha et al (2016) found that social capital within local business networks performed a range of functions, from building trust, overcoming the collective action problem and rectifying information asymmetries, to enabling goal conflict to be resolved, free-riding avoided, transactions costs lowered and uncertainties reduced. Johannisson (2007) specifically suggested that human and social capital is more important than financial capital in smaller settlements. Exchange between actors can be a seedbed for change and more intense than in larger settlements. Looking at small towns in the US, Besser (2009) outlined the way that social capital contributes to LED, particularly in places that were relatively homogeneous and experiencing economic problems. They argued that local capitalism, in terms of local ownership of business, could be important partly because local business leaders contributed to social capital and civic engagement. These business leaders generated both more bonding and bridging social capital;

bonding social capital here refers to close links between largely homogeneous actors, while bridging social capital is weaker links between actors who can be heterogeneous. Emery and Flora (2006) also saw bonding and bridging social capital as important in turning a downward economic spiral into an upward one. Their case study was from Nebraska and highlighted the importance of social capital leading to leadership and capacity building, capturing funds from the transfer of wealth and fostering entrepreneurship for LED.

Meanwhile, looking across European countries, Muringani et al (2012) found that bridging social capital was more important in LED than bonding social capital. While formal support mechanisms were important in implementing social entrepreneurship, other informal mechanisms were more important in the emergence of such entrepreneurship. They particularly identified new social values, social networks and entrepreneurship attitudes. Motoyama (2020) identified an informal function of local government as creating such linkages as 'connective tissue'. Local government may find this challenging, as it requires contact with a greater number of small firms and individual entrepreneurs, rather than a few larger firms as with inward investment strategies. Johannisson (2007) also pointed to the importance of a policy based on shared norms, organic structures and an identity that is embedded in local stories. As they state: 'the prosaic and routine everyday local life is both the ends and the means of entrepreneurial processes and of community development' (Johannisson, 2007: 23).

This points to the importance of looking beyond market-based activities and exchange that is based on monetary metrics. Social capital encompasses social relationships, common norms, a sense of reciprocity and mutuality as well as trust between parties. These cannot be built within market contexts alone.

Experiences of planning for neo-endogenous and community economic development

The European Union based its signature economic development policy for rural areas (and later fishing areas also) on the idea of neo-endogenous development. LEADER was a pilot programme of the European Union from 1991 to 1994, was a formal programme from a first phase starting in 2007 and became embedded to the extent that it formed the second pillar of the Common Agricultural Policy over 2014–20. LEADER was anchored in local action, place-based policy and public participation and worked through Local Action Groups. In the 20 years of the LEADER programme, around 2,600 partnerships were established across Europe, with some €8.6 billion of funding from 2007 to 2013.

Ray (2000), Bosworth et al (2015), Biczkowski (2020) and Marango et al (2020) have all studied LEADER projects. They emphasised that these encompass both exogenous features through economies of scale and concentration of economic activity, as well as endogenous features through harnessing local resources for development, including local entrepreneurialism. The combination maximises the value of local resources and competitiveness, creates networks that extend beyond the local area and capitalises on non-local demand. This enhances the competitiveness of local firms. It requires local actors to combine with actors operating at a distance, at higher tiers or on larger scales and also needs local community-led initiatives to integrate with external processes and networks. Local project managers at the heart of these connecting networks are vital, particularly in transferring knowledge around the locality, but experiences show that NGOs can also be vital intermediaries here.

There are challenges in this approach. Gkartzios and Scott (2013) pointed out the possible tension that may emerge between meeting local needs and competing for these extra-local resources, while Marango et al (2020) saw that limitations in local knowledge and local buy-in could affect the success of a LEADER project. For Goodwin-Hawkins et al (2022), the key challenge was to overcome the constraints of existing local capacities while avoiding the influence of local power differentials and elite capture. Shucksmith et al (2021) considered the LEADER programme in terms of its contribution to spatial justice, in terms of both distributive outcomes and processes of inclusion and suggest that LEADER displayed a tension between networked and hierarchical modes of governance. Looking specifically at England, they argued that LEADER had shifted decisively towards the hierarchical. Rather than being embedded in local action, it had been directed, controlled and constrained by government, particularly at national level. This may be a consequence of the particular nature of the UK. Eisenschitz and Gough (1993) identified the UK as uniquely international, concentrated, urbanised and proletarianised, and these features may have influenced the limited potential for neo-endogenous solutions noted earlier.

The follow-up to LEADER within Europe was community-led local development (CLLD), introduced in 2014. Again, this was based in bottom-up, community-based action, but emphasised the strengthening of synergies between local actors across the public and private sectors. It comprised participation and consultation by the local community as well as an integrated approach across sectors and scales. It thus aimed to have both the benefits of local communicative action with top-down direction, expertise and resources. It also focused on quick gains to build support (Saracu and Trif, 2019). While there was much overlap with LEADER, CLLD did not work with Local Action Groups but, rather, called for spaces for community participation in a more flexible way. The CLLD approach also involved explicit interfacing of local and expert forms of knowledge.

In their study of CLLD in the UK, Marango et al (2020) identified clarity over the scope of decision-making powers of the local group as important. They found that CLLD cases they studied were motivated by a long-term perspective and improving quality of life, alongside social cohesion. However, they also found limited linkages to formal spatial planning at the local authority level, although CLLD groups were able to engage in neighbourhood-level planning. They grounded this in the unwillingness of local authorities to listen to the CLLD groups. Neighbourhood planning in the UK, by contrast, is led by a neighbourhood forum which is more likely to be coterminous with the CLLD area. This means that the local knowledge of the CLLD project is unlikely to benefit the local planning process at broader-than-neighbourhood scales. It is important to note here that English local authorities are relatively large, often comprising several 100,000s of people; whereas neighbourhood forums are more flexibly designated and can be at the scale of a few thousand or 10,000s of people.

In the US, this kind of LED is known as community economic development. Spicer and Casper-Futterman (2020) identified three different types of community economic development. In extractive or concessionary community economic development, mainstream commercial activity is required to 'pay up' for community benefits; this is close to growth-dependent planning as outlined in Chapter 1. There is localist or 'made here' community economic development, as well as transformative community economic development which challenges conventional capitalism with forms of democratic economy; the latter is closer to the social economy that will be discussed in later chapters. Localist community economic development is most akin to neo-endogenous development. It has a particular flavour because it arose as a response to top-down and often brutal urban renewal programmes of the 1960–80s and it focuses specifically on low-income groups. From the 1980s onwards, community economic development evolved in a context of the growing dominance of a neoliberal ideology, in which community-based initiatives could be readily co-opted by a struggling and constrained state. This has led to a debate as to whether community economic development is filling in the gaps in existing capitalism, reforming that capitalism or potentially transforming it. Spicer and Casper-Futterman argued that there is potential for using community economic development to resist both neoliberal pressures and the underlying globalisation trend; the example that they give is of the Green Worker Cooperative Academy in New York (see Chapter 5 on cooperatives). Others, such as Pike et al (2006: 51), saw community economic development as potentially limited by a low level of local disposable income, weak education infrastructure and poor skills.

More positively, Lønning (2018) provided a case study of successful community economic development in northern Norway. The success here rested on the existence of an umbrella organisation, a minimum of very engaged and resourceful people and a focus on broad community involvement balanced with one-to-one working with individual people. In addition, there was a focus on not doing planning or finance per se but, rather, for a very specific purpose and with a clear overall vision. They emphasised the need to replace key individuals over time to maintain success. In the Swedish context, Meijer and Syssner (2017) argued, like others, for the importance of social capital in community-based development, but also saw benefits in leveraging local history, a feature of the County Durham case study discussed later. As in other cases of neo-endogenous development, they emphasised the central role that a key policy officer can play, acting as the manager of local networks.

Eisenschitz and Gough (1993: 169) argued that 'successful initiatives [in LED] are therefore typically very delicately poised', and experiences with LEADER, CLLD and community economic development reinforce that point. All these examples point to the limitations of relying only on local resources and the need to link to broader networks related to funding, market opportunities and/or public sector support. Local action is needed in cognisance of the need for such networks to make community-based LED a reality.

Focus on Shildon, County Durham

Shildon is a town of about 10,000 people in the former borough of Sedgefield, now within the Durham County Council municipal area in North East England (see Rydin, 2023 for more details, including sources). It is one of a number of small dispersed settlements in the county that had their origins in the earliest days of the industrial revolution. As such, Shildon is both a distinct urban area, albeit it a small one, and part of a network of urban areas of different sizes that together make up the urban structure of the county. In many of these settlements, the countryside (as dominated by agriculture and open space) is never far away, and yet neither the county as a whole nor the Shildon area itself can be simply described as rural.

Shildon presents itself as the birthplace of the steam railway and was effectively a railway town until the closure of Shildon Wagon Works in 1982–84 with the loss of 2,600 jobs. Always a fragile economy since the decline of coal mining, the closure of its railway works was a major economic and social blow to the town, but not the only one. While employment at the railway works was overwhelmingly male, the fake fur company Astraka employed many women in the town until its closure in 1988. Shildon is, thus, a classic example of de-industrialisation on a small scale. The current local planning response is a mix of the more traditional growth-dependent planning combined with attempts to attract investment from outside (although largely in the wider region rather than in Shildon itself) and a form of culture-led regeneration that does engage with local identity, local communities and the heritage of the town. There is space, though, for elements of a more endogenous approach too.

Conventionally, local planning seeks to facilitate new development that businesses – both local and inward-migrating – will need, that is, the provision and improvement of sites and premises, operating alongside selected subsidies and business advice/mentoring and so on. In 1990, Roberts et al (1990*b*) studied the area and detailed this as a positive response to the loss of employment in the town after the closure of the railway works. Roberts et al (1990*b*) described the provision of space for industrial activity in Shildon as 'the leading edge of the practice of local economic development' in the 1980s (p 145). It has been claimed that the Sedgefield and Shildon Development Agency had helped nearly 150 projects in its early years, including 80 start-ups, and that 12 companies were established in the old wagon works. By the 1990s, it was being reported that about 70 businesses were operating in and around the historic wagon works, significantly increasing the number of firms in Shildon from only six or seven companies, and that these businesses were increasingly diverse. Yet Pike and Tomaney (1999) note that while the number of small and medium-sized enterprises (SMEs) in the area had grown, employment in SMEs had fallen.

By 2004, the focus for LED had shifted to the wider subregion beyond the town and the key development agency, the Sedgefield and Shildon Development Agency having moved its offices from Shildon to Newton Aycliffe in 1994. This wider focus continues to be relevant. The present policies of the 2020 County Durham Plan protect business/industrial land and allocate new sites. Business Durham – the county's economic development arm – owns and markets spaces on a number of industrial parks towards the south of the town and almost 100 firms are registered on these parks. But the overall approach is to remove Shildon from competition with other nearby settlements, particularly with Newton Aycliffe, which is only two miles away and has one of the largest industrial parks in the North-East. The County Council sees Shildon as an economy dominated by SMEs and micro businesses and places it in the context of the wider local economy with the clustering of business promoted elsewhere, hopefully offering the potential for some Shildon residents to benefit from the employment generated. A key example of this is the opening of a train manufacture and assembly plant by Hitachi in the latter 2010s on the Merchant Park in Newton Aycliffe. The 2020 County Durham Plan (Durham County Council, 2020) saw this as 'having the potential to act as a catalyst for further growth and investment within the sector and bring wider benefits to Newton Aycliffe and County Durham as a whole' (S.4.35).

The Shildon Regeneration Framework of 2013 (Durham County Council, 2018) explicitly positions Shildon as a low-rent business prospect, with smaller, more flexible premises, and the county council recognises that the local economy of Shildon is dominated by small and micro businesses. The unemployment rate in the Shildon area is above the national average but still relatively low, although this has to be seen in the context of low participation in employment by Shildon residents: 17 per cent are retired and 9 per cent are long-term sick or disabled; over 35 per cent of households have one person in these categories. In addition, some 4 per cent are long-term unemployed or have never worked. As of the 2011 Census, over 35 per cent of the population in the parish of Shildon aged over 16 years had no formal qualifications. This speaks to problems of deprivation and the prevalence of a low-wage economy in the town. The Index of Multiple Deprivation for 2019 covers Shildon in four sub-areas. One is in the 30 per cent most deprived areas in the country, two in the 20 per cent most deprived areas and one in the 10 per cent most deprived areas. Thirty per cent of the population live in socially rented housing and thirty-nine per cent had no car available to the household. Low wages are matched by relatively low house prices, but this is reportedly in the early 2020s attracting more economically marginal residents, with private landlords buying property for tenants reliant on social benefits.

Local planning documentation identifies a further problem arising from the proximity of Shildon to several other places, notably that it generates travel to shops in other centres. The lack of a distinctive offer from Shildon town centre is blamed for this inability to compete with other retail centres. Certainly, the kinds of retail outlet in the town are limited: among the 97 retail units, there are 'bespoke' shops such as butchers and cobblers, but no major supermarket, for example. The 2018 County Durham Town Centre Survey puts the split of the high street at: 44 per cent retail (A1), 5 per cent professional services (A2), 7 per cent hospitality (A3 and A4) and 9 per cent hot food takeaways. The 2013 Shildon Regeneration Framework saw one 'solution' to this 'problem' as building more housing to attract households with above-average incomes and a greater ability to spend in the town, in effect a gentrification policy (S.6.12). As a result, there has been new housebuilding on two main locations, both on the edge of the town (indeed, one beyond the edge). It is questionable whether such a housing-led approach would build local wealth within Shildon; new residents taking advantage of the relatively cheaper housing are likely to work elsewhere and still spend the majority of their money outside the town, given the limited consumer offer within the town.

However, it could be argued that Shildon's retail offer is meeting important local needs. The County Plan cites a vacancy rate in terms of units of 14.4 per cent, just above county average but below nearby Bishop Auckland; vacant floor space was just over 10 per cent, less than half of that at Bishop Auckland. The 2016 Masterplan Update (Durham County Council, 2016) suggests a vacancy rate of 8.3 per cent for 2016, that is, only eight units in total. Thus, while the high street may be a low-value offering, there are relatively few vacancies.

Shildon need not be seen through the lens of a monetised focus in which higher wages, higher house prices and higher retail sales are positive indicators. Rather, its specific character as a low-wage, low-house-price and even low-employment location with a reasonably abundant SME sector could be recognised. This puts a value on aspects that have a low monetised price or cost, such as the highly affordable housing, but also on the non-monetised flows within the town that support provisioning and enable access to goods and services. Here the abundant social capital of the town has a key role. The Shildon Town Council is a significant local body, particularly since Sedgefield Borough Council was dissolved in 2009. The Town Council has a civic hall and is responsible for cemeteries and burials, parks and green spaces and allotments, including the main park, Hackworth Park. It meets monthly and fosters community events throughout the year, including projects such as a health and well-being garden, a 'fridge for all', food banks, a credit union, support for young people not in employment, education or training and park improvements. It also coordinates Shildon Children and Young People's Action Network, which brings together providers of youth services. It was particularly active during the COVID-19 pandemic.

The Town Council is contributing to the foundational economy, understood as meeting everyday and providential needs. In this task, it is joined by numerous civil society organisations, such as the churches. Shildon Alive! provides food banks and community meals and a shop that sells food waste from supermarkets at low prices. The Town Council is limited by its ownership of land and assets, its reliance on key personnel, particularly a few active councillors, and a specific remit; but they do have local knowledge and can foster a sense of local identity. They are supported financially by Durham County Council's Area Action Partnership approach. Shildon falls within the Bishop Auckland and Shildon Area Action Partnership, where a small team work with elected members, representatives from business, social housing and the voluntary sector and the wider public. Funding is provided for a variety of small projects such as: Guerrilla Gardening; Coundon Gateway, a road safety project; From Plot to Plate; Brusselton Incline restoration; Salvation Army kitchen appliances; Eldon Bank road safety; IT upgrade and support for community newspaper; Jubilee Fields Community Centre heating upgrade; Shildon footpath improvements; and Shildon Station artwork.

Also interesting is the approach to culture-led regeneration in the town focused on the Locomotion museum that opened in 2004. Locomotion houses part of the national railway collection and is now part of the national Science Museum Group. It has incorporated renovation of historic railway buildings on its site and in 2020 was slated as the new home for the world's first iron railway bridge, the Gaunless Bridge designed by George Stephenson. This is part of an expansion plan, called Vision 2025, which will almost double the visitor space. There will be a new building, and older buildings will be renovated, with better interpretation of the site and 40 more locomotives going on display in addition to the bridge. The aim is to increase but also spread visitor numbers so that they are not concentrated on a limited number of steam days.

This development is notable for being closely linked with the heritage and identity of the town as well as building links with local business and local communities. The fact that about 90 local companies trade with the museum opens up the possibility of developing the local supply chains around this key anchor institution, an institution that has a wider-than-profit perspective but – in the local context – relevant purchasing power. There are also proposals to provide some local business space within the Locomotion site, although the space is limited and has to fit with the museum's brand. Suggestions include a bike hire hub for visiting trails on local disused railway lines, a holiday rental in a historic building and a pop-up cafe. The 2020 County Durham Plan (p 82) suggests that this could revitalise the town centre; however, it remains questionable how significantly these expansion plans will impact on the market economy of the town. The development at the Locomotion site will be small in scale and the museum has limited potential to act as an anchor institution as compared with, say, a hospital, local authority or higher education institution. Crucially, there are physical barriers to the footfall into Locomotion benefiting the wider town. The town centre lies about 10–15 minutes' walk uphill from the railway station, where the museum is located, separated by largely residential areas and a substantial park.

However, the Locomotion museum itself is developing a form of community engagement that will bring its economic activities into synergy with the social capital that already exists within the town, potentially reinforcing one another. There are plans for an intensive period of community consultation to ensure that people's local histories are incorporated into the overarching narrative of railway history that will be presented through interpretation efforts at the museum. The current links with the Shildon Railway Institute are being expanded by appointing community champions and establishing a range of activities that will link the museum's business with local history and identity and community action. And the physical development at the site is being carefully designed to provide facilities, such as play spaces, for local residents as well as for visitors. In all these ways, the expansion of Locomotion may build social capital alongside market-based economic activity, both leveraging the history and culture of the town.

The role of planning in economic development for small local firms

Neo-endogenous development poses a challenge for local planning because some of the key ways it operates are not embedded in the local environment, built or otherwise. They relate to networking across scales, innovation through mobilising local resources and local social capital. The question is how local planning can promote this through the tools it has at its disposal and combine with LED policy. Eisenschitz and Gough (1993) argued that, at least in the UK, such policy has often overemphasised built environment solutions as in the provision of premises or the improvement of places: a property focus within LED 'has come to be considered almost axiomatic' (p 36). Standard policies have come to include information and advice, advertising and small-unit provision. These have become 'so common as to have little geographical leverage' (p 51). Negative consequences of a property-led approach can be increased rents and loss of opportunities for smaller, less profitable businesses (pp 101–103). Raco and Moreira de Souza (2018) showed how small businesses are often adversely affected by urban regeneration, which increases the uncertainty facing such businesses, increases costs – particularly rents – and can be associated with deteriorating local government support.

This suggests that a different approach is needed that promotes local entrepreneurial capacities through linking firms to the resources that extra-local networks can bring. In a study of micro and small enterprises in the Italian clothing and footwear industry, Buciuni et al (2022) examined how they tap into global value chains and partake in the global economy. They identified the difficulties that smaller enterprises can face in establishing these wider links. They noted that participation in domestic value chains can enable such participation in global chains, particularly where they upgraded through shifting from lower- to higher-value activities in terms of the products, the processes, the capacities and/or the nature of the chain and links between sectors. So, local policy needs to find ways to help local firms find these connections elsewhere nationally and, potentially, globally. Linkages between local firms can help in forging these broader networks of connections, and this can be achieved through co-location and through common facilities, both potential foci of local planning. This is evident in the experience of the Maker Movement and of co-working spaces.

Fiorentina (2018, 2019a, 2019b) provided a detailed analysis of the Maker Movement in Italy. This movement has its origins in a new entrepreneurial style that emerged in the San Francisco Bay Area around 2006. It claimed to democratise innovation and small-scale manufacture through the provision of spaces as accelerators, incubators and shared service accommodation. Knowledge spillovers remained largely dependent on social capital in the locality and relationships of trust between firms, but the provision of such premises had a role to play. Van Holm (2017) looked at maker spaces in Georgia, US offering tools, training and space but also generating new ideas, enabling prototyping and leading to planned and accidental entrepreneurship. He found four contributions to economic development. First, there is the creation of cultural change by encouraging entrepreneurship. Second, small businesses can be supported to grow through provision of services. Third, workforce training can be offered, and fourth, this may result in better workforce retention.

Lowe and Vinodrai (2020) also studied the Maker Movement, in a case study of the Carolina Textile District project in Carolina, US. This project connected textile manufactures in the more remote areas of the state with a new generation of urban-based textile designers and innovators. The Carolina firms provided both samples for marketing and scaled-up manufacturing. The connectivity with the urban Maker Movement provided access to high-quality technology not available locally and digital marketing platforms that local firms had less experience of. But this was also a place-based strategy using local public institutions to generate local maker spaces, seeking to create a new generation of local entrepreneurs and leveraging 'produced-in-place' sensibilities through 'made here' marketing. These all supported local employment, innovation and sourcing. Thus, the strategy combined place-connecting actions with maker–manufacturer links. The outcomes had been about 150 SMEs benefiting in Carolina and over 1,200 clothing and textile designers and makers utilising the Carolina manufacturing capacity. The Carolina Textile District also acted as an intermediary, seeking to de-risk connections over space by screening contacts and providing local training and education.

Turning to the provision of co-working spaces in business hubs, Merrell et al (2020) examined different kinds of hubs, both honey pots that involve business-to-customer links and hives which focus on business-to-business links, in North East England. Honey pots were seen as especially useful in rural areas, where they could attract footfall to a space through a mix of activities such as cafes that then supported a target market for other businesses, typically in the arts and crafts, tourism, food and drink and retail sectors. The physical infrastructure could support knowledge exchange, the entrepreneurial process and wider community cohesion. Even a micro-cluster could be beneficial; they did not have to reap substantial economies of scale. One benefit could be the provision of new links to extra-local networks that are central to neo-endogenous development through one member of the cluster. Goodwin-Hawkins et al's (2022) work on rural service hubs in Austria, Finland and Wales offered similar insights. They saw such hubs as mobilising social innovation, networks, scale and proximity.

Thus, the planned provision of hubs offers the advantages of access to customers, knowledge, networks, skills, amenities and collaborations. Fiorentina (2019a) differentiated: the social incubator, which is privately or publicly owned and originates from bottom-up action; the start-up incubator, which is usually publicly owned and instigated top-down; and the real estate incubator, which is privately owned and provided due to commercial incentives. All such co-working spaces could build networks and offer firm-to-firm training and, as such, they can be a good use for vacant property. The planning approach that she recommended includes maintaining a database of such vacant property and putting in place a new lease structure that enables small and new firms to operate readily from such property. Hubs also need planning protection from redevelopment for other purposes.

Digital hubs have a particular role to play (Price et al, 2022). They can cover co-working or networking spaces, innovation spaces, spaces for demonstrating emergent technologies and/or points of access for public broadband. Price et al provided a typology of four kinds: public internet access points; incubator and co-working spaces; advice, training and support spaces; and sector-specific spaces. They emphasised the need for the space to have a scale appropriate to the local needs, and to offer a mix of space, services, skills and staff. Such digital hubs also rely on the provision of information and communications technology (ICT) infrastructure, another role that planning can play alongside ensuring integration of hubs into the wider range of infrastructure (transport, energy and social infrastructure, such as educational facilities).

Another approach is to require the provision of affordable workspaces as part of new developments. These are intended to provide premises for smaller local firms so that they can retain their role within local labour markets and business networks. However, Ferm (2014, 2016) has done extensive research on the use of planning gain mechanisms to deliver such affordable workspaces and is highly critical of this approach. In the London context, she noted that the negotiation of such space within new developments was not able to control the eventual occupier of the facilities. Often, the provision and management of such workspaces was contracted out to a specialist firm, given that most developers do not have expertise in this area. The requirements of the planning agreement negotiated were fulfilled, provided that the space for workspaces within the new development was built and offered out. However, the workspace delivery company often filled these premises with firms external to the locality and in different sectors to existing small businesses.

Thus, affordable workspace conditions on new urban development can hasten rather than constrain the displacement of local small firms by other businesses. Ferm and Jones (2016) saw the underlying cause of such displacement as the difference between the value of these sub-prime industrial and commercial sites as compared with the value of housing land, particularly in cities where there is a shortage of housing and very high investment interest in buying new housing. They critiqued the then London Plan in this context for anticipating and then actually planning for the decline of existing industry, rather than seeking to protect and provide for it. Ferm (2016) has argued that there are competing discourses

around commercial displacement, so that such displacement can be presented –
within the growth-dependent planning paradigm – as a positive move.

She considered that this undermined the unique character of many urban areas
that is based in a mixed-use structure and which can be destroyed by development
leading to a single dominant use in an area, citing Jane Jacobs's phrase: 'the self-
destruction of diversity'. While Jacobs did see this as potentially forming part of the
evolution of cities, the rate and scale of change in modern urban areas precludes
the adaptation that is part of evolution. Small firms can be vulnerable to such
sweeping change, as they are often locally dependent on existing relationships
between buyers and sellers, trust between businesses and creditors and/or a local
labour force (Ferm, 2016). Raco and Tunney (2010) showed in the case of small
firms on the London Olympic Park that trust and reciprocity – key elements of
social capital – were essential for their survival. This can be destroyed in larger-
scale redevelopment, and thus planning should seek to avoid this where possible,
certainly where there is an existing local business structure.

A more place-based approach to support neo-endogenous LED can be found
in the focus on local high streets, locations which are often erroneously seen as
purely retail. Research has shown that these are, in fact, a mixture of retail, service
providers and manufacturers, with a high level of involvement of smaller and
independent businesses (Vaughan, 2015; Rydin, 2019). It is this mixture that is seen
as central to the vitality of such streets and their immediate hinterlands. In some
of her key works, Jane Jacobs has long emphasised how urban neighbourhoods
required numerous small businesses to support the networks of exchange and
encounter that make for a lively area. She discussed how the presence of such
small businesses underpins connections within the wider community and helps
build social capital (Jacobs, 1961).

Zukin has continued this line of work in her study of high streets across the globe
(Zukin et al, 2016), as has Hall in London (Hall, 2011). Very similar themes of
the positive impact of small interconnected businesses and communities emerge.
This suggests a role for local planning – both in making plans for such areas and
regulating change through new development – in protecting the spaces available for
such businesses and preventing their demolition, amalgamation and redevelopment.
In addition, forms of local area management can improve the physical environment
and provide for accessibility by foot, car and public transport, as well as fostering
a sense of local identity. Research on neighbourhood planning for hyper-local
retail and business areas has shown how diverse local approaches can support such
identity creation (Rydin, 2019). There is analogous work on the role of markets
in providing locations for small, independent retailers, servicing local residents and
also creating unique and colourful locales that cement specific spatial identities.
Research into the Grainger Market in Newcastle, UK (Newing et al, 2023) has
demonstrated how such markets are important to more vulnerable consumers,
including the elderly and those living in more deprived neighbourhoods. Not
only do they provide cheaper food, but they also provide other household goods
and clothing in a diverse and affordable offering.

The essence here is to plan on the small scale for a mixture of land uses and to protect existing employment land that is occupied by businesses providing employment, where this is in short supply (Ferm and Jones, 2016). This raises questions on how housing supply should be expanded, an issue returned to in Chapter 6. The key point that Ferm and Jones made is that housing development has been used as an economic development tool but this has undermined the existing structures of local business. Token inclusion of non-residential uses or large-scale commercial development has affected the viability of existing business ecosystems, ironically often under the banner of urban sustainability. Yet it is the pattern of smaller plot sizes and mixed land uses that has been shown to be most resilient (Ferm et al, 2021), as compared to larger plot sizes, greater separation of land uses and developments which face inwards, away from the street frontage.

Disruption of existing small business is to be avoided wherever possible. Such firms, particularly within the manufacturing sector, are highly place dependent and often tied to specific localities. They rely on the local labour market and, in the case of services, often local clientele also, with proximity to customers being important. The interconnections between local firms and their suppliers and customers forms a delicate business ecosystem which is not captured in many broader-brush zoning policies and which requires a more nuanced approach, one influenced by detailed knowledge of how this ecosystem works and what local businesses need (Ferm et al, 2021). Fiorentina (2023) echoed this with a call for integrated place-based solutions that are targeted towards but also anchored in local needs and the identity of place. Regeneration needs to move away from large-scale redevelopment towards a focus on existing social and institutional infrastructure also, including work on building trust, the capacities of communities and local imaginaries and identities.

Thus, the role that local planning could play in supporting local businesses and providing an alternative to growth-dependence involves the provision of suitable premises for local businesses, and also hubs or co-working spaces offering a range of facilities and services as well as the opportunity to meet and exchange knowledge. Such knowledge covers both technical and also economic aspects such as links to customers and the wider supply chain. Planning can also protect existing premises and hubs from redevelopment for other purposes and ensure an adequacy of infrastructure provision to support these smaller businesses. Such infrastructure should be technological (for example, fast broadband) and also social (as with appropriate training and education provision). Less attention should be paid to increasing the value of land in the locality as opposed to meeting the needs of existing businesses. Above all, a place-based approach is required that builds on the existing characteristics of an area and how the delicate business ecosystem is formed out of many interrelationships, some to external organisations (customers, suppliers) but many rooted in the detail of local relations with labour, customers and other firms. Such an approach can also leverage the unique identity of the area, but this needs to be based in the imaginaries of local people and firms, rather than using a manufactured sense of authenticity as a brand for redevelopment and urban change, as Zukin (2010) has highlighted.

5

Economic democracy and cooperatives

Introduction

Chapter 4 looked at the role of small local businesses within the economic development of their localities, arguing that such firms are not subject to the same pressures for growth as larger and footloose firms and yet play an important part in the foundational economy. While such firms are characterised as market actors, the discussion emphasised that they are embedded in local civil society as well as local market dynamics and thus have a hybrid character. In this chapter, the focus is still on organisations that produce and distribute goods and services of various kinds, but they are organisations usually characterised as within the social economy. As Chapter 3 outlined, the term social economy is a broad one, encompassing many different kinds of organisation. The focus here will be on cooperatives, as one of the earliest but still extant social economy organisations. Chapters 6, 7 and 8 and will broaden out to consider other types of social enterprise, especially as they develop housing, manage community assets and operate infrastructure. But here, Chapter 5 looks at producer and consumer cooperatives, partly through a more detailed look at the cooperative movement in Sweden, where it has long been important.

Origins of cooperatives

Cooperatives can be worker cooperatives or consumer cooperatives, but the history of cooperatives is generally told from the perspective of the workers' cooperative. These arose in the 19th century in industrialising countries as a response to exploitation within the factory system under early capitalism. While Karl Marx led a movement based on the revolutionary replacement of private capital with state direction, other critics of capitalism, such as Proudhon and Bakunin, suggested the cooperative as an alternative ideal form of production (Rothschild, 2009). As history tells us, Marx won that argument within the left-wing political movements of the time, but cooperatives have remained a subsidiary thread within counter-capitalist movements. The earliest cooperatives were probably found in rural areas in the US, and since that time there has been a continued trend there towards farmers' markets and hubs that involve cooperative principles (Matson and Theyer, 2013).

However, many cite Rochdale, UK as the first exemplar urban cooperative (Fairbairn, nd provides a history). The Rochdale Society of Equitable Pioneers was set up in 1844 in North West England. Prior to the cooperative being established, there was already a Rochdale Friendly Cooperative Society, a mutual society of about 60 flannel weavers which set up its own retail store in the town, alongside a branch of the Owenite movement, espousing the principles of Robert Owen. The Rochdale Society was formed when many of the original flannel weavers dropped out and a partnership was formed between the remaining weavers, a group of Owenites, some ex-Chartists and some temperance (anti-alcohol) campaigners. The objectives were to undertake manufacturing in common and also run a retail store, provide housing, offer some land for food cultivation and, eventually, support a home-colony and a temperance hotel. The Society thus had a mix of social and economic purposes from the outset. Organisationally, it had to fit within the Friendly Societies Act, pertaining at the time, in order to get legal recognition and protection.

The Rochdale Society developed the core idea of a cooperative as a member-based business where members are also owners, have rights and are able to control the cooperative. It opened its store in 1844, adding a newspaper room four years later and then growing rapidly. Above the ground floor, it housed a Dissenters' chapel and a school. As other local savings and educational institutions failed, the Rochdale Society came to develop 'not so much a monopoly of business as a monopoly of community support and leadership' (Fairbairn, nd: 10). The example of the Rochdale Society led to other cooperatives being set up, partially integrated into a wider network. The greatest challenge that these businesses faced was wholesaling, which led to the Cooperative Wholesale Society or CWS being formed in 1863. By 1878–79 there were 1,200 cooperatives in Britain, of which 584 were affiliated to CWS.

Over time, the cooperative movement became more retail focused and this drove further growth. By the start of the First World War in 1914, the movement peaked at 1,385 societies with over 3 million members in the UK. The number of societies fell to just over 1,000 during the Second World War but the membership was in excess of 8.7 million. The retail focus matched the Fabian emphasis on consumption as a unifying interest, Fabianism being an influential political ideology of the time. Consumers were also attracted by 'the divi' or patronage refund which could be 10 per cent of retail spend or even twice that. The influence of the Rochdale model was more widespread, however, through the promulgation of the Rochdale Principles worldwide. These principles encompassed: unity or association, economy, democracy, equity, liberty, responsibility and education. For example, these influenced the North American farm cooperatives that developed over 1880–1940.

Nowadays, a cooperative can be defined as a member-owned, managed and controlled organisation that is guided by a set of values that shape everyday operation. These encompass mutual aid by members for each other, self-responsibility for the cooperative by the members, democracy whereby the members guide the organisation, equality between members and solidarity in that members collectively work for each other (Bastida et al, 2022). These values inform working practices, but they also lead to an ethical basis for the cooperative grounded in honesty, transparency, social responsibility and concern for others.

Practically, in a cooperative the employees own shares in the organisation, profits are shared between employees and these employees participate in the general management of the organisation.

Experiences of cooperatives: producer cooperatives

Mondragon in the Basque country of Spain is often discussed as the most important current example of cooperative enterprise. This was originally founded in the 1930s by a priest and five of his students as a response to the lack of investment in the local area after the Second World War. The first cooperative was established in 1956, growing over time to about 150 cooperatives involving 150,000 members–workers–owners, although numbers are now lower; in 1986 a figure of just over 30,000 was reported (Gibson-Graham, 2006). The early focus was on developing internal markets through incorporating supply chains. Since then they have also moved into consumer cooperatives and have developed principles of environmentally responsible production.

Importantly, the cooperatives operate in a network together with a common cooperative bank that provides seed funding for new cooperatives as well as health and pension cover and cooperative schools (Rothschild, 2009). The bank is capitalised by deposited surpluses from the cooperatives (Gibson-Graham, 2006). There is also a second-degree cooperative, Caja Laboral Popular, that supports enterprise development, that is, the creation of new cooperatives. It offers social insurance, research and development capacities as well as education and training (see later).

The Basque model encompasses job security, so that if one workers' cooperative cuts employment the aim is to re-employ those workers in other cooperatives in the region. Workers' pay tends towards equity rather than market levels. Wages are decided by a Cooperative Congress, with a principle of regional solidarity so that they do not outprice local labour. Wage differentials inside individual cooperatives are limited, originally to 1:3 and more recently to 1:6 (Gibson-Graham, 2006). A share of the surplus is also put into individual workers' capital accounts as a form of forced saving; it cannot be withdrawn while they are in employment. Workers also get extended training, not least to enable worker participation in workplace-level decision making. Such training covers technological developments, cooperative values, social skills, leadership and teamwork. There is a Mondragon General Assembly and all worker-members are entitled to vote at this.

Each cooperative is managed by a number of elected councils. The cooperative manager is appointed, but only for four years, and the governing council of each co-op meets each day before the workday begins, clearly indicating where the main influence derives from. In larger co-ops there is a separate management council. One important decision was to limit the size of future co-ops where possible to 500, although this has not prevented growth through partnerships (see later). There is also an elected president for each co-op. The key feature of the Mondragon complex of workers' cooperatives is that they are integrated into local networks to leverage common social capital and local knowledge. Locally rooted consultancies and universities reinforce this, and training attunes managers to the local context.

However, growth at Mondragon has led to changes in working practices (Bretos et al, 2019). Gibson-Graham (2006) suggested that expansion has largely been in non-cooperative structures and that 50 per cent of the Mondragon workforce are not cooperators. Furthermore, workers' cooperatives have expanded their remit in a bid to maintain competitiveness, given that they now operate in global markets. This often involves partnerships with straightforwardly competitive firms overseas. Bretos et al (2019) estimated that there are 30 multinational cooperatives controlling about 140 production subsidiaries abroad, none of which are themselves cooperatives, as well as 45 production subsidiaries in Spain, of which 15 are cooperatives. These multinational cooperatives have tended to adopt the mainstream management practices of total quality management, lean production and subdivision into mini-companies. The concern is that operating on a global scale in this way may alter management priorities and shift cooperatives away from local concerns and agendas. For example, globalised cooperatives at Mondragon have created more employment than those that stayed localised, but this can be at the expense of very poor labour conditions overseas.

The importance of the Mondragon case should not lead to the wider Spanish cooperative movement being ignored. Looking at seven Spanish cases, Urbano et al (2010) stressed the importance of both formal and informal institutions for cooperatives. Formal institutions set the mechanisms of creating and maintaining a cooperative in place, but the informal institutions do the vital work of generating and embedding new social values, of developing entrepreneurial and socially responsible attitudes and of building social capital through relationships, linkages and common norms.

Ortiz-Miranda et al (2010) examined rural agricultural cooperatives in Valencia, Spain, both large and small, with the smaller ones being concentrated in the olive oil and dried fruits sectors. They saw the different forms of capital – social, cultural, environmental and capital linked to local knowledge – as essential to the success of the cooperatives but characterised them as being embedded in the locality and hence immobile. Problems could arise from two sources. First, there might be constraints on investment because of the incentive structures associated with common property ownership, the different time horizons of cooperative members and the difficulties of working with a portfolio of assets. Second, there could be problems in taking and implementing decisions arising from the principal–agent problem, where one actor sets the goal and another is tasked with implementation. This led to difficulties with monitoring, following up on decisions taken, conflicts of interest between actors and the choice of how to weigh different members' interests. As Ortiz-Miranda et al (2010) state, 'internal tensions seem to be an inherent feature at the very heart of cooperatives' (p 665).

Meanwhile, Bastida et al (2022) studied 142 workers' cooperatives in Galicia, Spain. They found five drivers for enhanced entrepreneurialism in the cooperatives, a form of entrepreneurialism also oriented towards social cohesion. First, there was the importance of the cooperative principles which provided the core motivation for joining the organisation. Second, there was the use of a governance model and, further (third), the perception of that model as favouring equality. Fourth, there was the individual social orientation of members and, finally, the influence of external support such as financing and consulting. However, Bastida et al also emphasised the importance of a supportive policy framework at local, regional and national scales. These cooperatives were important in reducing unemployment by actively seeking to avoid job losses and re-employ workers and in providing a pathway to employment for disadvantaged and excluded groups. Flexible working practices were sometimes favoured which supported inclusion in employment. In particular, this could support gender equality, with the business model of cooperatives more readily fitting with women's lives and also their values. The challenges were issues with raising finance, given that banks were often less willing to lend to cooperatives, along with issues of equality in decision making, and restrictions in how profits could be used. Bastida et al saw a tension between business strategy and democracy emerging from time to time.

Cooperatives are also strong in other countries. While there were mutual aid societies in Italy in the 19th century, traditional cooperatives emerged after the Second World War. Three ideological roots can be identified: the secular–socialist movement; working class left-wing movements; and the social solidarity tradition within the Catholic Church. By the 1960s they had become more focused on production within a competitive market environment, usually with a hierarchical structure. Ten of the 50 largest Italian agrifood enterprises are cooperatives, mainly in the marketing and processing fields. At the other end, 66 per cent of cooperatives have a turnover of less than €2 million, representing only 5 per cent of total turnover in the sector.

Social cooperatives emerged in the later 20th century (Fonte and Cucco, 2017) as a distinct strand of social enterprise separate from traditional workers' cooperatives. The new model was more closely embedded in the local economy and focused on solidarity-oriented initiatives. Alternative food networks were central in this shift, as was the passing of a new law in 1991 (Law No 381) which approved the regulation of social cooperatives and defined them as pursuing social integration and the common good. Typically, these social cooperatives either offer welfare services or operate commercially, targeting disadvantaged groups for labour. More recently, social agriculture has emerged as a category combining agricultural production with services such as health, education and recreation within the frame of an inclusion agenda.

However, experience with these new forms of cooperative points to certain tensions, such as between farmers' individualism and common values. The generation of genuinely shared values is central to success, as is the avoidance of overly complex organisational structures. Knowledge of how to cooperate is necessary and could be considered part of local social capital, that is, inherent in the community as a whole rather than linked to individuals' interpersonal skills. There is also a clear split between larger and smaller cooperatives. Larger cooperatives tend to emphasise profit generation and are more managerial and expansionist in ethos. The smaller cooperatives operate on a multi-stakeholder basis, are more associational and rely on or at least use volunteers while seeking to meet wider social goals.

Looking at Nicaraguan cooperatives, Fisher and Nading (2021) argued for cooperatives as a form of commons (p 1232). Furthermore, they were not seen as recipes but, rather, as historically generated, immanent projects. This underpins the diversity of forms that cooperatives can take and means that real-life cases can be quite different from the cooperative of socialist imaginaries, including those expressed through the Rochdale Society principles. Fisher and Nading looked at two cases, a women's sewing cooperative and a recycling cooperative and saw two themes as being at their heart: the centrality of cooperation itself and the idea of commoning as represented in self-management or *autogestión*. However, beyond this, individual cooperatives will interpret and apply the nine Rochdale Society principles in different ways.

Thus, the sewing cooperative developed a critique of how Mondragon cooperatives relied on sweat equity and social capital, and instead built their own model, based on principles of kinship and direct labour. While the women's sewing cooperative had become the first worker-owned free trade zone in the country, after ten years they opted out, partly because of the lack of orders from their US partner, Clean Clothes, but also due to the pressures on hiring labour that this partnership created. Instead, they favoured limiting the membership of the cooperative. This is in the context where the Nicaraguan General Cooperative Law of 1971 prohibits members of the same family being co-members in a cooperative, so as to prevent conflicts of interest. Creating kinship is thus a critical act and involves creating a boundary around the cooperative: 'constructing a commons always involves some degree of enclosure' (Fisher and Nading, 2021: 1242).

The recycling cooperative developed in a different direction. The background to the formation of the cooperative was a conflict between municipal waste management contractors and groups of informal recyclers, given that recyclables were seen as valuable. The cooperative established itself more formally in a warehouse where recyclables could be sorted with a fleet of trikes used to transport the recyclables. Cooperation was organised by a set of formal rules to guide both the labour of sorting and so forth and the distribution of rewards from the business. However, this failed, and instead a more flexible approach was adopted. As Fisher and Nading put it, this resulted in the cooperative operating on the boundary between flexibility and disorganisation.

Despite these examples, the overall share of cooperatives within the total number of firms or workers remains relatively low. This was analysed by Elster (1989) as being due to problems of economic viability, which are fundamentally related to the incentives that cooperatives produce – incentives which can lead to labour efficiencies. Elster also pointed to the apparent preference of workers for employment in capitalist firms, given that they do not wish to participate in decision making, may feel they lack the necessary skills or face costs in participating. He saw the influence of the cooperative founder as central in successfully setting up such firms, although the impact of multiple cooperatives within an area in overcoming thresholds for establishing further cooperatives needs to be acknowledged.

Once established there are a number of challenges that a cooperative faces. These include the shifting mix of stakeholders, which can alter the balance within the organisation's mission; changes in external conditions that affect the availability of finance; the tendency towards organisational slack, due to a mix of desired goals leading to inefficient management; and change in leadership, particularly where this affects the value base of the organisation (Murtagh, 2019: 102). It is also important to recognise that cooperatives can be of different kinds. Mens et al (2021) distinguished early pioneers from niche entrepreneurs and boundary spanners and, further, from intermediate or facilitating agents. Each will have their own distinctive set of incentives and criteria for success, although viability is always a requirement.

Experiences of cooperatives: housing cooperatives

Housing has proved a fruitful area for using the cooperative form. Here the emphasis is on using cooperatives to provide housing services and manage residential properties; Chapter 6 looks at the role of community land trusts in developing new housing. Ganapati (2010) suggested that part of the reason for the growth of housing cooperatives lies in the values associated with building a community and utilising collective management. He also acknowledged that there has been an impact from the withdrawal of the public sector from housing provision, under conditions of fiscal austerity and the ideology of neoliberalism. In some countries, the public sector has failed to engage at all with the need to provide housing outside market processes. In these circumstances, community groups and non-governmental organisations have looked to housing cooperatives to fill the gap in adequate and affordable provision that has arisen.

In her study of housing cooperatives in Washington DC, US, Huron (2018) provided an account of the issues involved in establishing and maintaining a joint housing venture based on the limited equity cooperative model. In this model, the cooperative owns the building and site, and occupiers may either own a variable share of the equity or only rent their apartment and pay a fee to the cooperative for management and maintenance. Huron saw the creation and maintenance of a housing cooperative as an act of commoning, putting the emphasis on the dynamics of cooperatives and their operation (see Chapter 10 for further discussion of commoning).

The decision to create a housing cooperative often arises from a crisis, as when the private property owners wish to evict tenants and sell on for redevelopment. Not only does the moment of crisis create the impetus for change but it also has a strong effect in changing the collective action problem that can otherwise inhibit a group of people from acting together. In such a crisis, the costs of not acting collectively are significant and clearly apparent, and this outweighs the costs of active participation. That said, the work that a cooperative demands is extensive. Huron (2018) detailed this in relation to setting up a cooperative, in this case enabling tenants to take over their existing rental properties. The tasks included: form a tenants' association; find a lawyer; find financing from public and private sources; select a developer; form a cooperative association and write corporate by-laws; make seemingly endless decisions about the renovation; draw up house rules; search for new members; and so on.

Huron drew on Elinor Ostrom's (2007) work on common property regimes. While these were devised largely for rural contexts and environmental resources, Huron (2018) argued that Ostrom's requirements for an institution that can successfully manage a common pool resource were also applicable to urban contexts, such as cooperatively owned and managed housing. These included the presence of clearly defined boundaries alongside rules that are well matched to the local context. Affected individuals should be able to participate in making and changing the rules, and external authorities must respect the right of community members to draw up these rules. A system for self-monitoring community members' behaviour in relation to these rules should be in place alongside a system of sanctions. Access to low-cost conflict-resolution mechanisms should be available. All aspects of appropriation, provision, monitoring, sanctioning, conflict resolution and other aspects of governance should be organised in a nested structure, with each activity occurring at the appropriate level.

The significance of Huron's work is that she highlights the challenges and tensions involved in such cooperative commoning, as well as the benefits. The more obvious benefits are the provision of affordable and stable housing. There is the possibility of some limited accumulation of wealth but, while many emphasise the purpose of property ownership as being to realise value through sale on the open market, cooperative members seem, rather, to be motivated by the control that this gives them over their home. This control is three-fold: control over the physical space of the building; control over decision making; and control over others in the building through creating and enforcing rules of behaviour. The last point can considerably increase the quality of life for occupants in a well-run housing cooperative.

This control also enables the occupants to improve the housing units (which are often in a highly dilapidated state by the time they are converted into cooperative ownership). Such improvement, combined with the price caps that cooperatives exercise, breaks the relationship between price and housing quality that is assumed by the private market, in that cheaper housing is assumed necessarily, and indeed rightly, to be of poorer quality. More generally, involvement seems to enable improvements in people's own lives. The provision of affordable housing enables occupiers to divert energies into other aspects of their lives and even experiment with how they might live. The release from financial anxiety and the pressures to earn enough to pay the rent enables cooperative members to work less, to spend more on their family and to make personal decisions in a new way.

Finally, the cooperative can create the sense of community, closely linked to the opportunity for participation in self-governance of the housing. Interestingly, while it may be assumed that the community pre-exists the cooperative, Huron (2018) showed that the collective work involved in creating the cooperative at minimum reinforces the community and may even create the community where none existed before (see Chapter 7 for more discussion of community). The commons of the cooperative housing shapes the community, just as the community shapes the cooperative.

Turning to the challenges, Huron (2018) listed: financial challenges; the often-difficult question of whom to include and whom to exclude; the challenges of working collectively; and the temptation that can exist of dissolving the cooperative in favour of a market-rate ownership structure and the apparent (but sometimes illusory) benefit of realising cash. The financial challenges included keeping a viable cashflow for the cooperative and managing arrears that may arise. In addition, reconfiguring the physical layout to be more suitable for the occupants often resulted in fewer but bigger and better laid-out housing units, which might reduce the total rental and fee income into the cooperative. Then there was the periodic maintenance and upgrading that would be required, the finance for which may be limited by an over-enthusiasm for keeping rents and fees low. Ultimately this may imperil the finances of the cooperative.

The question of deciding access to the cooperative highlights Ostrom's point that all commons have a boundary. In some of Huron's cases there was a tendency towards allowing residents' relatives to take up new vacancies. This was seen to build trust within the community but could also result in an upward pressure in terms of occupants' income. Building a stronger, more bonded community could reduce the extent to which the housing cooperative was meeting housing need. Such decisions are just one aspect of the day-to-day work of maintaining a cooperative, which can be tedious and onerous. Huron (2018: p 111) described this as 'the low-level, continuous work of maintaining their commons for the long haul'. It is also highly communicative work, and communication takes time and patience (p 122). Researchers seem to agree that women bear a disproportionate share of such work, and often do not get the recognition that this deserves. Again, the domestic domain is assumed to be the realm of women's work.

Huron usefully emphasised that the decision to establish and run a housing cooperative may be a pragmatic one rather than part of an ideological project. To quote her (p 155):

> Commoning, my research shows, is a rational choice often made by people with a relatively narrow range of choices: people without access to capital, for whom capitalism is not working. Ultimately, if we understand the commons for what I argue it really is – a pragmatic practice to be pursued, within and between and against capitalist practices – then we can be quite hopeful about building postcapitalist

worlds. Because these worlds are already being built all around us right now, out of necessity.

Focus on the cooperative movement in Sweden

Sweden provides a good case study because it has a long history of a comparatively strong cooperative sector, operating across producer, retailer and consumer sectors, as well as in housing, where it encompasses both new development and ongoing management. Each of these will be reviewed before drawing out some common threads.

In terms of context, it is worthwhile noting that Sweden is a relatively small country with a population of just over 10 million. It industrialised relatively late for Europe, but thereafter it developed very rapidly, shifting from an economy heavily based on agriculture, often organised around family farms and with limited exports, to one that had a strong engineering sector and was increasingly oriented towards external markets. This was not completely interrupted by the two world wars, where Sweden remained apart from the conflicts, largely avoiding destruction of its cities and infrastructure and (controversially) maintaining international trade, including with Nazi Germany. Per capita national income (as measured by conventional monetary metrics) grew so that Sweden became one of the wealthiest countries in the world, a sharp contrast to the 18th/19th centuries, when famine drove a massive exodus of the population, largely to North America.

But Sweden has also been notable for its social democratic politics and its apparent ability to score highly in the 'happiness stakes'. The rapid industrialisation of the later 19th century and early 20th century led to a growing working class which was effectively organised into trades unions. These gained political leverage through the franchise, and the result was a compromise between the industrial classes and organised labour at the expense of landed interests, under the banner of social democracy. Such landed interests had been in long-term decline since Sweden ceased to be an imperial power from the early 19th century. Social democratic politics have dominated Swedish government until around 1990. It produced the so-called Nordic model in which relatively high taxation funded an extensive welfare state. This went with social norms oriented towards equality, particularly gender equality, and aligned with broad cultural norms of favouring homogeneity, avoiding exceptionalism, seeking sufficiency and avoiding conflict.

The result has, at least during the postwar period, been impressive in terms of avoiding extremes of inequality alongside poverty and providing high levels of public service provision. This has gone with a political culture that emphasises local autonomy and the expression of social capital within communities. However, since 2000 there has been a notable rightwards shift in Swedish politics, with growing neoliberal tendencies in public policies that have reduced support for the welfare state and expanded the involvement of the private sector in traditional public sector-led activities. Alongside this, there have been stubborn difficulties in responding to the generous in-migration that the Swedish government permitted in the wake of the 2015 Syrian crisis. While taking many more migrants per capita than any other European country, the Swedish government and society failed to achieve integration, so that unemployment, lower income levels and poorer housing conditions persist within these migrant communities. This has been associated with some (relatively contained) urban unrest, but, more worryingly, also with the growing penetration of gang culture and associated violence as well as increased electoral support for far-right parties, notably the neo-fascist Sweden Democrats.

So, in this context, how has the social democratic policy of supporting cooperatives fared? The Swedish Institute (1983) define a cooperative enterprise as having a direct connection to both the needs and interests of its members, and these members – who may be workers, customers, suppliers or residents – are actively involved in the activities of the organisation. Thus, joint action and mutual self-help are integral to a cooperative. Key principles include open membership, independence from political parties and religious denominations, democratic administration, not searching for maximum returns on investment, using capital for development and independence, engaging in educational activities and being based on cooperative teamwork.

The cooperative movement in Sweden can be dated from the mid-19th century, with the formation of the Lagunda and Hagunda district goods purchasing company, but the main wave of cooperative formation came in the 1860s and 1870s, in both the consumer and producer sectors. A significant factor enabling this was the Swedish Freedom of Commerce Decree of 1864. Also important was the ideological support of the cooperative movement by trades unions, the farmers' movement, the nonconformist churches, the temperance movement and social democratic political parties. Leadership in cooperatives often overlapped with involvement in these other movements.

The agricultural sector was an early adopter of cooperatives. A number of organisations working on behalf of groups of farmers were established in the 19th century, evolving into farmers' associations which undertook collective purchasing of supplies on behalf of their members. The first national association was formed in 1895, to be followed by others, with some subsequent consolidation in the 20th century. By the late 20th century, farmers' cooperatives had come to dominate agricultural output, supplying some 75 per cent of the total. They cover diary and meat production as well as forestry, supplies and credit. This is reflected in the medium size of members, on average cultivating about 26 hectares (64 acres) of land. It can be argued that the existence of the cooperatives enabled smaller farms to survive financially.

The advantages of being a member of a cooperative are that sales are guaranteed, prices are more stable (through management of total supply of goods) and product development and marketing is supported. The philosophy is expressed by the Federation of Swedish Farmers or LRF (Lantbrukarnas Riksförbund) in terms of aiming for higher prices, lower costs, limited interest payments on share capital, 'equal price for equal performance' and ensuring that surpluses are distributed so that no member benefits at the expense of another (Swedish Institute, 1983). The role of agricultural cooperatives is built into national agricultural policy but the hand of the state is light. Cooperatives operate within a market context, using collective buying and selling power to maximise incomes. Outside of the agricultural sector, workers cooperatives have not been widely adopted, and traditionally the trades unions have been sceptical. There was some growth though from the 1970s, mainly from small businesses which found themselves in financial difficulties and were then taken over by employees. They are not numerically significant, however.

Consumer and retailer cooperatives have, however, long been important within Sweden. Between 1896 and 1899 more than 200 consumer cooperatives were founded, and in 1899 these were organised under the banner of a national organisation, the Swedish Cooperative Union and Wholesale Society, KF (Kooperativa Förbundet). However, the early initiative for consumer cooperatives came from the local level, particularly in rural areas and small towns, where it could be difficult to obtain food and clothing and where levels of indebtedness were high. They were supported originally as a form of philanthropy but then came under the influence of the growing labour movement. The reformist as opposed to revolutionary approach of trades unions fitted with the growth of consumer cooperatives. Such cooperatives cover both goods and services; for example, insurance has been subject to cooperative provision since 1908 when Samarbete was formed, followed in 1914 by Folket. The two cooperatives companies were merged in 1925 and now trade under the name Folksam. Other examples include cooperatives for motorists, oil consumers, funerals, banking and travel.

Today, KF act as the national organisation of numerous self-governing consumer cooperatives. In the early 1980s, such cooperatives had almost 2 million members, over 20 per cent of the total Swedish population at the time. KF work with over 80 different purchasing departments, using their substantial purchasing power to get good deals for their cooperatives and hence consumers. Such deals are both national and international, sometimes involving collaboration with cooperative movements in other countries. KF have moved into food processing through mills, bakers, meat packing, brewing and canning. They also own factories that sell to local cooperatives and more generally, including even overseas; the goods involved are wide ranging and include paper, cardboard, vegetable oils and fats, sanitary and household earthenware, car tyres and plastics. Nordic cooperatives collaborate in the manufacture of chocolate too.

These consumer cooperatives are legally independent units owned by their members with very diversified retail outlets operating under various marques such as Domus, OBS and Servus. Traditionally, the trading surplus in a consumer cooperative is split between interest obligations, payments into the reserve funds and a payout to customer-members in proportion to their purchases. There have been periods of difficulty for consumer cooperatives (Böök and Ilmonen, 1989), due to the changing nature of retailing, and they have been faced with the need to change distribution practices, particularly during the 1960s and onwards, when a downturn in economic performance became apparent. The result was a greater reliance on outside finance and a loosening of bonds between members and societies.

Housing has also been a traditional focus of cooperatives in Sweden and remains so today. The first housing cooperatives were founded by workers in the 1870s as mutual building groups; that is, by pooling members' savings and loans, they sought to build new homes for members. These early experiments were often unsuccessful, sometimes making substantial losses. Many were taken over by commercial firms. The situation changed in the 1920s, when tenants' organisations were the driving force for creating new, viable housing cooperatives. The Tenants' Savings and Building Society, HSB (Hyresgästernas Sparkasse- och Byggnadsförening) was set up in 1923 in Stockholm, with a national organisation following the next year. Key factors in establishing the cooperative form for housing provision were the impact of the abolition of rent control in 1923 and progressive ideas about good housing for workers, including items such as bathrooms, nurseries, common laundry facilities and modern refuse collection (Bengtsson, 1992). HSB continues to be influential today, alongside The Cooperative Housing Organisation of Trades Unions, Riksbyggen, which was founded in 1940. In the late 1980s HSB comprised some 3,000 cooperative housing associations with nearly 400,000 members of which two-thirds were in HSB accommodation and the rest on waiting lists. Riksbyggen comprised over 1,000 associations providing accommodation to over 190,000 households.

These housing cooperatives (Bengtsson, 1992) provide both one-family houses and multi-household flats in apartment blocks, as well as day care centres, schools and shopping centres. Members hold a standardised lease which provides indefinite rights of abode for households but with joint ownership and management of the housing estate or block. The tenant-owner cooperative or TOC owns the whole estate, with households as members and owners of their own subsidiary property right. Members buy their property right, known as a *bostadsrätt*, with a mix of down-payment and a share of the loan for the whole development. HSB administers its own savings bank, which provides loans, while Riksbyggen has agreements with local savings banks. Members regularly repay their share of the loan for development and of ongoing operating expenses. They have the democratic right to be involved in management decisions and can sell their cooperative leases at a market rate. In addition to TOCs organised within HSB or Riksbyggen, there are some independent housing cooperatives which are quite heterogeneous.

Bengtsson (1992) has analysed the relative success of housing cooperatives in Sweden where one sixth of all Swedish dwellings are cooperatively owned. The majority of these are in multi-householder apartment blocks, largely because, for a long time, owner-occupation in such housing units was prohibited by law (owner-occupied flats were legalised in 2009). By contrast, the Tenant-Owner Act of 1930 established a common tenure pattern for cooperatives. This established a strong institutional context for supporting TOCs as the dominant cooperative form and downplaying rental cooperatives, where policy support was provisional and both the legislative framework and financial arrangements were not supportive. Just as with central government agricultural policy, cooperatives were recognised within post-war Social Democrat housing policy, alongside public rental housing. Within the Million Programme of 1965–74 (which saw 1 million new homes built), 160,000 of these were within cooperatives. Local councils also often support cooperatives with land or loans. Indeed, Sweden adopts an official guideline of 'tenure neutrality' in relation to housing finance and taxation.

Over time, however, there have been shifts which are pushing housing cooperatives closer to market housing. In the 1980s, banks and other financial institutions started to accept a TOC certificate as collateral for long-term loans, thus widening the sources of finance available to cooperative members. The negative side-effect of this has been a significant increase in prices for cooperative developments (Bengtsson, 1992). Similarly, transfer control has been largely abandoned. Transfer control refers to control by the housing cooperative over the sale of tenant-owner rights to favour those on waiting lists, focus on households in need and/or to prevent price speculation. From 1969, HSB permitted market transfers, Riksbyggen having already made this decision. Thus, from the 1980s, prices in cooperative housing rose and pushed many lower-income households out of this sector, particularly in the larger cities. As a result, cooperative housing has become increasingly middle-class, although Bengtsson (1992) argued that HSB was never really a working-class organisation.

In a later paper with Sørvoll (Sørvoll and Bengtsson, 2018), Bengtsson argued that housing cooperatives shifted to being more market oriented and profit seeking in the post-war period of the 20th century. This was due to the operation of two logics. On the one hand, there was a logic of conflicting members' interests, which diluted the idea of the cooperative as serving a collective interest; on the other, there was the logic of competition and growth in which housing cooperative organisations saw themselves as competing with other housing providers and sought to increase the scale of their operations. The shift was most apparent in the 1980s and 1990s, when the housing cooperative sector moved decisively away from relying on the local and national state and instead became more enmeshed in market dynamics. The legalisation of owner-occupied flats in 2009, putting them on a par with single-family houses, further spurred this on.

An earlier study by Vogel et al (2016) reached a similar conclusion. They found that almost all housing cooperative developments were now initiated by commercial developers rather than members and that these developers control most aspects of the 'interim' phase of planning and production. This includes building design, building performance and building-related resource use. The transfer to the long-term building owners occurs only after planning and production is completed and then the developer steps back completely. This means that the developer has no incentive to secure quality in the built-in systems and ensure their performance over the building's lifetime; this includes energy efficiency and carbon reductions. Vogel et al pointed to poor energy efficiency and problems of indoor mould as a result. This means that regulatory control of such features is essential to ensure residents' health and environmental sustainability.

Vogel et al (2016) proposed a number of governance changes to remedy these problems. First, members should be empowered in the design stage and not just involved in management. Second, the types of companies that can be involved in cooperative housing development should be restricted to those that can demonstrate a longer-term perspective. Third, there should be a representative of the cooperative association in the board that governs the interim stage of planning and production. Finally, the information made available to potential residents about the technical aspects of the housing should be widened and there should be at least five-yearly monitoring of the technical systems and operating costs of the built stock.

The role of planning in the social economy

This discussion of cooperatives has highlighted a number of features. Taking worker cooperatives first, they clearly operate with a strong value set oriented towards worker democracy and, thereby, protection of livelihoods and living standards for employed workers. However, that said, they are not that distinct from other market-based firms. They have to respond to market pressures for the goods and services that they produce, and, in some cases, this has led to internationalisation and growth. The relevant distinction here is not between market-based firms and cooperatives, it seems, but, rather, between small and locally embedded providers of goods and services for profit, on the one hand, and firms or cooperatives which respond to an international market and seek growth accordingly.

Customer cooperatives exist largely to ensure that a range of goods and services are provided in areas that might be otherwise under-supplied and to keep the costs of such goods and services down. This clearly contributes to social sustainability, including of areas that exhibit low market demand for reasons of depopulation or low household incomes. Where customer cooperatives grow to serve a wider market, then they become less distinguished from other retailers and could come under organisational pressure to expand their scope and to encourage greater levels of consumption. Housing cooperatives are often relatively small in scale, as they link local communities with a specific stock of housing. However, as the Swedish example shows, they can also grow in scale. Given that they meet an essential need on an ongoing basis rather than being concerned with speculative housing development, growth here is not necessarily a problem.

This suggests that cooperatives, per se, are not necessarily aligned with concerns to limit economic growth. Worker cooperatives can be impelled to grow, except insofar as they are concentrated in the small, locally embedded sector, where they are akin to the firms discussed in Chapter 4. It is interesting to note here that, in the case of Swedish agricultural cooperatives, it seems that the possibility of joining a cooperative enabled smaller farms to survive. Thus, a strong cooperative sector may support and expand the share of the smaller, locally embedded firms.

Customer cooperatives can also grow and promote consumption, but they may also be oriented towards meeting essential needs at a local scale or, in the case of housing cooperatives, potentially at a wider spatial scale. Again, this depends on the organisational motivation of the cooperative. It does seem that cooperatives are likely to contribute to social sustainability, in terms of protecting the livelihoods of workers – through security of employment, pay and working conditions – and of customers – through affordable prices and the range of supply of goods and services.

However, there has been little to suggest that cooperatives as an organisational form are well aligned with environmental sustainability. For example, there have been studies of sustainability and wine cooperatives in both Spain and Germany. Ferrer et al (2023) studied the Spanish wine sector, where cooperatives dominate. They situated their work within a European literature that suggested that cooperatives were more oriented towards the social component of sustainability than the environmental one. Through a survey of over 400 wine producers, they found that investor-owned firms (that is, not cooperatives) were more likely to engage with corporate social responsibility agendas, including reporting, to produce ecological or organic wine and to measure the carbon footprint of their activities. Ferrer et al argued that this was because investor-owned firms incorporated sustainability across the range of their activities, including marketing, human resources and finance. By contrast, cooperatives tended to see sustainability in terms of innovation, links with others in their networks and management activities. The greater average age of cooperative members was also seen as a barrier to change, which a significant shift in environmental sustainability performance would require.

Similar conclusions arose from a German study by Richter and Hanf (2021) which found that social sustainability was taken for granted by the cooperative sector but less so environmental sustainability. Again, the key barriers were the high average age of cooperative members, the problems of succession, the slow pace of decision making within cooperatives and the tendency to invest in tangible assets rather than a less tangible output such as reduced carbon footprint. A wider study by Preluca et al (2022) looked at a range of worker cooperatives in the UK, with six case studies. While involved in very different sectors, the findings were similar: the strength of cooperatives lies in the learning capacity and values that readily contribute to social sustainability, while environmental concerns such as better waste management or engaging with the circular economy were constrained by costs and relationships within the supply chain.

With this in mind, what should the role of planning be with regard to the cooperative sector? It is clear that some aspects of the support that this sector needs are not within the purview of local planning. For example, national policy and legislation can require the support and fostering of cooperatives, which clearly would set in place structural conditions for the growth of the sector. Basáñez (2019) analysed how the Spanish constitution, together with statutes at the level of the autonomous regions, encourages the cooperative sector through a fairly general formulation advising more participation in company decision making and greater facilitation of access to the means of production by workers. This is contrasted with the situation in Italy, where a tighter connection between the mutualist organisational form and promotion of cooperatives is more constraining. Ganapati (2010) made it clear that national policy structures can influence the extent to which the cooperative sector is supported.

Furthermore, many of the factors that shape the success of a cooperative once founded are internal to that organisation. These include management capacity, governance capacity and the ability to access markets. A variety of training needs emerge, including with regard to finance and marketing (see, for example, Ibourk and El Aynaoui, 2023). The local state can provide a facilitative context, if it wishes to, although this is not assured, as Bianchi (2022) discussed. He showed how the state can play various roles in relation to social enterprise: it can be antagonistic, co-optative or supportive and has been found to move between these roles even with regard to one cooperative organisation.

For cooperative enterprise to be effective, the social economy frame needs to be accepted by a wide range of policy makers, since it requires the cooperation of governance structures (Chaves-Avila and Gallego-Bono, 2020). That this does not always happen was highlighted by Chaves-Avila and Savall-Morera (2019) in their review of the promotion of the social economy in Spain. This means that local planning needs to integrate the social economy into local economic development policy and spatial planning. In part, this is a question of making support and premises available to social enterprises and protecting the premises and sites that are already contributing to the diverse local economy. This is an extension of the planning approach suggested in Chapter 4 for smaller commercially oriented businesses.

However, the example of Preston in Lancashire, England suggests that a more pro-active approach can also be taken which puts social enterprises like cooperatives at the centre of the strategic effort. Preston has become renowned for turning its back on market-led urban regeneration after a number of failed attempts to attract inward investment. Instead, it has espoused a community wealth-building approach (Manley and Whyman, 2021; Thompson, 2023). This seeks to retain more of the wealth created through commercial means within the local economy. The starting point was procurement by public anchor institutions, such as the local authority, local hospitals, local educations institutions and so on (see also Chapter 4). By buying from local suppliers, this has strengthened the local economy through the multiplier effect of local business owners and local workers having more finance; paying the living wage was also promoted. Where possible, the emphasis has been on more of the supply chain being localised through using regional suppliers.

Another key feature of this approach has been the development of cooperative businesses to fill the gaps in this supply chain. This has been supported by community finance and the Preston Co-op Education Centre. The council have not so much developed a coherent strategy as encouraged and persuaded local actors to align themselves with their objectives. Local anchor institutions have been urged to support the development of cooperatives in Preston. The council have also adopted an open-minded attitude to the use of council buildings, and this could help cooperatives at important early points in their development.

This Preston 'model' is not a model, according to Manley and Whyman (2021), but, rather, a 'hotchpotch' of initiatives backed by a desire for proactive and positive change. The action of the local council, notably its leadership, has been the expression of this desire. Thereafter, the aim is that communities of stakeholders will self-organise through communities of place, interest and practice. They can articulate the need for local anchor institutions to act with the locality in mind, through emphasising that they have sunk capital into the area, are not spatially mobile and thus are unlikely to relocate. They therefore need the locality to thrive. The council also has a direct financial role to play in that it can support financing for cooperative development by using a proportion of its pension fund. In the longer term, a regional bank is proposed that would expand cooperative support finance. However, Thompson (2023) emphasised that the nature of Preston City Council as a second-tier local authority under Lancashire County Council gave it limited powers, budget and remit within the English local government system. It therefore has to rely mainly on anchor institutions and persuasion of partners to enact its approach.

That this can fit within a place-making approach is shown by Webster et al's (2021) research into cases in Italy, the US and England. Here, the Roman and Bolognese cases were linked to social infrastructure and are thus more relevant to the discussion of community assets in Chapter 7, but the Cincinnati Union Co-operative Initiative (CUCI or Co-Op Cincy) in the US sought to bring together union solidarity with cooperative governance. The combination of outreach, and use and creation of social capital, alongside fostering a positive business culture, operationalising networks and generating income, were seen to lead to wider change within the city. In effect, the cooperatives (and unions) became the springboard for urban change through their distinctive working practices, married with an outward-facing approach.

The Rochdale case in England saw the history of cooperatives (see earlier) in the town being leveraged through the Rochdale Stronger Together Initiative. As in Shildon (see Chapter 4), the Rochdale Pioneers Museum and the Co-operative Heritage Trust were used to mobilise a strong sense of local identity in pursuit of urban change. In part, this worked by building networks through cross-stakeholder partnership in projects and using the Rochdale Borough Social Enterprise and Co-operative Forum to make links to the voluntary sector. But there were also planning-specific actions involved, such as the designation of a Heritage Action Zone and the development of housing in the town centre using the Co-operative Forum. Empty premises were used as interim spaces for emerging cooperatives and the Co-operative Development Hub sought to encourage young people to consider creating cooperatives. The overall aim was to use a mix of resources – the built environment as permitted by planning regulation; heritage including as designated by local planning; and network-building as fostered by local planning – to encourage innovation towards a more diverse economy in Rochdale.

Thus, local planning can contribute to the role of cooperatives within the social economy and diverse economies more generally by focusing on place, leveraging heritage and local identity and ensuring that space is utilised so as to build local economic linkages, which will involve provision of affordable and appropriate premises and locations for building connections between cooperatives and with local firms and institutions.

6

Housing development and community land trusts

Introduction

Housing is a basic human right, and yet, in places across the world there are many who do not have access to habitation of a decent quality. Planning systems have come to play a particular role in the stories about why there are enduring housing crises. They are blamed for delays and failures to release land for new construction and for regulating inappropriately. Paradoxically, planning regulation is seen as being both too stringent and deterring development, but also too lenient and allowing substandard and even unsafe housing to be built. This narrative is situated within the assumed frame of the dominance of market-led housing and the problem is seen as lying in the relationship of planning systems to private sector development. This chapter begins by unpicking this narrative and showing how it is situated within prevailing neoliberal tendencies concerning planning. This opens up the opportunity to consider alternative approaches to housing provision that are community based. In particular the chapter will focus on community land trusts (CLTs), a model that has global application, with an extended discussion of CLT-Brussels.

The dominant narrative of housing and the market

In a market-based economy, housing provision is predominantly left to the private sector. Simply put, this means that private sector companies are responsible for finding and buying sites for development and for organising the construction process. The resultant housing may be sold to landlords who let the property to tenants or to an owner-occupier. Rents and house prices will be set by the market. The problems with relying on the private sector in this way have long been apparent. The private sector tends to provide housing where it is profitable to do so and to favour more over less profitable ventures. This has, over time and over space, led to lower-income groups or groups with unstable livelihoods being unable to find affordable housing. Sometimes such groups fall into the unregulated and informal sectors, where the standard of housing is low and security of tenure is uncertain, or they are homeless, a category that covers the range from street-living to sofa-surfing.

The problems of an inability to find a decent home at an affordable rent or price are evident in many towns and cities. One historic solution has been to bring in the public sector to provide housing instead of relying on the market. The 20th century in particular saw waves of public sector housebuilding in many countries, and in communist countries, of course, public housing was the norm. However, in the 21st century the advance of neoliberal thinking and the movement of many formerly communist countries in Eastern Europe and Asia towards espousing private ownership of housing has meant that public housing has become a much less favoured tenure. In the UK, for example, public housing was sold off to tenants at substantial discounts or transferred to separate organisations for management. New housing at 'affordable' rates (often not that much discounted on market rates) is largely provided by private developers, sometimes in partnership with housing associations, and the share of such 'affordable' housing is highly dependent on the profitability of the private market-led housing that is being built under growth-dependent planning.

What is the role of the planning system in a context of greater reliance on the private sector to deliver housing for all? Planning systems usually have a degree of responsibility for identifying the location of housebuilding sites and/or regulating housing construction. Neoliberal ideology has come to frame the ways in which planning systems perform these responsibilities. In particular, there has been widespread critique of planning processes as constraining the supply of land for housebuilding and/or raising the costs of such building through regulatory demands (Monk et al, 1996; Ball et al, 2022). This has been seen as a cause of the high costs and limited availability of housing for all social groups. The solution becomes framed as the allocation of more land for housing, the issuing of more development permits and the relaxation of regulatory requirements. Planning is the problem, and less planning is the solution.

Furthermore, planners are encouraged to work with private sector actors such as landowners and developers. The identification of sites for development often falls to these actors, rather than planners determining which are the best locations from a strategic perspective, taking into account infrastructure provision and investment and relationships to other land uses in the vicinity and across the urban area. In some countries, developers can be the authors of plans for new development. In the UK, planners become embroiled in lengthy discussions and obscure calculations apparently designed to determine whether enough land has been allocated for the development sector over a given period of time and to ensure that expectations for the numbers of houses to be built are met (Layard, 2019; Rydin, 2021).

New housebuilding does not necessarily imply spatial growth. It depends on the impact on overall urban population, where the development takes place and at what density. However, often new housing is on land that has not been previously developed and/or occurs at higher densities. Both of these features usually increase development profits by increasing the total development value and/or lowering costs. As a result, the urban area grows and/or becomes more dense and urban population increases. Similarly, new housebuilding does not need to imply economic growth. If the development sector maintains a steady level for the value of economic activity, then there is no growth. However, again, there are commercial pressures to increase company turnover as well as profit and share prices, and this necessitates a push towards increasing development activity.

Thus, the narrative that planning systems should enable more housebuilding in order to resolve current housing crises typically does feed into urban growth and economic growth agendas. This is despite the fact that there is little evidence that this helps solve the problems of housing availability and affordability, particularly for lower-income groups with limited purchasing power in the marketplace and in areas where market conditions render new housebuilding less profitable. In this context it is appropriate to consider the role that alternative modes of provision can play. This chapter considers the work of community land trusts, both an umbrella term and also a rather specific form of social enterprise. As will be seen, their value lies in the way that they breaks the link between occupying and owning a stake in one's own home and the increase in development value that arises from urbanisation in an area.

Definitions of community land trusts

The ideological antecedents of community land trusts (CLTs) are varied. Among those cited by researchers are Henry George and his views on landownership and value accumulation, Ruskin's idea of a Guild of St George, the garden city movement in England which was based on ownership of the land by a trust, *Gramdan* in India, *kibbutz* in Israel, *ejido* in Mexcio and *Ujamaa Vijini* in Tanzania. Within current forms of community-based housing, Vestbro and Horelli (2012) distinguish: co-housing, where different households share at least common facilities; collaborative housing, where a group come together to build housing units; collective housing, where the group own the overall housing ensemble in common; communal housing, where different households live together; a commune, which typically covers more than housing and has a strong ideological component; and cooperative housing, which takes the specific legal form of a cooperative.

Bunce and Aslam (2016) clarify that CLTs are non-profit, non-governmental organisations (NGOs) that own the title to land and make decisions about its uses through membership-based representation for the purpose of long-term stewardship. They suggest that there are four key aspects. First, land is viewed as a common socio-cultural and ecological heritage rather than as based in individual rights. Second, this land is permanently removed from land speculation through restrictions on resale. Third, the title to the land is held by the NGO (the trust) and only the building is owned or leased by residents. Fourth, ground leases are a central component and form a contract between the homeowner or tenant and the CLT.

Thus, the defining feature of a CLT is that the ownership of land and building is split. The land is held collectively and permanently by the CLT in trust for the future and the benefit of the community. The building – a house or set of apartments – is owned separately through a leasehold, either by a landlord who then rents it out or by an occupier. The landlord or the owner–occupier thus owns a property interest. This has the potential to accumulate in value over time, but either the resale value is restricted or the interest has to be sold back to the CLT. This ensures that housing remains affordable and does not simply move into the private market on first resale, to accumulate at the full market rate. CLTs differ from other forms of shared ownership in that there is this separation of ownership of the land and of the building. This affects how increments in the overall asset value are shared between the trust and the individual resident. Usually the resident, where they own a right in the building as opposed to just renting it, takes a relatively small share of increments. This contrasts with shared ownership, say, where the housing organisation and the resident split the total value of the housing unit in set proportions and share in the increment in value according to those proportions.

Cahen et al (2022) have argued that CLTs are more than a way of distributing property, providing housing and sharing increments in asset value. They see CLTs as centrally involved in matters of care, for people and for place. These relationships of care are related to the collective nature of part of the ownership, and this differentiates CLTs in a further way from shared equity models, say. Partly that care relates to looking after the physical environment of the CLT (see also the case later in Puerto Rico) and partly it relates to the ways in which CLTs support residents through education, training, advice, repairs and help in times of difficulty. That said, it is possible to overemphasise the sense of community within a CLT. Kruger et al (2020) have studied this and actually found relatively little contact between existing residents within CLTs. Rather, there are stronger contacts between residents and the officers of the CLTs and, interestingly, a sense of connection with future residents, through the perpetuity of collective landownership and a sense of stewardship.

Experiences of community land trusts

CLTs in the US

While there are variety of conceptual roots that can be delineated for the CLT concept, it is generally accepted that, as a practical model for delivering housing, the first examples can be found in the US. The first example (Meehan 2014) was in a rural location and concerned a project enabling African American farmers to access productive land; this was in Albany, Georgia in 1969. Thereafter, the CLT model was mainly found in urban areas. While they can encompass mixed-use development, they have become more housing focused. DeFilippis et al (2018) saw the rise in the importance of CLTs in the US as linked to the decline in support for community development from the 1980s, particularly at the federal level, and the resulting orientation of organisations such as community development corporations towards development based on commercial grounds. That said, CLTs in the US have also become increasingly professionalised, aiming for measurable outcomes rather than any broader political agenda.

DeFilippis et al (2018) found five reasons for the shift from a more politicised agenda around community control to housing delivery. First, the CLTs themselves had mission statements focused on affordable housing delivery; second, this was reinforced by the attitudes of CLT practitioners. Third, a growing number of CLTs were operating over larger geographical areas and moving beyond the scale of the neighbourhood, with the tight community ties which that might imply. Fourth, CLTs were increasingly situated within elite-driven and technocratic housing policies driven by local government. Finally, CLTs had become a sector represented by advocates and researchers, rather than the communities themselves. Since 2007, this has been accelerated by incorporation of the National CLT Network in the US into the Cornerstone Partnership, set up by the Ford Foundation to promote affordable housing. These two organisations merged in 2016 to form the Grounded Solutions Network. The housing provision focus has meant that CLTs are promoted on the basis of delivery alongside the potential individual wealth creation and avoidance of foreclosure, but also opening up the possibility of transitioning to standard fee simple ownership. This downplays both the possibility of non-housing land uses within CLT projects and their role in community empowerment.

Williams (2018) provides a case study of the Rondo CLT in St Paul, Minneapolis. This provides 34 affordable senior housing units, but it also includes 9,300 sq ft of affordable commercial space. Interestingly, to enable communities to access this space, the CLT provides entrepreneurship classes also. For Williams (2018), the essence of a CLT was seen as the interaction between two factors. First, there had to be a place-based population with the will to operate collectively, often arising from a history of threats of displacement and of local gentrification. Second, that needed to mesh with an institutional arrangement with authority over the shared resource of land. Leadership had to be created to represent the wider community. Williams identified three tensions in the ongoing operation of a CLT. First, there was the need for skilled professional support and how that meshed with the democratic involvement of the community in decision making. Second, there was the tendency to pursue organisational and geographical growth rather than remaining rooted in a locality, with consequent attention to local need. Third, there was the necessity of relying on external funders, which could act as a constraint on other activities, particularly those involved in political mobilisation.

The Dudley Street Neighbourhood Initiative (DSNI) in Boston, Massachusetss, is another widely studied CLT, which has operated since the 1980s. Engelsman et al (2018) detailed how this CLT was located in a redlined neighbourhood, where banks refused to approve mortgage loans. There had been deindustrialisation and disinvestment in public services, with landlord–initiated arson being common. In this context the DSNI was established. Dudley Street is unusual, in that it was granted the power of eminent domain or compulsory purchase in order to access the land, as compared to the more usual routes of donation or market purchase (Meehan, 2014). Perhaps because of the legal complexities of this, it took a long time to establish the CLT and there were fears that a decline in the general housing market might undermine interest in the units that the CLT would provide. The way in which the DSNI limited the increase in housing unit prices was by constraining resale prices to no more than 5 per cent over ten years, a limitation that directly challenged the idea that house prices should keep pace with inflation or even accumulate in real terms (Meehan, 2014). Over 1994 to 2008, Dudley Neighbours Inc built 207 homes within the CLT framework (Engelsman et al, 2018).

Engelsman et al (2018) also contrasted Dudley Street with Cooper Square, New York, finding some key differences that highlight variety within the CLT sector. Cooper Square was based in an area with a history of working-class activism and resistance to proposed development plans. As far back as 1959, residents set up a Cooper Square Committee to represent the community and used this to draw up a community-based plan which was adopted in 1970; by 1984 the first housing under this plan was built. Two years later a revised plan for an urban renewal area was proposed and, under Mayor Dinkum, CLTs became a key focus. In 2015 the Cooper Square Mutual Housing Association was established, over time coming to manage 377 residential units in total.

Looking at six CLTs across the US (Burlington, Boston, Durham, Athens, Portland and Minneapolis), Lowe and Thaden (2016) examined how their activities contributed to broader societal transformation. Interestingly, all the CLTs provided – in addition to the core housing provision – homeowner education, review and approval of loans, support with home repairs and financial counselling. Champlain Housing Trust in Burlington, Vermont also provided a senior and childcare centre, while Athens Land Trust in Georgia included urban agricultural projects and explicitly sought to foster intergenerational interaction. Lowe and Thaden argued that there did not need to be an explicit political attempt to disrupt neoliberalism but, rather, that challenges could arise from the interaction between residential betterment for a disadvantaged community, the exercise of community control of land and the way that the CLT preserved assets in an area. The strategic implementation of stewardship practices by the CLT could in itself challenge the dominance of the conventional housing market. However, strong community engagement was needed for all these aspects to operate and such engagement depended to a great extent on the local political environment. It also helped if there was recognition of the residents' life cycle, and that people would move in and out of deeper engagement with the CLT project.

This research was a response to the argument put forward by DeFilippis et al (2019), that most CLTs are not engaged in transformative political action but are, rather, 'affirmative', to use Fraser's term (1995) term. Studying CLTs in Minnesota which were oriented towards providing owner-occupation opportunities, DeFilippis et al (2019) found that members often resisted seeing CLTs as political but, rather, saw them as providers of affordable housing. This partly arose from the emphasis of funders on provision of housing units and efficiency in such provision. The most important dimension of a CLT was that it retained subsidy within the scheme by keeping housing affordable and limiting asset accumulation. But DeFilippis et al (2019) did see that access to home ownership within a CLT structure could be transformative for certain groups, and First Nations were cited here in the North American context.

A study of a CLT in Minneapolis (Hackett et al, 2019) found that involvement in the CLT gave residents a more secure housing tenure, and Hackett et al reference research on how CLT members experience less foreclosure and less financial distress, while benefiting from modest wealth accumulation at low risk. This housing security also contributed to a deeper sense of ontological security, thereby opening up a greater range of life possibilities than previously considered. Part of this is due to the additional services that a CLT may provide, such as education and personal support; together this creates a culture of security within a CLT. There is also the sense that members are part of something bigger, of a group. The values this gives rise to are captured as autonomy, responsibility and control.

Finally, Kim and Eisnelohr (2022) provided a case study in Rolland Curtis Garden, Los Angeles. This was a high-price neighbourhood and the CLT was seen as a way of protecting a site for low-income households – a more effective way than the prevailing use of affordability covenants that limit prices, but only for a period of time, with the potential to create an affordability crisis when covenants run out, whereas the CLT offered a solution in perpetuity. This example needed legislative change to permit mortgage financing on CLT properties. The research identified the depth of collaboration that was needed between the CLT and a professional affordable housing developer, each bringing different resources to the scheme. The developer understood the finances of residential development, while the CLT could generate meaningful community engagement.

CLTs in the UK

CLTs have become increasingly popular within the UK. Collective housing organisations can take a variety of forms, including a company limited by guarantee, a community interest company (CIC) or a community benefit company (BenCom), but these do not provide the asset lock that a CLT does; that is, the CLT preserves the ownership of the land into the future. CLTs tend not to develop land themselves but, rather, often collaborate with housing associations or developers, requiring forms of governance that go across these different organisations.

Moore (2021) looked at eight CLTs in England and explored the relationship to place attachment. They found that the motivations for forming a CLT were 'clearly grounded in a desire to maintain and preserve a sense of place expressed through the affective bonds and social ties of community members' (p 25). Moore argued that a successful CLT needs to be *of* place and not just *in* that place. Thus, the CLT here was going beyond a focus on housing provision, but still concerned with the local community-in-place, not a broader political agenda. This does not mean, however, that the CLT model is not implicated in giving local residents more control over planning housing in their locality. Furthermore, the ties of place attachment are sometimes mobilised to access resources, such as access to land or support from professionals.

The East London CLT in Mile End, Tower Hamlets has become well known as a London example (Bunce, 2016). Again, the focus here is on ensuring access to affordable housing in an increasingly expensive part of the city. Due to the nature of the local land market, the main difficulty was acquiring the land. Thus, the CLT was first established as a campaigning organisation to access land. The East London Communities Organisation, TELCO, was formed in 1994 as part of the umbrella organisation London Citizens. London Citizens was involved in discussions of how to ensure affordable housing as part of the legacy of the 2012 Olympic Games in London. They were asked by the Olympic Delivery Agency and the London Development Authority (a London-wide regeneration agency under the guidance of the Mayor of London) to initiate a CLT pilot project outside the Olympic Park to test it out. Their request for a donation of land from the London Development Agency in Bow was refused, although the local council was in favour. This led to the formation of the East London CLT in 2007 to lobby for a suitable site.

In 2008, East London CLT decided to aim for the old St Clement's Hospital site which was now owned by the Homes and Communities Agency, a national body aimed at providing affordable housing. Unfortunately, the Homes and Communities Agency wanted to sell the site at market price through public tender to raise funds. The East London CLT asked the Mayor of London, then Boris Johnson, to intervene and he required the Homes and Communities Agency to include community landownership and affordable housing provision within the evaluation criteria for the bids for the land. Jenny Jones, the Chair of the Planning and Housing Committee of the Greater London Authority (and a Green Party representative) also lobbied strongly in favour of the CLT getting the land. East London CLT entered into a partnership with a developer, Igloo Regeneration, and a housing association, Poplar Harca, and together they put in two bids during 2011.

In July 2012, it was learned that East London CLT's bid had been rejected in favour of one by the developer Galliford Try. However, the London mayor asked the developer and the CLT to work together with a view to providing affordable housing for rent through a housing association (the Peabody Trust), with the CLT managing 23 housing units for affordable ownership. This was a much smaller scheme than originally envisaged, where Igloo would have built up to 300 housing units with a proportion sold to the CLT. The current organisational form of the CLT follows the tripartite structure common in US examples. One third of the board members are residents, one third are civil society organisation representatives and one third are public officials. In addition, £1 buys lifetime membership of the Trust for East London residents more broadly.

Liverpool's experience of CLTs is grounded in a history of community mobilisation and promotion of the cooperative form of collective housing provision (Thompson, 2020). In 1974 in England, funding for social housing was increased and cooperatives became eligible. In Liverpool, Co-operative Development Services supported local cooperatives in bidding for this money.

This led to a short-lived cooperative housing movement in the city – short-lived because, over 1983–87, the Trotskyist Labour local government municipalised them all. During the decade after that a neoliberal housing policy dominated in the city, with designation of housing market renewal areas where widespread demolition was encouraged in order to restructure the local private housing market. URBED, a private regeneration consultancy, sought to develop a CLT model that would work within the housing market renewal programme, but this was never implemented.

However, there were grassroots attempts to use the CLT model to resist demolition. One notable example in Liverpool was the Homebaked CLT. It combined a cooperative bakery with a range of other community support and facilities: a meeting room, a source of subsidised food, a range of therapeutic activities; and skills training. It was established as a CIC in 2012 and considered shifting to a BenCom so that community shares could be offered, thus raising finance. While these are non-residential activities, Homebaked did move into housing, with a four-bed shared flat above the bakery and subsequent plans to renovate the whole terrace.

As with social enterprises more generally, Scotland has a strong record of engaging with CLTs. Skerratt (2013) looked at 17 CLTs across Scotland and found them to be rooted in processes of positive, proactive change rather than defensive responses to external pressures. They were as much about building skills and capacity as providing specific facilities. As such, they are often much broader than just providing access to housing, covering other kinds of building, tourism, hunting and fishing rights, forestry, renewable energy and other basic infrastructure. It should be noted that in Scotland it is possible to place an occupancy condition on housing in rural areas, restricting occupancy to those with a local connection (Moore and McKee, 2014).

There has been central government support within Scotland for the growth of CLTs alongside other social enterprises (see Chapter 5). In 2000, the Scottish Land Fund provided £13.9 million to be spent over 2001–06. The Land Reform (Scotland) Act of 2003 provided opportunities for communities to register an interest in buying land through either the Community Right to Buy or the Crofting Community Right to Buy. Thereafter, the Growing Community Assets Fund provided £50 million over 2006–10, with subsequent further tranches of budget. In 2012, the Scottish Land Fund was reinstated with £6 million. All of these measures ease the central problem of being able to access and afford the land at the core of a CLT project. Subsequent policy shifts have set this in the context of a broader emphasis on community empowerment and land reform. Such support is vital, as Skerratt (2013) estimates that land purchase can take from two to seven years, putting a strain on the CLT's ability to persist over time and remain committed.

Skerratt (2013) also showed how the skills and capacities needed by CLTs vary in three key stages: before the land purchase or transfer; in the years immediately after accessing land; and over the longer term. The key strategies that Skerratt identified as important are five-fold. First, there is a need to communicate with the wider community. Second, a broad board membership is helpful. Third, there should be deliberate delegation of tasks to spread burdens and utilise capacities. Fourth, where possible, staff should be employed rather than relying entirely on volunteers, who can be subject to burnout and competing demands on their time. Fifth, there is a paramount need to identify and secure revenue streams for the CLT from rents, fees or other payments. To enable this, CLTs need to sit within multiscale networks of contacts and resources, rather than trying to go it alone. Individuals within the CLT need to connect with a variety of groups at the local level and then with contacts beyond the locality.

CLTs across the rest of the world

CLTs are now found across the world. Europe has a strong tradition of collective forms of housing provision outside of the market or the public sector (Thompson, 2020). Whereas the UK has less than 0.2 per cent of its housing stock in cooperative forms, equivalent figures elsewhere range from 5 to 8 per cent in Germany, Spain, Belgium and Austria and up to 17 per cent in Sweden. In the later discussion, the use of CLTs in Belgium is covered, but varieties of CLT can be found outside of Europe and North America too.

There is an interesting example of a CLT in Kenya, in Tanzania-Bondeni, Voi, where the model was chosen as a solution for an area of informal settlement (see Bassett, 2007 and Midheme and Moulaert, 2013). The settlement was characterised by insecure land rights and some squatting. In the 1990s, the government proposed upgrading the area. A residents' committee was elected and they chose the CLT model over two alternatives: individual titles to homes and a mix of individual titles and a cooperative. The local residents chose the CLT model as the best way to protect themselves against dispossession and loss of land to outsiders. Bassett (2007) emphasised that the adoption of the CLT approach was possibly because of the high level of trust within the community, which rendered a collective tenure feasible. In addition, the local community had a history of working together to protect themselves and there was a wider national tradition of collective self-help movements, through a philosophy known as *harambee*.

However, there was a degree of central government opposition to the CLT model. In the 1960s, after independence, the government sought to extinguish all customary property rights in favour of individual rights. The latter were seen as more in line with the programme of economic modernisation and growth that the government was pursuing. Within such an agenda, individual rights would provide security of tenure to support commercial investment. This was quite at odds with the existing residents' idea of what would give them security. The community feared that upgrading the area would result in current land-occupiers being dispossessed and displaced by middle-class land-buyers looking for speculative gains on their investment. They feared that existing poorer households would be forced into distressed sales of their land.

Adopting the CLT model was not without challenges. The legal framework and institutional design can be complex, with collaboration between multiple actors needed. Midheme and Moulaert (2013) considered that the long-term success of such a model depends on community commitment and effective leadership. In addition, the capacity of poorer households to engage financially in the CLT was enabled by the project providing construction job opportunities to existing residents, thereby offering an income, together with staggered payments and subsidised housing development loans. In addition, planning standards for construction were set at what was considered an 'appropriate' level to bring down construction costs. Finally, members of the CLT paid a fee which went towards a development fund.

In addition, the Kenyan legal system posed challenges to a collective form of ownership. It limited the number of owners in a parcel of land, limited incorporation to profit-making enterprises and had a 'rule against perpetuities' which restricted the permanent alienation of land. Furthermore, the land registry bureaucracy was used to dealing with individual titles to land and was slow to deal with any alternative. Change required two Acts of Parliament, leading to the use of two separate legal instruments to set up the CLT: the creation of the Tanzania-Bondeni Settlement society; and a trust deed with the trustees subsequently registered as a CLT. This CLT applied for a head-lease from the Commissioner of Lands and then issued subleases to members/residents. Under this arrangement, when a member of the CLT left, the CLT had a pre-emptive right to repurchase.

Over 4,000 families were provided with housing under the CLT. However, despite the requirement that members would improve their homes over time to come into line with municipal building by-laws, there were still problems of poor housing conditions in the settlement. Some 20 per cent of the original structures needed improvement at the time of Midheme and Moulaert's (2013) research. Furthermore, there remained legal challenges with the complex structures and the land administration bureaucracy remained unenthusiastic. These were being addressed by more recent changes to the constitution, law and policy in Kenya to render them more supportive of CLTs.

CLTs can also be found in Central America. Veronesi et al (2022) provided a case study of the Caño Martín Peña CLT in Puerto Rico. This concerned a settlement that was considered vulnerable to flooding risks. The CLT enabled the tenure of about 1,500 households to be regularised, which was the primary concern of residents. It enabled them to challenge proposed plans to reduce flooding risks that implied their dispossession and resettlement. The CLT regulated the resale of improved plots, limiting the transformation of a site with a low monetary use-value into a financial asset. The status of collective land as a challenge to prevailing landownership regimes was central to this case. The community lobbied for the creation of a law in 2004 to enable the creation of the CLT in the first place. In 2009 the government sought to repeal this and take the land back into their ownership, but the community fought this and won.

Meanwhile, in Australia CLTs have been found to be particularly effective in providing a form of housing for Indigenous people that meets their specific needs. Crabtree (2014b) looked at the ways that CLTs supported a difference-based policy for Indigenous groups who value home ownership for a sense of stability, autonomy, and the ability to bequeath that land to family or the kinship group. This was valued over asset accumulation and wealth creation. A CLT ensures that title and housing opportunities are retained for future generations and can also underpin the provision of spaces for commercial and social enterprises.

Focus on Community Land Trust-Brussels

Community Land Trust-Brussels (CLT-B) was created in 2012 to provide housing for lower-income households in Brussels, Belgium. It developed the first CLT project in Europe. It comprises a non-profit organisation which is charge of the daily management of the development projects and a Foundation of Public Utility, which is the landowner. CLT-B identifies with the core CLT model, seeing it as a flexible 'kit' that has four key elements.

First there is the hybrid ownership model. To allow for the horizontal division of the overall building, CLT-B use the existing legal forms available in Belgium: *droits démembrés* or *droit de superficie*, also known as property dismemberment or leasehold estates. This latter property right is of limited duration (currently 50 years) but can be renewed. A monthly lease fee is paid by the owners of the flats to CLT-B, currently around €10. CLT-B works with partners to make mortgages available to those who wish to buy. The main mortgage provider is the Brussels Housing Fund.

Second, there is the maintenance of permanent affordable prices for the homes by capping the resale price of flats. Generally, sales are permitted at only a small percentage increment over purchase prices. Alternatively, prices may be indexed or linked to average local incomes. The CLT-B website gives the formula for resale as: the initial investment by the resident *less* the costs of development *plus* 25 per cent added value *allowing for* any work performed by the resident with the knowledge of CLT-B.

Third, there is the management of the development by the community. This is achieved through the tripartite board comprising public stakeholders, project residents and members from the wider community who have paid a nominal sum for membership. Residents are also involved in the design and ongoing management of the housing projects, and community infrastructure is integrated into the design where possible to meet neighbourhood as well as residents' needs. However, some co-design processes have been very lengthy – up to seven to nine years in duration – which has led to CLT-B trying to strike a balance between community engagement and timely development. They now involve future residents at the time when planning permission is applied for, running the resident selection process at the same time. More general workshops are run as an input to the design rather than as partnerships throughout the development process; typically, this will mean three workshops before the architect is chosen and three afterwards. In addition, a community engagement plan is requested as part of the tenders for the design and build processes. Communities are also involved in the tender selection. What in the early stages was a more experimental approach to engaging with communities is now becoming more standardised.

Finally, there is the value of stewardship for the future. CLT-B combines development of new housing projects and community work with the residents. The community work comprises a variety of activities including after-school tutoring, bicycle training and job coaching. Partnership with local organisations that are embedded in the localities is central to this working well. CLT-B also plays a wider role in supporting CLTs elsewhere in Belgium, and indeed across Europe. However, in terms of environmental sustainability, the work of CLT-B relies on the regulatory frameworks set down by Brussels City Region, where energy efficiency standards for new build are close to Passivhaus levels and where a broader policy of circularity within construction processes is being promoted.

CLT-B homes cost on average 40 per cent less than market houses in the same area. About 64 per cent of residents are single-parent households. Future residents have to meet certain criteria to be considered. This includes: not being a current home owner; earning below a stipulated maximum income level; ability to service a loan through their current income; and ability to pay a deposit of around €2,000. CLT-B provides training for residents-to-be through a compulsory group where participants prepare for their purchase, learn about co-ownership and life within a CLT building and learn also about the local neighbourhood. As of 2022, the waiting list for future residents was oversubscribed and closed.

CLT-B in 2022 had five completed developments and five in the pipeline. Their features are summarised in Table 6.1.

The sites chosen for the developments are not strategically planned; rather, they arise often from happenstance, where a site becomes available. CLT-B started with a pilot project, Le Nid. Work began in 2010 on developing the plan for

Table 6.1: CLT-B developments

Verheyden – Le Nid	Completed	Anderlecht	7 flats
Mariemont – L'Écluse	Completed	Molenbeek	9 flats
Vandenpeereboom – Arc-en-Ciel	Completed	Molenbeek	32 flats
Indépendance	Completed	Molenbeek	21 flats
Calico	Completed	Forest	56 flats
Project Transvaal	In progress	Anderlecht	15 flats
Project Abbé Cuylits	In progress	Anderlecht	9 flats
Project Anvers	In progress	Schaerbeek	14 flats
Project Tivoli	In progress	Laeken	22 flats
Project Liedts	In progress	Schaerbeek	6 flats

Source: CLT-B website

redevelopment of a disused parish centre on a mixed residential/industrial road near the railway line that also backs onto a hospital. The framework for a CLT development was tried out – with funding from the Brussels City Region – but construction did not begin until 2016, with residents gaining access in 2020 to a high-quality residential development of seven flats with a common area and garden. Arc-en-Ciel was a second pilot project, begun in 2013, with ownership of the land passing to CLT-B in 2015 but construction occurring only from 2018. This project was subject to an extended co-design process that has been recorded by Aernouts (2020). The site is near a park and a metro station, set back a little from the road by a small *place*. Residents occupied the building in early 2020. Because of the delay in starting construction on these pilot projects, the first inhabited CLT development was L'Écluse, which occupies a noisy corner site next to the canal. CLT-B again received a subsidy from Brussels City Region to buy the site in 2014. Construction proceeded more rapidly, with residents taking ownership in 2016.

As can be seen from Table 6.1, the projects are generally quite small. They all incorporate community space for collective activities and an outside garden where possible; in the case of Indépendance this is on the roof space. The aim is also to include non-residential spaces for neighbourhood use. This may be small commercial spaces or space for institutional uses. Calico accommodates a birthing centre and a hospice, while Liedts includes a seniors' day centre and an office for a local NGO. In Project Transvaal, the location next to a football field will permit use by a community NGO using sport to facilitate social integration. Project Abbé Cuylits will support a self-run temporary socio-cultural centre which will run activities such as a cooking atelier, an upcycling atelier and a homeless shelter. Meanwhile, Project Anvers has a strong ecological dimension by accommodating a park warden's office for the adjacent park, funded by Brussels Environment.

CLT-B has become an exemplar in CLT development in Europe and a recognised partner in planning housing and development in the Brussels City Region. It aims to grow, although its target of 1,000 housing units remains modest within the overall Brussels housing market. It is worthwhile considering the special features that enabled CLT-B to reach this position.

First, there is the history of housing activism in the Brussels area, which had produced a rich network of housing NGOs. A number of community-based organisations formed the unofficial Ministry of Housing and signed a charter. Together with a key Green Party politician, they supported the idea of exploring the CLT framework. This was seen as plausible, given that Belgian law allowed for the ownership of land separate from the building upon it. Long-term leases allowed for rights over periods of 99 years or 50 years, with the possibility of extension. This fits also into a political background where the Socialists and Greens, who dominate the politics of Brussels, have worked together on housing and espoused a fairly similar ideological position. Housing policy is relatively progressive, partly because of the evidence of considerable housing poverty within the city and a desire to keep all social groups in the city rather than pushing them into segregated areas on the periphery.

Second, the Brussels City Region government has had devolved powers with regard to housing and a policy of supporting home ownership, a policy that CLTs fitted into. In 1997 Brussels City Region formalised the policy in the Housing Code. In 2022, CLT-B was specifically mentioned in the Housing Code, so that they are now an official social housing provider and can benefit from a reduced tax burden on their developments. This shift means that CLT-B can also broaden their involvement in housing provision. They have founded a cooperative, Fairground, that offers more flexible ways of providing housing, including through tenancies rather than ownership. Their relationship with the Social Rental Office (AIS) is important in providing a way to maintain links with tenants. This contrasts with the local management structures that each CLT establishes for co-management of the co-owned housing. This move into social renting is encouraging CLT-B to consider establishing a social housing management organisation that is better suited to dealing with low-income households.

Third, Brussels City Region have also provided funding for CLT-B developments through the Housing Fund. The Housing Fund in fact provides funding in three ways: through support for the land purchase; through grants for the construction costs over and above the finance provided by residents' mortgages; and through providing these mortgages to residents at preferential rates. The Housing Fund have been a major partner for CLT-B acting as the main project developer, but CLT-B has moved on to partnering with a range of organisations in their developments.

Fourth, the local planning frameworks provided a structure that CLT projects could fit into. These frameworks are termed Neighbourhood Contracts. They are part of the city renewal strategy and provide a detailed plan for a local area. They combine physical development with participatory processes and social action. For example, the social economy has had a place within Neighbourhood Contracts since 1991. Municipalities (there are 19 within the Brussels City Region) propose areas for a Neighbourhood Contract and Brussels City Region makes a selection every four years. Funding comes from Brussels City Region, but the relevant municipality is in charge of managing the renewal and often provides land for some of the development. This is a major source of sites for CLT-B. However, municipalities vary in the scope of their landownership portfolios. They can get finance from Brussels City Region to buy land and then sell this on to CLT-B at a lower price, as much as 25 per cent discount. The financial support for social forms of housing development in Brussels City Region is rather advantageous, but the process at each stage requires public tender to ensure a degree of competition for land and construction contracts. This public tender can involve a restriction on reselling housing on the open market, which implies a CLT framework.

The emphasis historically has been on the so-called 'poor crescent' around the west of the city. This has meant that the land prices were low to start with. As attention moves from the limited supply of brownfield sites to sites in suburban areas, there has been local opposition. It should be noted that Neighbourhood

Contracts are intended to provide a range of housing options, both for lower-income households and also for middle classes to prevent them moving out to suburban areas or outside Brussels City Region altogether. Increasingly CLT-B have sought to be a part of larger-scale development projects that municipalities are leading on. Rather than picking up leftover sites, they aim to be a key partner from the outset.

Fifth, CLT-B has worked with social groups from African communities, particularly from Ghana. Within these communities a housing tenure that involves ownership is often an aspiration. In addition, these communities have faced discrimination within the Brussels housing market, which encourages them to look for alternatives. They are able to benefit from experience with the *tontine* method of group saving, which aligns with the CLT approach. A number of NGOs have been working with these communities and can partner CLT-B in the development process, particularly in terms of making contact with and working with local communities.

The role of planning in promoting community land trusts

We have seen how landownership is key to the successful operation of CLTs. Ready transfer of land to the CLT organisation, either from the private sector or a public sector landbank, smooths the path to speedy development, whereas in cases where this transfer becomes protracted not only is development delayed but that delay puts a strain on an organisation that typically has limited resources and where commitment can be eroded by the sense of not achieving the CLT's objectives. Such a land transfer is also central to the economic model by which households achieve an affordable home and yet the residential development as a whole is protected from increases in land value that would undermine the mission of providing affordable housing into the future.

This implies that CLTs would be supported by the availability of a public landbank or the use of compulsory purchase powers (also known as the exercise of eminent domain) to achieve these transfers smoothly. Legal recognition of the landownership rights of a CLT and of the legal form of a CLT could also be important in supporting the sector, as would standardisation and/or dissemination of models for CLT structures and legal contracts, so saving time in learning about these new forms and avoiding forms which have proved to create problems in their execution.

Such institutional supports largely fall within the categories of land policy and business policy. What is the distinctive contribution of planning, particularly at the local scale? Planning seeks to coordinate urban change, including new urban development. A key means of achieving such coordination is through the use of a plan, that is, a spatial depiction of future patterns of land use and development in an area. This centrally involves allocation of land and sites for new development, such as housebuilding. Aligning the vision in such a plan with the land transfers needed to implement a CLT scheme is necessary if planning is to play a role in promoting CLT development. How effective such alignment will be depends on the kind of plan and the nature of the planning system that it sits within.

Nadin and Stead (2013) summarised the variety of planning systems found within the European Union as the regional economic planning approach, the comprehensive integrated approach, the land use management approach or the urbanism tradition. The UK falls within the land use management approach, while Italy falls within the urbanism traditions with a strong emphasis on urban design (Bragaglia et al, 2023). But, more important than the style of planning system is the extent to which resources follow a plan that has been drawn up. In some circumstances, there will a range of resources – financial, legal, regulatory, legitimacy – that follow from the proposals within the plan. This can include the designation of land, and indeed the designation of land for CLT development. In these cases, the plan can have direct consequences for the pursuit of CLT housebuilding. Hopkins and Knapp (2018) termed such plans as 'comprehensive'.

But, in many cases, particularly where neoliberal ideology and austerity budgeting have had an impact, the plan may not be associated with resources and may therefore carry less power. Planning theory has debated how planners can draw up plans in this context so as to have influence even when they do not control resources. Completing their typology of existing approaches, Hopkins and Knaap (2018) distinguish advocacy, communicative and collaborative plans. Advocacy plans are explicitly one-sided and seek to present an under-considered viewpoint, highlighting the difference from existing plans and strategies. Since advocacy plans are not drawn up by actors with decision-making authority, any development land proposals they contain remain just that – a proposal.

Much more significant is the emphasis on communicative and collaborative approaches, both of which have been highly influential within planning thought. Communicative plans involve facilitated deliberation between stakeholders tending towards consensus. This is held to create sufficient legitimacy to persuade decision makers to conform, perhaps adaptively over time, to the recommendations of the plan. Collaborative plans are linked to a place and to the civic and political institutions of a place. As such, they emerge from a context of relative power and are more likely to influence regulatory and investment decisions. In either case, the involvement of stakeholders, agencies and political authorities in the development of the plan itself is central, so that they are organisationally aligned with the plan's objectives. However, such involvement can skew the plan towards the objectives of the more powerful stakeholders, that is, those holding more resources. It can therefore be difficult to deliver something as specific as CLT development through such a plan. It can remain on the shelf as a record of communicative or collaborative activity but not produce the land transfers that the CLT requires.

Hopkins and Knaap (2018) developed a different approach in the face of these difficulties. This is based on two key insights. First, planning takes place in the context of the four 'I's: interdependence (actions are not separable), indivisibility (continuous marginal adjustment is not efficient or not possible), irreversibility (history and dynamics matter) and imperfect foresight (uncertainty cannot be eliminated). These all inhibit planning as straightforward, single-actor rational problem solving. As a result, there are pressures towards greater stakeholder involvement to overcome the problems these may pose through collaboration, knowledge exchange, negotiation and so on.

However, the second insight is that the result is not one plan but, rather, multiple plans produced by multiple relevant actors. Thus, it is better to conceive of planning as 'a network of autonomous plans' (Hopkins and Knaap, 2018: 278). Hopkins and Knaap see these plans as signalling to each other more or less effectively. The need for and benefit of land allocations and transfers, say to CLTs, thus needs to be conveyed from plan to plan. Elsewhere this has been referred to as plans being in dialogue, artefactual dialogue (Rydin, 2021). The conclusion to be drawn is that the essential land transfers that CLTs require may be difficult to deliver through conventional planning actions and that instead prioritising land policy, with an explicit emphasis on property and landownership, may be necessary.

Beyond the making of plans, however, planning systems typically encompass a form of regulation. Such regulation can be particularly important in ensuring that new developments meet the highest environmental standards and contribute to reduced emissions and other forms of environmental impact. The foregoing discussion makes it clear that while CLTs can deliver on a central aspect of social sustainability through providing affordable and secure housing, they do not intrinsically align themselves with environmental values. This conclusion is akin to that for cooperatives and, to some extent, for small local firms. Strong environmental regulatory standards remain a necessary form of state action in the current context of ecological and climate crises.

7
Community assets and social enterprise

Introduction

This chapter considers the range of facilities found within the built environment that can be considered to constitute social infrastructure and are often termed 'community assets'. Such social infrastructure is vital to the functioning of an area and the quality of life of its residents. It is also an essential element of the foundational economy. Moore and McKee (2014: 522) use the terms community asset to 'refer to physical assets such as land and buildings that may be controlled, managed and owned by place-based community organisations'. For clarity, this should be distinguished from the recent adoption of the term within community asset-based development, which refers to the idea that community development should be based on the assets (that is, the positive features) of the community, rather than rooted in a deficit model of what that community lacks. The kinds of community assets discussed here encompass libraries, nurseries, shops, public houses, community centres and so on. In line with the ideas of diverse economies and with the agenda of certain policy approaches, communities have often taken an active role in the ownership, management and delivery of such community assets and the functions that they support. Moore and McKee thus identify as key commonalities the assets being tied to a specific geographic area where the community groups running them have objectives relating to a broader social purpose than just profit, seeking to enhance local well-being.

Hence, this chapter looks at the role of social enterprises, based at least in part on community effort, in relation to community assets. It considers the different forms that social enterprises can take and what their experiences have been, with a focus on such activities in the Western Isles of Scotland and western Ireland. Because both 'social enterprises' and 'community assets' place the concept of community centre stage, the nature of this concept is examined, leading to a discussion of how planning policy and practice can set the context for social infrastructure delivery through diverse economies.

Forms of social enterprise

Murtagh (2019) provides a neat definition of social enterprises and the social economy that they constitute: they are collectively organised, profit seeking, but deploy the surplus for social and environmental purposes (p 66). He discusses how they are engaged both in monetised trading but also in non-monetised forms such as local currencies, mutual exchange systems, service credits, time-based currencies and barter markets. Following Defourny and Nyssens (2013), Murtagh sees social enterprises as operating in a place where all three logics have influence: that of for-profit activities associated with the market; that of redistribution associated with the state; and that of reciprocity associated with community. As Murtagh notes, there can be tensions between the social welfare logics and the commercial logics (Murtagh, 2019: 104–105). However, he critiques the idea that the tensions between these logics are all equal; rather, he sees the market logic as necessarily often prevailing. This could be read as neoliberal hegemony or, more pragmatically, as the need for social enterprises to be viable. As outlined in Chapter 3, Murtagh (2019: 93) provides a four-fold typology: a not-for-profit model; a corporate social responsibility model; a more-than-profit model; and a multi-stakeholder model. The last is often expressed as the ideal type within the social economy.

What this discussion highlights is the way that social enterprises are – like small firms, cooperatives and community land trusts (CLTs) already discussed – hybrid organisations. Bloom and Chatterji (2009: 114) define social entrepreneurs as 'individuals who start up and lead new organisations or programs that are dedicated to mitigating or eliminating a social problem, deploying change strategies that differ from those that have been used to address this problem in the past'. These change strategies can involve enterprise and trading, even while the social objectives remain at the core (see also Blundel and Lyon, 2015). They are influenced by market pressures and the need for profit from the provision of services and goods, but also community dynamics and values. This tends to lead to limited profit distribution and a reduced reliance on paid workers, including some volunteers. A level of economic risk is accepted but the goal is ultimately to benefit the community.

The initiative comes from within civil society, usually in the form of a localised community. The resulting organisation usually exhibits considerable autonomy, with governance arrangements that are highly participatory and democratic. Decision making is driven not by capital ownership but by social values. (Murtagh, 2019: 95). A key feature of organisations within the social economy is, thus, that they combine a social logic based on their core mission with a commercial logic, so that they generate sufficient financial return to sustain the venture. This means that growth is not a straightforward impetus to such organisations. Scaling up may be relevant, but this can be *in situ* or involve an initiative elsewhere.

Organisations within the social economy can take a variety of forms. Curry (2022) lists voluntary groups, mutuals, charities, land trusts (see Chapter 6), credit unions, local exchange and trading systems and cooperatives (see Chapter 5). These are given specific institutional and legal form within particular contexts. So, in the UK, cooperatives exist alongside BenComs and community interest companies. The community interest company (CIC) was introduced in 2005 and must meet two tests. The first is that it benefits the local community and not just the members of the company or its shareholders. The second is that it must involve an asset lock, whereby assets are held for the benefit of that community in perpetuity. As

Chapter 6 discussed, such an asset lock is a key feature of CLTs in their endeavours to provide affordable housing and workspaces.

There has been growing interest in expanding the social economy. For example, the European Union have made the social economy a priority because they see it as a pathway to achieving social, societal and environmental benefits, including reductions in carbon emissions, while at the same time delivering inclusive employment which is fair and dignified. There are also dedicated strategies for expansion of the social economy in Scotland and Spain (European Commission, nd). But Murtagh and Boland (2019) comment on how social enterprises vary across different countries, with their distinctive social, political and economic structures and particular histories. Northern European models are described as more corporatist, while Mediterranean countries tend to foster more independent charitable organisations. In the UK and the US, entrepreneurialism and enterprise is emphasised, while in Latin America there are links to liberation theology. Thus, there is diversity within the social economy sector, which nevertheless demonstrates some common features and experiences.

Experiences of social enterprises

A first common thread within social enterprises' experiences arises from their character as hybrid organisations. Doherty et al (2014) identify hybridity as *the* key feature of social enterprises, that is, the unique ways of combining financial sustainability and social purpose. This defines all aspects of the operation of the social enterprise, including the management of the mission, the acquisition of financial resources and the mobilisation of human resources. It also means that there are likely to be tensions and even possibly trade-offs between the different dimensions of hybridity. For Bloom and Chatterji (2009) this relates to three drivers for success in social enterprises: the generation of earnings to ensure financial stability and back the sourcing of start-up capital; replication by identifying a more dispersed set of beneficiaries; and using available economic incentives to stimulate market forces. Blundel and Lyon (2015) relate this to the ability of social enterprises to make entrepreneurial adjustments, essential for their long-term survival and potential to scale up. But, alongside these market-oriented concerns, the generation of social value remains at the core of social enterprises' activities.

Second, the literature repeatedly points to the importance of operationalising networks and forging partnerships if social enterprises are to last and be successful (Di Domenico et al, 2010). Blundel and Lyon (2015) see network relations as important to realise the opportunities identified by social enterprises, and Bloom and Chatterji (2009) emphasise the building of alliances to enrol potential allies in the enterprise's mission. Looking at the food sector, Curry (2022) examines the case of community food hubs in rural areas, both producer and consumer hubs. He concludes that partnerships are key to their long-term success. These are the best way of ensuring that the enterprise does not become dominated by a market logic, although Curry does see a partnership between consumer and producer interests as providing a workable model. Links to non-food interests can also buttress the position of community food hubs, emphasising the benefits of multitasking.

Goodwin-Hawkins et al (2022) studied rural service hubs across Austria, Finland and Wales as part of the ROBUST project. Their research showed how such hubs need to be part of multiscalar networks and incorporate urban–rural connectivity. This emphasises the importance of not thinking of such local initiatives in purely local terms. Thus, the endogenous development model on which such initiatives are based (often using the LEADER programme within Europe) is critiqued. Goodwin-Hawkins et al argue that endogenous development can be limited by local capacities, can disguise local power differentials and be subject to elite capture. Instead they favour an approach that includes a place-based strategy with participatory roots, alongside operationalising multilevel networks and multiscalar linkages. Indeed, they go further than conventional neo-endogenous frameworks (see Chapter 4) to explore the importance of social innovation alongside networks, moving across scale and proximity. They see services which are based in the community but with these wider linkages as particularly important in local development.

For example, they describe the Cletwr Community Shop and cafe in Tre'r Ddôl, Ceredigion, Wales, which was set up in 2013. The village had lost multiple services, including the garage, post office, school and chapel. Residents came together to reopen the garage as a social enterprise. They established this in the form of a company with membership open to all local residents. They have 40 members and an elected management board. In 2017 they opened a new sustainable building utilising a variety of funding sources from the local county, the Welsh Government, UK Government and EU grants. They offer food retailing, internet connectivity, cash withdrawal, parcel drop-off, a mobile library as well as a place for meetings with the police, councillors and MPs. They have formed an oil-buying syndicate to leverage the cost advantages of scale and are engaged with local food growers. This is all cemented by a strong local identity, here associated with the Welsh language.

Another example Goodwin-Hawkins et al cover is the Allerleierei farm shop and cafe in LaBrutzhöhe, Styria, Austria. Some 20 miles east of Graz, this is a traditional spa town, now largely based on commuting to Graz. The area is active in the Slow Food movement, and in 2015–16 the local council restored the main square in the town and the market building became a community centre with business space. The founding partners of Allerleierei were a local hotelier, a restaurant owner and an organic fruit and vegetable farmer. They rented some of the business space and offered local farmers the opportunity to sell their produce there; LEADER funding was used. Now they operate with a circular economy model to reduce waste and offer a wide range of regionally sourced supplies and a cafe. In 2021 they became a franchise of the AckerBox system, already operating in nearby locations, which uses old shipping containers to provide a 24-hour self-service shopping facility.

A third aspect of social enterprises' experience is the building and utilisation of community capacity. This variously includes sufficient staffing (Bloom and

Chatterji, 2009), managing the nature of a relatively small and partly volunteer workforce (Blundel and Lyon, 2015) and actively working with the interactions between resources and capacities within the local community. Hobson et al (2019) emphasise the need for institutional thickness in order for community ownership of local assets to be successful. Otherwise, they point to struggles in establishing local control of the asset and an over-reliance on a small pool of individuals – individuals who may move away, become ill or no longer wish to be involved. A critical mass of community capacity is essential.

Fischer and McKee (2017) provide a salutary story in this regard from the Scottish Highlands, from which they deduce three key lessons. First, the interactions between the resources and capacities within a local community are vital for understanding the situation of a social enterprise. Second, capacities within a community may not only be low but can be negative, with destructive potential. It can be extremely hard to overcome such negative capacities through standard approaches to capacity building. And third, the social capacities that emerge from interactions between people are powerful microstructures that can constrain individuals' ability to engage in community action. Fischer and McKee define these capacities as personal, organisational, infrastructural and cultural.

There therefore needs to be a critical mass of community capacity, but this can be built, for example through training. Skerratt and Hall (2011a and 2011b) looked at a very large number (347) of village halls across Scotland. They found three sources of complexities for local communities managing these assets: that the buildings themselves may be a liability because of their condition; that the financial asset base is often not robust; and that the human assets are vulnerable in terms of succession and governance. Skerratt and Hall particularly emphasise the importance of evaluating the community capacity for ownership before asset transfer, and also of considering the complexities of the specific asset and its ownership. Ongoing support is essential, with an emphasis on long-term investment, not short-term costs. Nevertheless, Skerratt and Hall see such assets as potentially enhancing cohesion, resilience and sustainability for the local community. The key is utilising the full range of financial, built, social, human, natural, cultural and political capital where possible. In particular, training for volunteers was important. This tends to cover food hygiene, first aid, funding raising and legal compliance (which might all be considered essential prerequisites to managing an asset), but often omits sufficient training on business planning, meeting management, governance or people management. Skerratt and Hall emphasise that the range of skills needed for running community assets covers the property itself and also funding, finance, legislation and committee matters.

One notable problem is that a reliance on volunteering can render the staffing of social enterprises unreliable and liable to erosion over time. Gieling et al (2019) studied the relationship between place attachment and volunteering. They distinguish social, cultural and environmental dimensions of place attachment and, through survey research of over 5,000 Dutch residents, found that social attachment was the best explanation of volunteering levels, whereas general place attachment had limited explanatory power. This points to the frequency and depth of social contacts – a key part of social capital – as important in maintaining this vital resource of volunteer effort for social enterprises. In other research, they found that cafes and local supermarkets were particularly important in building social contacts and that primary schools, community centres and sports centres were less so. This may, of course, be specific to the Dutch case.

Bricolage has been identified as a useful way to think about the work that faces social enterprises. Blundel and Lyon (2015) point to the importance of 'bricolage' as an approach that enables social enterprises to assemble diverse resources. Such resources may come from: philanthropy, donation and volunteering; commercial trading and other income; and/or public sector grants and contracts. Bricolage is also emphasised by Di Domenico et al (2010). From the literature on social enterprises, they identify the importance of 'making do', refusing to be constrained by apparent limitations and being 'creative under pressure'. Bricolage is particularly relevant to the first and third aspects here. Looking across eight UK cases, Di Domenico et al identify the additional importance of creating social value, enabling stakeholder participation and successfully using persuasion.

Finally, there is the importance of communication, including lobbying and persuasion about the value of the social enterprise agenda. Bloom and Chatterji (2009) emphasise the need for good communication to produce public support and lobbying to generate supportive public policy for the long-term success of social enterprises. Curry (2022) also sees campaigning to garner local and more widespread support as necessary for such entities.

Community and place

The elements of diverse economies that are constituted by community assets managed by social enterprises are rather different from those involved in the small, localised firm sector, the cooperatives and even the CLTs discussed in Chapters 4, 5 and 6. This is because the collective concepts of 'community' and 'place' loom larger here. There is more of an inherently collective dimension to social enterprises owning and managing community assets. Firms, cooperatives and CLTs provide their goods and services and also engage with their labour largely through traditional market mechanisms of one-to-one exchange, even where the employed workers also are part-owners of the cooperative and the homeowners have a stake in the CLT. This contrasts with community assets within the social economy, where the goods and services provided are typically a mix of individually consumed and collectively consumed goods and services. Similarly, labour does not comprise only employed workers but also includes volunteering and other non-market ways of participating in providing goods and services.

And, while the previous chapters emphasised the role of local planning in ensuring that firms, cooperatives and CLTs have access to appropriate premises and land at a viable cost, this has a different significance in the case of community assets. Here, the ownership of a property right in the premises is not only important in providing a degree of security but is also linked to close identification and even emotional attachments with the premises being occupied. Furthermore, it is more than the individual building or site that is relevant here. There is often an attachment to the area within which the building is located, an emotional relationship to the place and the role of the building in creating a sense of place.

For these reasons, social capital plays a more important role with community assets. Previous chapters emphasised that the boundaries between the market and civil society are porous and that small firms, cooperatives and CLTs are all reliant to some extent on local social capital. But this is stronger with regard to community assets because the idea of running such a community asset often arises from within the local community and there are considerable calls on local social capital to support the planning for and running of these assets. Through the nexus of community assets operating by using market and voluntary labour to produce and distribute both individual and collective goods and services, such assets are integral to a dynamic process of creating and maintaining social capital.

But the very topic of community assets owned and managed by social enterprises based in a community necessarily raises the issue of what is actually meant by the term 'community'. There is considerable nostalgia in discussions around community. Brent (2009) referenced Phillips' definition (1993: 3), which sees communities as defined by a specific group of people who live in a common territory and share a common history and also values; they participate together in activities and exhibit a high degree of solidarity. This is a highly restrictive view of community that rarely exists in modern societies and, in any case, has considerable drawbacks for members. The strong bonding social capital that characterises such cases does not just create a positive sense of community but can be used to monitor behaviour and impose restrictions on what is considered acceptable and to exclude people.

Thus, there has been a shift towards a view of community based less on this idealised model and rather on different kinds of networks between people. These networks can define communities of interest (where a common interest drives the connection), communities of place (anchored by networks within a bounded spatial area) or communities of identity (where the actors in the network share a common sense of themselves along some axis). Again, a nostalgic view might wish to see these three different kinds of community combine so that a group of people within a given place see themselves as sharing common interests and identifying closely with one another, perhaps even seeing their main identifier as being residence of that particular place. However, in practice, people live much more mobile lives than this suggests and are usually members of multiple communities in terms of interest, place and identity. Many aspects of interest and identity are not rooted in one place, or people juggle a mix of place-based and non-place-based identities.

Bradshaw (2008) contrasts completely post-place communities, which are highly fluid, dynamic and with relationships often conducted virtually, with *Gemeinschaft* and *Gessellschaft* communities. *Gemeinschaft* communities align closely with the nostalgic idea of a single, stable community bounded by strong bonding social capital and rooted in residence or place (the nostalgic ideal); *Gessellschaft* communities are considered looser in that they involve bonding and bridging social capital, that is, stronger and weaker ties which link people who are unlike each other as well as those who might be considered homologous to each other. In practice, people in any locality are likely to see all three types as being relevant to them. Evans (2009) offers a looser typology of community as networks, suggesting that these can be variously termed diverse, restricted, friend-focused or family-focused. Romero and Harris (2014) emphasise the salience of the context and the inevitable fuzziness of any boundaries; they also point out that policy often helps to shape perceptions of community.

So, community is a rather fluid concept. Brent et al (2009) take a view of community that emphasises various aspects of collective life, including morality, territory, action, identity and control. They suggest that the meaning of community depends on the situation and the actor, combining these in different ways. Drawing on the literature that sees the idea of community as potentially cloaking flows of capitalism and globalisation and their impacts, Brent et al (2009) point out that 'Life is in constant flux and solid social structures evaporate' (p 206). In this context, the idea of community offers solidity, autonomy and protection, but it can do so only temporarily and sometimes this is achieved only by actively excluding other groups of people and activating prejudicial ideologies. The very use of the language of 'community' can act to neutralise political issues and social divisions, as well as the exercise of power. This may seem a very negative view of the idea of community, but Brent et al do see potential in using the concept, seeing it as offering possibilities and new imaginaries, even if these are not fully realisable. It involves accepting that community activities are messy and conflictual, rather than seeing community as a salve for conflict. Parkinson and Howarth (2008) see social enterprises as drawing their legitimacy from a form of morality that emphasises geographical community and collective action, but also power struggles.

Many see that the materiality of place makes a difference even within such a deconstructed notion of community. Evans (2009) suggests that specific physical features can contribute to strong identification with a place and, while place may not encompass all aspects of everyday life, the physical features of that place will shape some aspects. The layout, social and other infrastructure and pattern of land uses may mean that people make heavy use of local facilities, making connections with people in these contexts (schools, gyms, shops and so on), even while they work outside the local area and have family and friendship networks that are widely spread. This means that even those with networks only partially rooted in a place may develop strong place attachments. This term refers to the psychological investment in a place that develops over time and is encouraged by the perceived distinctiveness of the place, continuity in residence or other engagement with the place, and ways in which the place contributes to a sense of self-esteem (Evans, 2009). Evans thus distinguishes manifest neighbouring, based on face-to-face interactions, and latent neighbouring, which captures the broader sense of belonging to and responsibility to an area.

Brent et al (2009) also argue that place has a role to play. Place can be both a meaningful part of identity and a site of community activities. 'One cannot separate out boundaries of space as being purely physical from boundaries of community as being social or symbolic' (p 219). Place is connected with narrative and meaning, in part shaping the discourses circulating in a locality. But place always remains a site for physical contact and the social relationships that may develop from such contact (although this cannot be assured). So, Brent et al (2009) conclude that 'Community exists as an imagination of relationships' (p 220) and is 'a combination of thoughts, dreams, actions and materiality' (p 228). Even where these are incomplete, split, changeable and ambiguous, they are no less important for this. Within this, community action is 'time-based, coalescing around certain moments of excitement and mobilisation' (p 233).

The importance of 'newcomers' in local community initiatives is highlighted in Healey's study of community action in her village in Northumbria, England (Healey, 2022). This is a feature also found by Creamer et al (2018) in their research on 'incomers' and their involvement in community-led organisations in rural Scotland. The conclusion seems to be that incomers or newcomers can be particularly active in community initiatives and, while they may retain their somewhat pejorative label for years to come, this is not necessarily resented. This again challenges the idea of a community as rooted in a common history. Rather, social enterprises can be a focal point around which diverse residents in the area can come together to form a community based in joint practice. Indeed, Sonnino and Griggs-Trevarthan (2013) see social enterprises as niches where values are turned into such daily joint practices. This both generates and enhances social capital, itself a key motivation for social entrepreneurship. The community-running of such social enterprises constitutes an active and continuous effort to bond and bridge people in the face of dynamics emphasising difference and separation.

Focus on the Celtic periphery of the Western Isles, Scotland and western Ireland

The Celtic periphery refers to the more rural areas of Scotland and Ireland, and the focus here is on three locations: the Isle of Lewis within the Western Isles, Scotland and two Irish rural locations in West Kerry, County Kerry and Connemara, County Galway. All can be described as 'fragile economies'. They have been based in primary production and are now slowly diversifying, with some of the primary production and processing moving into the hands of large companies, including multinational companies.

The main economic sector in the Western Isles remains primary production, notably fishing, but there are other niche products such as Harris Tweed and local gin distilling which serve international markets (Highlands and Islands Enterprise, nd). Alongside, there is considerable employment in the public sector, notably local government, education, health and care. Productivity is below 88 per cent of the UK, but it is really questionable how meaningful this figure is. The Isles of Lewis and Harris are notable for having employment rates, economic activity and self-employment above the regional and national level, and unemployment below. However, incomes levels are low and many households combine different sources of income. Fuel poverty is also present. The population of north–west Lewis has declined from about 2,500 in 1979 to near 1,600 in 2019, and over a third are aged more than 65 years. While there has been some recent repopulation, there are labour shortages in the islands both for the public sector and the fishing industry (which relies heavily on overseas labour, most recently from the Philippines).

Ireland as a whole has a very high proportion of rural residents; for example, over 77 per cent of the people in County Galway (where Connemara is) live in rural areas (Galway County Council, nd). Much depends on how far a rural area falls within the influence of a local urban area. Thus, much of Connemara is not far from the small city of Galway, which is quite an active urban economy. The urban economic influence for West Kerry is much more limited and this affects its economic statistics. The data for County Galway suggests average income levels and a high proportion of employment in the public, education and health sectors, with some manufacturing; but it also suggests that the household income in rural areas is quite low. For the area of West Kerry, lower household income and greater reliance on pensions is recorded; there is little industry and, again public sector, education and health employment is significant.

The role of social enterprises in these locations was highlighted in Stöhr's edited volume on local economic development across Europe (Stöhr, 1990). In this, Bryden and Scott (1990) reported on four cooperative enterprises within the Celtic periphery. One of these was considered a failure at the time; Co-Chomunn Nis was based at the northern tip of the Isle of Lewis, having been founded in the 1970s as a community cooperative to run a shop, a mobile food van and various agricultural support enterprises, including supplies and contract hire of machinery. However, the various ventures faced competition on the island and were not profitable; this was compounded by management deficiencies and the cooperative was wound up in 1985.

But the story of the other cooperative on the Isle of Lewis is more encouraging. Pàirc Co-op was set up in 1978 with £10,000 from 300 mainly local shareholders and matching funds from the Highlands and Islands Development Board. Like Co-Chomunn Nis, they invested in a local digger for hire and agricultural supplies, as well as a local delivery service; all proved unprofitable. However, the co-op found two profitable enterprises to support. One was local hand-knitting, partly for an overseas market; Bryden and Scott (1990) reported 60 knitters working. This was supported by the Hebridean Knitwear Association, set up in 1985, who particularly facilitated connections with designers and agents abroad. The other enterprise was in seafood. Early attempts to farm rainbow trout faced competition and foundered, closing in 1984. Then the enterprise moved into producing young salmon smoults through the Pàirc Hatchery and mussel farming and salmon through Pàirc Salmon set up in 1985 and 40 per cent owned by the co-op. The co-op also had a laboratory that offered a local service. Much of this had been consolidated into Atlantic Sea Products, which operated as a commercial business; in Bryden and Scott's (1990) view, this opened the co-op up to risk.

The Pàirc Co-op continues to function at the time of writing. It became a limited company in 2001 and registered as a charity in 2007. In 2010 it established a wholly owned subsidiary, Ravenspoint Trading Ltd, which runs a cafe and shop in the Ravenspoint Centre, a building which also provides a community facility; the Centre was extended in 2011. This asset allowed the co-op to rent space to local organisations such as a book trust and an archive. They also run a 14-bed hostel for visitors.

Bryden and Scott (1990) looked at two cooperative ventures in Western Ireland: West Kerry, a community co-op, and Connemara West, a community-owned development company. The West Kerry co-op is based in the *Gaeltacht*, the Gaelic-speaking part of Ireland. Bryden and Scott report that there was a dedicated development agency – Udaras na Galetachta – which provided a ready-made model for creating a co-op. CFCD (Comharchumann Forbartha Chorca Dhuibhne) in West Kerry was founded in 1967 and was based on land reclamation work, increasing the productive agricultural land for farmers and utilising detailed local knowledge of the soil. However, over time, the potential for this work decreased and commercial contractors came into the market. Similarly, a demonstration diary and a tomato-growing business proved unviable and closed in the later 1980s; a venture into fish farming was locally controversial. So, at this time, the cooperative restructured and refocused on cultural heritage and tourism.

These themes frame the work of CFCD today. They operate with four subsidiary companies and provide an enterprise centre, a family support centre, space for public use and a University Centre with links to the National University of Ireland. From 1983 they also ran information technology courses, but these stopped in 2003. They provide training through community employment schemes, which tends to focus on maintenance work. However, the main work of CFCD is on education in cultural heritage and Irish, for both school-age and adult students, and enrolments have grown over time. This is a very specific sector of the education market that CFCD have found a niche in. It fits with the policies in the Kerry County Development Plan (2021), which particularly supports cultural and linguistic intiatives, and also with the national government emphasis on education in rural areas, such as that operated through the regional technical colleges, which has particularly supported education and training for farmers.

The Connemara West Ltd (CW Ltd) initiative, which began in 1971, is wider in scope. Bryden and Scott (1990) identified it as focused on a number of projects in the 1970s. First, they set up a credit union, the Tullycross Credit Union Ltd. Second, they built nine holiday cottages to create an income stream, a project where 80 per cent of the local population were shareholders in the development company. Third, they worked with Ballinakill Community Council, which looks after the former St Joseph's Industrial School (a reform school which closed in

1974), purchased by CW Ltd in 1978 and used as a base for training courses. Fourth, they built a cultural centre at Tully – Teach Ceoil – in 1977, which generated revenue through courses and summer tourists. In addition to these main activities, CW Ltd has provided common office services for small businesses since 1980, and community education. When the local agricultural supplies store closed in 1983, CW Ltd were involved in helping set up a farmers' co-op and a new store.

Since the time of this analysis, CW Ltd and its associated activities have grown. The Industrial School at Letterfrack now has a variety of uses, including as a creche (since 2006), sports facilities, a hall for hire and Connemara Community Radio (since 1995). Conservation Letterfrack opened in 1999 and undertakes furniture and wood conservation and restoration, while GMIT Letterfrack is a training college in these skills, offering a BSc degree since 2005. The GMIT student library complements the community library provided by Galway County. Teach Ceoil has a well-established link with Aquinas College in the US, providing courses and letting out the cottages for student accommodation. Social housing projects have been completed, with 13 new houses in 2016.

By their very nature as social enterprises, these cooperative organisations operate as hybrid organisations across the boundary of the private/market sector and civil society. As such, they are an entanglement of monetised and non-monetised flows. Voluntary effort remains integral to such organisations based within the local communities, although they also have a set of activities aimed at profit making and underpinning the financial sustainability of the enterprises. Non-private ownership forms are central to supporting this.

In Scotland this fits within a long-term commitment to fostering community ownership of assets, and notably of land too. The Highlands and Islands of Scotland have experienced a long-term approach to community development. The key date is 1965, when the Highland and Islands Development Board (HIDB) was founded, to become Highlands and Islands Enterprise in 1991. This body has a wide-ranging remit and has had considerable funds allocated to it. While it aims to attract inward investment, it also has a strong social remit: in 1991, 25 per cent of its budget went to social and voluntary activities, village halls and sport and cultural activities in over 400 locations. According to Lloyd and Black (1993), it saw community development as complementary to 'inward investment, business development and economic regeneration' (p 78). From the 1980s to 2020, this was supported by European funds under various programmes (McCullogh, 2018).

But of most significance here is the focus on community cooperatives. Gordon (2002: 95) argues that this focus:

> has been very successful, on a number of different levels: it created new jobs, services and enterprises; very importantly, it built asset bases and revenue income to underpin development; it changed people's lives, was genuinely bottom-up, raised consciousness, reinforced the mutual cooperation tradition of the area, and inspired people elsewhere to do similar things.

It originated in 1977 with pilot schemes in the Western Isles. These followed the examples of the Irish community cooperatives. In 1996 the HIDB estimated there were some 2,700 social economy organisations in their area; by 2001 it was estimated this had grown to 5,000. Of those established by 1986, at least half were still operating in 2001–02. Paid employment was relatively modest at three to four people per organisation, but with another six or so volunteers on average. A key feature was that the organisations needed to be viable in order to turn a profit. If this could be projected, then the HIDB offered match funding, management and administration support for up to five years (tapering down), local field officers for advice and model rules. An umbrella association was put in place in 1985.

However, allowing for these frameworks, there are clearly local factors behind the success and longevity of such cooperatives structures. Whitelaw and Hill (2013), looking at Scotland and Sweden, pointed to the importance of the ability to access the relevant expertise and strong links into the communities for community social enterprises to be successful. Gordon's (2002) analysis of the HIDB-backed co-ops points out the importance of owning land and assets in providing financial security, a physical base and an expression of identity. But, above all, the HIDB approach

> reinforced the tradition of mutual cooperation in the Highlands and Islands, building confidence and capacity, and unlocking creative potential – as well as marshalling and deploying collective resources, financial and otherwise, which could be used to attract more funding, and to implement plans. In addition, the co-ops built asset bases and revenue income, to underpin their development. (Gordon, 2002: 109)

Above all, the approach fostered social capital within the communities.

Perhaps, the most significant change, however, is the more recent move into community ownership of the land of the Scottish community-based organisations. In 2003 the Pàirc Trust was formed; the Pàirc Co-op has a seat on the Trust's board. Mackenzie (2013) details the Pàirc Trust's application to buy the estate in some more detail. The application was approved by Scottish ministers in March 2011. This was significant because it was a hostile bid against the wishes of the landowner. The decision was subsequently taken to the courts by the landowner. They invoked an interposed lease which would retain for themselves the development rights over the land, because they wished to use the land for an onshore wind farm. This was opposed by the local population, who in a 2005 ballot had overwhelmingly (83 per cent of those eligible) voted against the wind farm development.

The community had formed the required company limited by guarantee in 2003 in order to purchase the common grazings of the Pàirc Estate, almost all of which is under crofting tenure. The landowner was an absentee landlord, Barry Lomax, resident in Leamington Spa, England. At this time the landowner had signed an outline agreement with Scottish and Southern Electric for 125-turbine wind farm; the interposed lease was set up in 2004. The hostile bid was made in

2005 after a ballot in 2004 that showed overwhelming community support for the buy-out. The wind farm would potentially generate £400,000 per annum for the community, which would be a major source of revenue, but this share of the profits did not unify the community behind the wind farm proposal.

Thus, in 2015 the Trust gained ownership of almost 11,000 hectares covering 213 crofts (small farms) and 11 townships (against the landlord's wishes and after a law case). As landowners, the Trust can develop plans for leveraging their assets, undertaking affordable housing, renewable energy and tourism projects; six housing units have been built and there is a wind farm trust. As of early 2021, they own the Kershader Resource Centre, which provides space for a playgroup and a community gym. This is a path that the community in Ness is now also taking. In 2004 a crofters' trust was formed under the name Galson Estate Trust, a first step in enabling the buyout of the land; the community took control in 2007, using an empty school as its centre and employing 30 people (Mackenzie, 2013). A new museum for the historical society is now housed in the school.

This has all been facilitated by a national framework enabling crofters (traditional tenant farmers working smallholdings), and now communities generally, to buy out land and creating common property landownership structures. The commitment to crofting in Scotland can be dated to the Crofters' Holdings (Scotland) Act of 1886, which emphasises the individual rights of crofters; the Crofters' Reform (Scotland) Act of 1976 gave crofters the right to purchase their crofts (Lloyd and Shucksmith, 1985). But in 2003 the Land Reform (Scotland) Act allowed communities (rather than individual crofters) to buy land and buildings, connecting land reform to the national policy for community development.

However, the significance of the social enterprise structure and the background shifts towards community asset and land ownership should not detract from recognising the way in which these community-based organisations link into national and even international markets. In Ireland, in particular, the community initiatives have fared well once they moved away from local agricultural sector support. They have found a variety of ways to generate a revenue stream based on culture, education and tourism and have used this market-based finance to support a range of community needs and activities. The organisational structures are quite complex but different aspects of their work intersect and it is clear that both must have effective management to achieve success. Financial support from national governments and the European Union, directly and indirectly, has enabled investment in projects and overcome short-term cashflow problems. It is also interesting that the Western Isles have been denoted as a pilot for community wealth building within Scotland (see Chapter 3).

In Ireland, community-based endogenous development has been successful to an extent (O Conneide and Keane, 1990), but, as with the Scottish cases, the direct employment effects are limited. The 2015 Galway County Development Plan, for example, expects little of local economic development in areas such as Letterfrack, seeing them as 'structurally weak'. However, once judged on the basis of their broader contribution to community services and infrastructure, these projects can be seen to have a greater local impact. That said, the context remains important, particularly the context of other infrastructure. In the Western Isles, for example, improved port facilities, better ferry services and enhanced digital infrastructure are all vital for any commercial or community activities to flourish.

The role of planning with regard to community assets

There are two clear insights emerging from this account of community assets being managed by social enterprises.

First, as with small firms, cooperatives and CLTs, there are a number of issues relating to the everyday functioning of social enterprises running community assets that would benefit from support by the local authority. These relate to the protection and transfer of ownership of premises as well as matters such as staff training, local procurement and knowledge of legal and business models, and have largely been covered in preceding chapters. For example, Earley (2023) showed that among the specific problems that community enterprises faced were knowledge of the options regarding the legal entity to choose, and problems of repair and maintenance that the buildings constituting the community asset required. Asset transfer could equate to the transfer of liabilities (Earley, 2023: 166). But the presence of volunteer advice centres, volunteer development agencies and development officers could prove very supportive. In addition, local authorities could support community enterprises through extending leases, say where a grant application required this, or absorbing loss of income while the group became established. They could run training seminars; the absence of training manuals for specific types of community asset was lamented. Generally, mentoring and contact with other volunteer-led assets could support groups, particularly when they were called upon to make decisions within a short time frame. Supported autonomy was considered by Earley (2023) to be the most desirable form of asset transfer, so that communities are genuinely empowered rather than burdened and supported in their ability to manage and control these assets.

Second, the national policy context makes a particular difference for these community-based enterprises operating at the margins of viability. Hobson et al (2019), in an English context, pointed to an increase in the number of community assets but, at the same time, a decline in the support from government for running them and managing services from them. In this context, community asset transfer can be seen as responsibilising local residents for public services in times of austerity and, thereby, tacitly supporting such austerity. Hobson et al contrast this with an agenda of community empowerment and genuine inclusion, where community assets can form the basis of resistance to corporate ownership or absentee landlordism, and/or to community dispossession, as when services and assets are lost to an area. Findlay-King et al (2018) looked at the transfer of leisure centres and libraries and similarly contrasted austerity localism with progressive localism, in which community groups connect to broader social and political movements aiming to transform policy frameworks at national and even international scales as a concerted challenge to neoliberalism. They found no evidence of such engagement with progressive politics but, rather, communities being empowered as an incidental or secondary effect of the state withdrawing due to austerity.

Murtagh (2015) examined community asset transfer in the UK under the New Labour government. Following the Quirk Report of 2007 (Department of Communities and Local Government, 2007), New Labour instituted an Asset Transfer Unit, an Advancing Assets Programme managed by the non-governmental organisation Locality, and a £30 million Community Assets Programme funded by the Lottery Fund. Murtagh critiqued that policy in terms of its claimed aims of being progressive and inclusive. He saw the absence of legitimacy as a key barrier to scaling up the quality and quantity of sustainable projects. In addition, ownership is essential for managing the asset and for securing finance. One danger – for local communities – is the transfer of assets that are not viable; here, partnership with state agencies is essential for sustainability. Murtagh also identified the importance of soft capital, capital that is patient, formed of loans on a semi-commercial basis and/or comprises a mix of loans and grants.

That different policy contexts are possible is illustrated by the Scottish example. The ReLocal project looked at how communities can be strengthened, taking the specific case of the Isle of Lewis (see also earlier). Currie et al (2019) emphasised the importance of national policy frameworks and funding opportunities, together with the role of key agencies operating beyond the local scale. In the case of the Isle of Lewis, the programmes supporting the purchase and management of community assets were really significant, as were the support provided by the Highlands and Islands Enterprise and the foundational legislation enacted by the Scottish Parliament. This support strengthened the competences and capacities of local actors, building the basis for autonomy in the future.

Given these points, what is the distinctive role that local planning can play? From a local planning perspective, the contribution of community-managed assets is more likely to be judged in relation to the creation, improvement and maintenance of social infrastructure in a locality than its relationship to progressive politics. Here the value of planning lies in the building of capacity in the local communities as a whole and taking a more place-based approach in terms of community assets and social infrastructure more generally. This involves building coalitions and focusing on place-making. For example, Dubb (2016) cited examples from San Diego and Cleveland in the US. They pointed to the importance of unusual local alliances between small businesses, social enterprises and non-governmental organisations, and also of local politics and policy embracing a new direction for change. The central theme in local policy needs to be improvements in local, everyday experiences which can drive comprehensive community-building efforts and new patterns of local economic development over time.

Hobson et al's (2019) work looked at two cases, both in semi-rural locations, in Churchdown and Brockworth, within Tewkesbury Borough Council, UK. The former was a renovated building used for youth work, elderly day care, sports and exercise, and information technology facilities and training. The latter offered youth services from a library location, alongside adult education. Hobson et al saw the advantages of asset transfer as the community accumulating and building reserves, while expanding the range of services and access to those services. This can contribute to community identity and pride and build social cohesion. Hobson et al drew two main conclusions. The first is that a transferred asset needs legitimacy within its local community to be regarded as of value, and for this the physical space needs to engage with as much of the community as possible. Social inclusion needs to be an aim, and constant use is important. Vacancy can undermine legitimacy but, used well, the physical building can help with the performativity of community, reinforcing identity. The second is that community capacity needs to be available for running the services associated with the asset. Individual 'trailblazers' are important, as are volunteers, where a wide pool is beneficial.

Webster et al (2021) also found examples of place-making based on local cooperatives in the Italian cities of Bologna and Rome. In Bologna, a regulation on civic collaboration for the urban commons created a variety of opportunities for engagement with plans for change in the city, but was more focused on the political and public spheres. Rome took a more neighbourhood-based approach, focusing on deprived neighbourhoods and seeking to involve a wider range of organisations. Within this, the rejuvenation of community assets such as parks and libraries played a central role. Unlike in Bologna, the efforts were much more grounded in community organisations, particularly the neighbourhood community cooperative. Concerns about the financial viability of this approach remained, however.

Looking at Toronto, Kamizaki and Rankin (2020) found a number of specific functions that local land use planning could play. First, a Toronto Strong Neighbourhoods Strategy was developed and renewed, with both social and economic indicators of well-being included. A new zoning designation was introduced – Residential Apartment Commercial – which allowed informal economies, including social enterprises, to be sanctioned in the inner suburban tower blocks where many low-income and recent immigrant communities lived. An initiative by the Thorncliffe Park Women's Committee to establish a community market was supported and this generated a range of spin-off community activities, including a community garden, an art-in-the-park programme, a sewing studio, a catering and café collective and a women's fitness programme. There were also collective day care services to support involvement in these activities. Kamizaki and Rankin (2020) concluded that the 'devil is in the details of market-oriented [community economic development], it seems, and concentrating merely on critiques of neoliberalism may result in overlooking the possibility for markets to be structured to provide care, extend democratic principles and articulate a progressive politics' (p 224). Other aspects of the policy approach in Toronto did include forms of planning gain from new development under the community benefits agreement umbrella, and leveraging the procurement of anchor institutions as in community wealth building (see Chapter 4). It seems that a mix of approaches worked best here, although it should be acknowledged that these did not challenge the pursuit of growth, rather looking to increase the social value that was also created and to move towards more equitable regional economies.

Local planning needs to have close regard to equity issues where community assets are concerned, as research has often pointed to the potential for gentrification. Earley (2023) studied the extent to which the use of community enterprises and community assets have contributed to gentrification in the areas where they have been adopted. Her conclusion was that the 'relationship between regeneration, gentrification and community assets depends on the type of asset, the nature of its use and the background and values of the individuals involved in both its governing board and as employees – their demographics, socioeconomic status and positioning in relation to gentrification' (Earley, 2023: 8). She argued that there is a need to diversify organisations' boards where possible, in order to understand better the diverse needs of the local community. Relying on volunteers produced boards and managements that reflect those with a higher level of social, economic and cultural capital and this could reinforce or even widen inequalities.

Findlay-King et al (2018) confirmed the widespread finding that the localism that resulted was highly dependent on local social capital and made a link here to entrenching inequalities: 'the community groups who are successful will be those who already have high stocks of social capital, operating in more favourable markets, and thus existing inequalities will be potentially entrenched rather than challenged through the asset transfer process' (p 168). Similarly, the ReLocal report warns against adopting a unified notion of community, pointing out that the ability to take advantage of this supportive context was not evenly spread across local residents and actors and could, in itself, create some level of inequality with the wider population (Currie et al, 2019).

Thus, local planning has to deal with the fragility of social enterprises involved in community assets while also trying to take account of the ways that their operation may generate inequalities. The fostering of social capital has to balance the ability to build on existing social capacities with the inclusion of larger sectors of the local community. The ultimate goal is an enhanced scale of social infrastructure, with the increased provision of goods and services to the locality that this offers. The hope of such social enterprises as a whole is that they will diversify the economy and extend the reach of non-market dynamics into even more diverse economies.

8

Community-based infrastructure

Introduction

The previous chapter looked at the role of community-based social enterprises in managing community assets as part of the social infrastructure of the locality, highlighting their need for active support and for local planning to ensure that local inequalities are not exacerbated by the reliance on the social economy in this way. This chapter turns to other forms of infrastructure, particularly the key services – such as energy, water, waste management and transport – that are necessary for both businesses and households. The availability of such infrastructure is central to the livelihoods and quality of life of communities. However, provision of this infrastructure has not been straightforwardly oriented to meeting the essential needs of firms and households. Increasingly it is oriented towards financial measures in the form of profits, share value, asset value and/or use of such assets to leverage debt income. There is a debate over the structural changes that have affected the infrastructure sectors and this sets the context for the search for alternative means of infrastructure provision that are less aligned with market pressures and the associated growth agenda.

The first part of the chapter discusses these debates and whether community-based infrastructure can be viewed as a response to structural change. It then considers how and to what extent community-based initiatives have emerged in relation to water, waste management, transport and energy infrastructure. This leads to a greater focus on community-based energy, with an extended discussion of such energy in France. The chapter concludes with a discussion on the role that planning systems can play. This involves recognition of the need to consider infrastructures at all scales, particularly in the light of environmental objectives.

The debate on the splintering of infrastructure networks

Infrastructure has often been regarded as a set of intrinsically public goods that need to be supplied at scale and to the public or a community as a whole. As such, where the public sector has the capacity, they have been invested in and provided by the public sector. Actually, many are not pure public goods in the language of economists, as households and firms may have to opt in to their use. However, they usually involve economies of scale, and the marginal costs of additional consumption can be low once the basic network is in place. Thus, in higher-income countries there has been a tendency to rely on the state to provide such utilities as publicly planned and supported services, even if chargeable at the point of use. In lower-income countries, the situation has been more mixed, with some limited state provision and a variety of more-or-less informal modes of provision.

There have, however, been a number of pressures that have moved infrastructure provision away from the public sector. These include the fiscal crises that the public sector has periodically experienced during the latter 20th and early 21st centuries, notably following the global financial crisis of 2008, which led to a period of austerity for the public finances in many countries. But, beyond these periodic pressures, there has been growing influence from neoliberalism as a political ideology, favouring market-based provision over direct public sector provision. This has further been affected by the economic shifts towards financialisation in which a growing range of activities have become the basis for creating financial assets that are traded in financial markets. This has affected infrastructure providers in many sectors, so that influences from the financial markets have been felt in the markets for the core services themselves.

In 2001, Graham and Marvin argued that a fundamental shift was occurring in infrastructure systems, which they termed 'splintering'. Their argument was four-fold. First, they posited that the modern infrastructural ideal from the mid-19th to the mid-20th centuries in industrialised countries had been monopolistic, integrated and standardised provision of a service through a network which was spread relatively equally across space. From the late 1960s onwards, this ideal was undermined, *inter alia*, by the factors already listed. So, and second, infrastructure services became 'unbundled' by a mix of economic liberalisation and the development of new technologies, particularly information technologies. As a result, coalitions of actors have been able to press for unbundling, that is, the separation of integrated infrastructure into different sections of the network and different service packages. Furthermore, unbundling allows for 'bypassing', whereby there is more emphasis on the more valuable sections and packages, resulting in the 'bypassing' of others, including more vulnerable users and disadvantaged places. The third part of their argument is that the result of these processes is the emergence of premium networked spaces, linked together to create 'global enclaves'. This further encourages more splintering and a widening gap between households and places in terms of access to infrastructure. Fourth, resistance to these processes may emerge from local authorities and communities, so that urban politics and the activities of urban social movements increasingly reflect these inequalities in infrastructure provision.

The UK was seen as a leader in breaking up a public sector-led system of integrated infrastructure planning and provision and allowing for greater private sector involvement, due to the influence of Thatcherism under Conservative governments from 1979 onwards. This sought to replace many areas of public sector provision with private sector involvement, on the premise that this would promote efficiency as private companies competed with each other; parts of the public sector were also required to engage in such 'competition' in the name of efficiency gains. Whether greater efficiency did result is a moot point; often, companies were competing for long-term contracts with the state which locked everyone in regardless of whether or not efficiencies were found in practice. Furthermore, such long-term contracts often proved highly profitable for the private sector partners without apparent commensurate benefits for the public sector or customers. The investments in network and service improvements that were promised have not always been forthcoming. In the 21st century this trend towards privatisation has been further influenced by the growing involvement of global companies in public service provision, so that a country's infrastructure can be owned and managed by overseas investors and utilities.

Community-based infrastructure might, thus, be seen as a part of the resistance to this splintering. However, Coutard (2008) provided a forensic investigation of Graham and Marvin's argument. He claimed, first, that the universalisation of basic infrastructure services is overemphasised. Instead, such universalisation depends on the will and capacity of the state (at central or local level), public control over land and urban development and a relatively prosperous population (in global terms). In the absence of these factors, splintering has long been the norm in some countries, particularly where widespread poverty prevails. Second, Coutard argued that the relationships between universal, homogeneous services and urban integration can be ambivalent. He pointed to examples from Santiago in Chile, Los Angeles in the US and Buenos Aires in Argentina, where the services akin to Graham and Marvin's (2001) modern ideal have gone alongside social segregation, urban sprawl and the emergence of premium networked spaces. Taking a broader geographical perspective than Graham and Marvin, Coutard found that the modern integrated ideal has failed to live up to its promises in many places, quite apart from any splintering that may be occurring.

Coutard (2008) further questioned the nature of resistance to liberalised utility services. Rather, he found that contemporary infrastructure systems often do not conform to the neoliberal privatised ideal but, rather, remain deeply politicised. Resistance must therefore be interpreted more carefully in this context. Finally, he found the terms 'unbundling' and 'bypassing' to be misleading when applied without consideration of specific geographical contexts. Even in Western Europe, where the analysis might be considered more applicable, the outcomes have not always been as Graham and Marvin (2001) anticipated. There have been some improvements in value for money of the services provided and the scale of inequalities has been somewhat contained. There does not seem to be a simple relationship between increased differentiation in service provision and increased segregation, inequality or fragmentation. So, there should be some caution in considering how to frame community-based infrastructure projects as resistance. In particular, it is worthwhile taking a broader geographical perspective when considering the potential of such projects and the challenges faced by them.

In higher-income countries where public sector provision of infrastructure dominated for well over a century there has clearly been a growing emphasis on community-based initiatives and what they can offer. But this seems to be only partly in resistance to structural trends. It also relates to the desire to support particular communities' needs and to align such infrastructure with a broader range of values, including environmental values expressed at the community scale. Smith and Stirling (2018: 67) provided an analysis of what they termed 'grassroots contributions' but could also be considered community-based projects. They defined grassroots contributions as:

> a diverse set of activities in which networks of neighbors, community groups, and activists work with people to generate bottom-up solutions for sustainable developments; novel solutions that respond to the local situation and the interests and values of the communities involved; and where those communities have control over the process and outcomes. (p 67)

They were particularly interested in the contribution of such initiatives to innovation, sustainability and, further, to democracy, and found four key benefits from such community-based innovation. First, there is its potential to generate more democratic processes of innovation. Second, they consider that such processes can then contribute to greater democracy more generally. Third, they can empower sociotechnical configurations that might otherwise be suppressed. And fourth, they can help nurture social diversity, which Smith and Stirling also see as important for the health of a democracy. These are more wide-ranging positive benefits of community-based infrastructure, in addition to their core provision of services. However, these can vary with types of infrastructure, and so the next section explores experiences with community-based infrastructure across different sectors.

Experiences of community-based infrastructure

Water projects

Water infrastructure is concerned with supplying usable water, both potable and non-potable, and with removing waste water. With the emphasis on reticulated water systems in higher-income countries and the past investment in piped water and collective drainage and sewerage systems, this has often been seen as collective supply and collective collection and disposal. Often there is no choice to opt in or out, as connections to the network are already provided to and from a building or street. However, are other options are possible. Water can be harvested outside (from rainwater) and inside (from grey waste water) to be used as part of the water supply. Localised purification means can be provided through reed beds and chemical means to enhance the potable supply. Drainage from a building or street does not have to be to the network but can be to local soakaways or treatment areas or dispersed via green infrastructure or sustainable urban drainage systems. And, of course, individual measures at the scale of the household unit, building or street can seek to reduce the demand for water in all its forms and for all its uses.

There has been extensive research into community-based water infrastructure, notably through the work of Eleanor Ostrom (1993; 2005; 2015), where water is conceptualised as a resource used in common and where management by the local community occurs through a common property regime. Much of Ostrom's research has been in lower-income settings. Here, community management is not only essential, as state or private sector provision of piped water is often absent, but is seen to offer considerable benefits to the communities themselves, since they are able to shape the governance of the water infrastructure to their specific needs. The common property regime can incorporate sets of incentives, that is, of relative costs and benefits that reflect the community and its key social and economic characteristics. Such a regime operates with agreed rules covering both use and conflicts over use, and this helps to manage the collective resource so as to avoid excessive depletion. In this way the so-called 'tragedy of the commons' is avoided (Ostrom, 2007).

Collective management regimes work well if certain conditions are satisfied (see also Chapter 5 for collective management in relation to cooperatives). These include clearly defined boundaries to the water resource system and rules about the use of the water resource that are related to local conditions and to other rules about inputs into the system. Those affected by the rules on water use should be included in making and modifying those rules, and monitoring should occur, either by the water users or by people who are accountable to the users. There are graduated sanctions on misuse of water resources and mechanisms for conflict resolution in low-cost local arenas. Users are able to devise their own institutions on the basis of long-term rights to the water resource, and the whole is nested within multilevel layers where the water resource is part of a system at a larger scale.

While community-based water infrastructure is less common in higher-income countries, due to the greater penetration of reticulated systems, in rural Ireland there are a relatively large number of community-managed water systems arising from the limitations in achieving coverage by the state utility. About 400 community-managed water systems provide drinking water to about 7 per cent of the population. Bresnihan and Hesse (2020) detailed how the expansion of these schemes dates back to the 1950s, when government capital grants supported rural groups in establishing access to piped water, often using volunteer labour. Bresnihan and Hesse reported that by the 1990s these accounted for almost 30 per cent of rural water supplies, some supplying a handful of houses, others estates of over 1,000 homes. The sustainability of these schemes was challenged by the abolition of domestic water charges within the public water network, putting community schemes at a disadvantage, since they needed the water charges to survive financially. Subsequently, the National Federation of Group Water Schemes negotiated for increased public funding to upgrade infrastructure, operational subsidies, related research programmes and strategies to protect water sources. This was partly in response to the failure of many community water schemes to meet water quality standards.

Following this, a Rural Water Programme was established in Ireland to support community schemes to reorganise and upgrade in pursuit of water quality and efficiency. Many community water groups now work with private water companies, the latter designing, building and operating water treatment facilities under 20-year contracts, while the community groups manage the source and water delivery within the locality, including collecting water charges. Bresnihan and Hesse (2020) saw a rhetoric of rationalisation being used to frame these changes, which have enabled community water groups to survive and remain viable. Metering is now being rolled out, but its advantages are seen in terms of reducing costs for the community groups by making leaks visible and hence remediable; it is not being framed as a way of reducing water demand as is common elsewhere.

Interestingly, a key feature of such community water schemes is that they utilise local knowledge of hydro-social cycles, that is, the water sources and flows in a given area as well as the sources and causes of water pollution, which are often associated with local agricultural practices. Engagement with local farmers – who are, of course, also part of the local community – has covered education and training programmes as well as persuading them to adopt new practices, such as fencing to reduce the amount of slurry reaching water courses. As Bresnihan and Hesse (2020) stated: 'Their efforts to protect source waters are localized and contingent on good relationships with farmers in the areas' (p 95). Their conclusion on these community water schemes was: 'While reliant on the state, they are self-organized, separate from, but entangled with broader processes within Ireland's water sector and economic development. As positive as their flexibility sounds, it also reflects their perennial vulnerability' (p 96).

Waste projects

Waste management is often conceived of as a service, but it requires infrastructure to collect, recycle, treat and dispose of waste materials. In higher-income countries this is seen as a function of the state, even if elements of this are privatised. For example, in England, private companies collect domestic and commercial waste under contracts either with the local authority or with commercial firms directly; they then engage with other private companies specialising in waste treatment, energy-from-waste generation or waste disposal (say, to landfill). Indeed, English waste management does provide a classic case of splintered infrastructure. The key environmental aims of minimising waste and encouraging reuse and recycling thus involve multiple private companies, individual households and businesses and local government also. Such activities are often considered more 'naturally' localised than is the case with energy or water, say, but waste can be transported over long distances (even internationally) for treatment and disposal.

Outside of low-income contexts, there are relatively few community-based waste infrastructure projects, although there are a wealth of local initiatives seeking to promote waste reduction or recycling through engagement with communities. Luckin and Sharp (2004) provided a review of community projects in England oriented to promoting waste reduction, reuse and recycling, situating this as part of the community waste sector and based in not-for-profit organisations. As with many social enterprises, Luckin and Sharp pointed to the importance of volunteer time and how this necessarily represents only a part of the local community. Nevertheless, they found that community waste projects did increase community engagement with waste management. They saw the tension between taking responsibility within waste regimes and expanding participation in waste management as inevitable. Another key finding was that community waste projects remained largely true to their social and environmental goals and were not distracted by the need to generate revenue in order to maintain their sustainability. This points to the inherent need to engage with the market but not necessarily at the cost of project values. Luckin and Sharp suggested that the institutional design of the project is really important in ensuring that the balance between social, environmental and economic aspects is maintained.

Looking to the lessons to be learned from experience in lower-income countries, Wijayanti and Suryani (2015) discussed a waste bank project in Surabaya, Indonesia. This was a social enterprise, a business owned by a group of people based within the locality who saw waste as a valuable economic commodity and therefore collected it. In the period Wijayanti and Suryani studied – the early 2010s – there was considerable growth in such waste banks in Surabaya. The key factor in their success seemed to be the receipt of money for waste reduction, due to the lower costs that the state faced in managing waste in the locality and reducing the amount going to landfill. Lusugga Kironde and Yhdego (1997) researched waste in Dar es Salaam, Tanzania and found a number of problems with conventional waste management associated with corruption, privatisation, poor relationships between the government and local communities, and community apathy. As a result, they recommended a shift from a state-led approach to a community-based model. This involved minimising waste generation through the involvement of women's and youth groups, and using small enterprises to encourage recycling and reuse. The remainder could then be separated so that the hazardous waste was sent to incineration, the biomass was used for composting and the remainder sent to landfill.

Such community-based waste initiatives therefore still rely on wider waste infrastructure. This needs to be taken into account when considering planning for community-based infrastructure.

Transport projects

Transport infrastructure is a mix of the underlying road, rail, cycle path or walking paths networks together with the collective provision of means of carriage, that is, public transport in the form of buses, trams and trains. Individually owned cars and bicycles make use of the collective networks but are private transport. However, these can be shared as with bike-hire and taxi firms, which bring an element of the collective into the use of motor vehicles and bikes. Rather than collective provision at the same time, this is collective provision separated out over time, as in several people using a bus at the same time compared with several people using a hire bike but at different times; it is part of the sharing economy.

Glover (2017) has studied community-based transport infrastructure and echoes Graham and Marvin's (2001) argument that such infrastructure in higher-income countries is made up of 'small islands of services run by regulated monopolies, using standardised infrastructure to provide reliable services in water supply, wastewater, electricity, gas, transport, communications and other requirements of metropolitan living' (Glover, 2017: 5), but there has been a shift away from the model of centralised infrastructure towards 'more disaggregated, poly-centric and varied approaches' (Glover, 2017: 5), known as distributed systems. Authority, resources and communication are dispersed and managed by a range of people across an entire system, leading to issues of integration (Glover, 2017). This has affected the transport sector, which has seen the rise of more diverse, deregulated and networked transport systems (see also Stehlin and Payne, 2022). Large transport bureaucracies have been broken up, with more interest in market-based approaches and the rise of contracting with the private sector. There has also been greater interest in collaborative consumption, such as the shared use of services and resources under commercial arrangements, through transport rental businesses operating at a variety of scales. Internet-based platforms have both enabled larger shared-use operators to grow and provided a basis for many smaller-scale renters to enter the market. These changes are now very apparent in the transport sector. There are also non-market variants involving gifting, exchange of used goods and sharing.

Community-owned transport fits into this context of change. However, it has been underdeveloped compared to energy, say, particularly where one is looking beyond the commercial activities of ride-sharing or bike rentals. Glover (2017) argued that it will work best where it adds to the flexibility of travellers through its integration into broader public transport networks. As such, it is likely to follow examples in rural areas that are demand responsive. These typically comprise mobility services that are available to the public using smaller-capacity vehicles. They offer flexible routes and schedules, as well as flexible destinations and origins, at least for some services. They seek to be responsive to the needs of individual passengers, often using online technologies. And, where possible, they could combine goods and passenger transport. Examples include not-for-profit car sharing as found in City Carshare in San Francisco, US, Moray Carshare in Findhorn and Forres, Scotland and Mobility Carsharing in Switzerland.

Glover (2017) considered that such community-owned transport can contribute to a convivial society because it is based on voluntary community associations and therefore involves social interaction. It creates a new institution for the benefit of members, who can articulate new strategies and projects to promote social connectivity and environmental protection. However, as projects are based in a local community, success depends on communication and understanding of members' mobility and other needs, and the quality of the response to these needs. Projects are likely to be generated where existing modes of collective transport – whether public transport or commercial shared transport services – fail to provide sufficient geographical coverage, leaving specific communities undersupplied. Scaling up beyond this may be limited.

Energy projects

Regarding energy infrastructure, in higher-income countries it has become the norm to connect to local, regional or national supply systems, which may themselves be supplied in part and at times by gas, oil, electricity or coal from further afield. However, there are also areas that are 'off grid' and thus meet their own energy needs from local storage of fuel (gas, oil) or local generation of electricity, biogas or other biofuel. There has been growing interest in more localised forms of renewable energy generation through smaller wind turbines, locally installed solar panels and micro-hydro schemes — all of which generate electricity — together with biogas, which produces gas for burning directly or for indirect electricity generation. Some of these may fall within the remit of an individual building, but there is the potential for locality-based schemes also. Unlike localised water schemes, localised energy generation has the potential for generating surplus energy and thus transporting this outside the locality, potentially earning a revenue stream via connection to a national or regional grid or a private wire.

In addition, the use of heating or cooling networks allows for thermal comfort to be achieved by using warmed or cooled air distributed through local networks; however well the networks are insulated, they have to be relatively localised, as the heat or coolth dissipates over distance. Air and ground source heat pumps are an even more localised version of this, providing thermal regulation from very localised sources — the air around a building or the ground on which it sits. As with water, there is also the demand management side, including potentially large savings in energy use from insulation and other ways of gaining efficiencies.

Energy is the area where community-based infrastructure has shown the greatest potential, in terms not only of meeting local communities' needs but also of making an aggregate contribution to the environmental agenda through the preferred focus on renewables. Using the example of a community micro-hydro project, Smith and Stirling (2018: 68) set out all the activities and processes that the community has to take part in, and indeed lead on, where community-based energy is concerned:

- The community has to constitute itself as a group and attract members.
- They have to learn about technology options.
- They need to raise funds for capital investment and ongoing maintenance and management.
- Permission needs to be secured for the physical development.
- Commitment, solidarity and stamina need to be generated and nurtured.
- A range of reasons for motivating members to support and engage in the project have to be articulated.
- Painful compromises need to be negotiated at times.

In order to achieve all these, there are a number of prerequisites. Knowledge has to be collected and generated, including knowledge about the local community's aspirations and needs, alongside more technical know-how and critical knowledge about the socio-economic limitations on grassroots activities. A number of procedures have to be activated in order to engage people within the community – including possibly participatory design – and to enable community members to access the more technical aspects of the initiatives – such as workshops, tools, mentoring and web-based platforms. It should be acknowledged that such initiatives are likely to prompt new identities for and social relations within the local community. For example, local people may see themselves at citizen scientists or grassroots entrepreneurs. Above all, these projects are resulting in new ways of thinking and doing, both within the community and in relation to infrastructure systems, alongside new skills also. Koirala et al (2018) – looking specifically at community energy infrastructure projects – saw these processes as creating a new kind of community: 'energetic communities' capable of integrating with wider infrastructure systems in a variety of ways.

A key example of success in community energy is provided by Samsø in Denmark. This is a small-scale community of only 3,800 people (Mundaca et al, 2018). The installation of renewable energy was the result of the village winning a national competition under the Danish Action Plan for 35 per cent share for renewables by 2030. This paid for wind turbines and district heating, with sufficient generation capacity to create a surplus that could be sold. Profits have supported a local energy academy. The increase in community pride and identity is less quantifiable, but equally important. The impetus for participating in the national competition was the economic shock arising from the closure of a major local employer, an abattoir. It was accepted that some change was needed on the island. Depopulation was a threat to the community, with people leaving for employment and educational opportunities. At the same time, the existing community was vulnerable to energy price shocks; they had also had a bad experience with a mini-combined heat and power plant that had led to high prices. The project was based on transparent information exchange from the outset, and widespread consultation. Connection to the district heating network was voluntary, given past experiences. The outcomes have included short-term and long-term employment and improved economic prospects. Shared ownership underpinned acceptance of the project, as did lower energy prices.

Sperling (2017) argued that the success of this project was due to a clear guiding vision, governmental support with technology and the whole implementation process, and expert assistance. Also important was the local history and tradition of cooperative projects within the community, and a strong sense of locality and community spirit. But the presence of a few entrepreneurial individuals and of links to wider networks was highly relevant. Throughout, intermediaries helped to align the different elements of the project.

However, this is just one example and it is important to recognise the sheer diversity of community-based energy projects, in technology, scale, the role of the local community and of other actors, the motivation of these actors, organisational features and the economic dimension (Seyfang et al, 2013; Hicks and Ison, 2018). Creamer et al (2018) saw this in terms of ambiguity with regard to all of: generation, transmission and distribution, supply and demand. And this feeds through to variety in terms of governance and ownership models. Thus, Creamer et al emphasised that community energy cannot be equated with concepts such as singular, bounded or localised.

Looking across 25 case studies from a variety of European and North American countries as well as Australia, Hicks and Ison (2018) identified two key features that influence a community energy project's evolution. The first is the importance of context. Community energy projects develop in different places at different times with different sets of actors. The second is that motivations for individual projects vary, and thus they cannot all be judged by the same criteria (see also Seyfang et al, 2013 and Brummer, 2018). That said, there seem to be four key factors to note: the level of community engagement; the governance structures for decision making and involvement of actors; the technology deployed and the implied scale; and the availability of finance. From this, Hicks and Ison drew attention to the way that voting rights are distributed and the associated balance of decision-making power, the distribution of financial benefits, important decisions about the scale of technology and the level of community engagement.

Walker (2008) discussed community energy projects in terms of actors involved, scale, nature of the place, networking, processes and sense of identity. Using this, Brummer (2018) identified benefits from community energy in terms of financial savings and returns, and also education, participation, climate protection (that is, environmental benefits), community building and associated self-realisation, meeting renewable energy targets and promoting innovation. The balance between these benefits varies. In Germany, education about and acceptance of renewable energy has a high priority, whereas in the UK, with its market-driven approach, financial benefits dominate. The US has more concern with meeting targets, but also community building and creating self-identity through such projects.

Brummer (2018) specified a number of barriers to implementing community energy. First, there are organisational issues, including the legal framework and planning requirements. Second, discrimination against large companies and incumbents (often for good reasons) can make community projects more difficult to achieve. Third, there can be a lack of institutional and political support, reinforced by – fourth – scepticism about community energy and the presence of nimbyism. Fifth, lack of resources and expertise can be problematic, and, finally, a saturation effect can be apparent. The UK was identified as primarily facing problems of resources and expertise, as well as the complexities of regulation around energy generation and marketing. For Germany, resources and expertise were also a hindrance, mainly in terms of the need for many volunteers, given the importance of cooperatives as the main way of realising community energy. In the US organisational issues dominated.

There are aspects of the analysis of community energy projects that reflect findings about community enterprise in general, particularly with regard to the level of community involvement, the need for buy-in and the use of extensive volunteering effort. But the financial dimension stands out where energy is concerned, both because of the need to regularise the distribution of costs and benefits within the project and also because many energy projects involve a degree of connection to the wider grid both for back-up power and to sell surpluses. Given that energy markets in most countries are highly regulated, this can give rise to complex contractual arrangements to establish the relationships between the various sources of generation and the distribution of energy to a variety of users. Once established, these contractual arrangements then influence the ongoing operation and sustainability of the community energy project (Rydin et al, 2015).

Reviewing a range of urban energy projects that had been able to maintain sustainability over almost a decade, Rydin and Turcu (2019) found that many projects ended because of short-termism in policy frameworks or because the primary goals of installing some technology (generation or energy efficiency) had been achieved. They did find a number of community-based projects that were ongoing but noted an overriding problem of limited capacity within the community to run these projects over time, as well as the need for a sound financial model to underpin their viability, and hence sustainability. Skills and knowledge were at a premium for these community projects as well as volunteering, leadership and generally the ability to leverage local social capital. A supportive institutional framework as established by national policies was also vital.

Looking specifically at German cases of community energy, Radtke and Ohlhorst (2021) found relatively low levels of engagement, particularly among women and young people. Perhaps because of the area they surveyed, they found a surprisingly high level of involvement by high-income academics. They considered that community energy projects have a potential for using and generating social capital that is only partially exploited. In Scotland, Van Veelen (2018) also found inclusion to be rather nominal and falling well short of any transfer of power or associated transformation of democracy.

A project in Feldheim, Germany which included community-owned electricity and heat grids supplied by local renewable energy was covered in a detailed case study by Mundaca et al (2018). This small village of only 200 people deployed a wide range of technology including a biogas plant, wind and solar power, a wood pellet plant and a battery system for storage. So innovative was their approach that new legislation was needed to permit it. Interestingly, Mundaca et al saw the impetus for this innovation in a local economic shock with the closure of an electronics factory after German reunification. The facilitating factor was a high level of social capital in the village, with widespread formal and informal consultation facilitated by intermediaries. The result has been long-term energy price security and independence from market volatility. In addition, some jobs have been created and a community centre built. The local income tax and the generous and stable German feed-in-tariff supported the project financially. While not all local people benefited equally, it was significant that the outcomes were perceived as fair by the community.

It is important, however, to recognise that community energy projects do not exist in isolation, except for completely 'off grid' examples, largely because of the financial dimension. This means that, as Creamer et al (2018) pointed out, community energy is both enabled and constituted by trans-scalar assemblages of actors and thus requires multisector participation and coordination. This connection through to networks at larger scales, for some, means that there is potential for community energy projects to contribute to system-wide change. But national frameworks can be a strong influence on the shape of these contractual arrangements and their success. Brummer (2018) noted the oft-quoted importance of the German feed-in-tariff in enabling households generating electricity from various renewable energy technologies such as solar panels to benefit from surplus supply or efforts at demand management within the household. The UK adopted a more limited form of the feed-in-tariff, relying instead on a more market-driven approach, with predictably poorer results in terms of household take-up. In the US, Brummer (2018) referenced the extraordinarily wide range of financial incentives, with over 3,900 numbered in 2017.

Focus on community renewable energy in France

France is notable for having one of the most centralised energy systems in Europe, not least because of the long-term dominance of nuclear power plants in electricity generation. However, there has still been considerable growth in the community energy sector and, in particular, the community renewable energy (CRE) sector, which is now well established. The European Union (EU) Directive on Renewable Energy (2019, amended 2023) defines CRE projects as citizens, social entrepreneurs, public authorities and commercial organisations coming together to jointly invest in, produce, sell and/or distribute renewable energy. Such CRE projects were given an impetus in France by the 2015 Energy Transition Law for Green Growth, and France was the first EU member state to introduce dedicated incentives to promote the involvement of local actors in renewable energy projects. These were termed participatory bonuses and they provided additional funding if participatory financing from citizens and local authorities reached the threshold of 10 per cent of the total or 40 per cent of the equity for a minimum of three years.

As a result of a supportive policy and legislative framework, the number of CRE projects in France grew four-fold over 2014–19, to some 240 projects (Vernay et al, 2023a). Dudka et al (2023) report that the projects developed under the Énergie Partagée umbrella increased energy production two-fold over 2016–19, with 50 per cent increase in the total capital invested and an over 20 per cent increase in the number of shareholders. By 2020, Sebi and Vernay (2020) assessed that over 70 per cent of CRE projects were solar projects and about 15 per cent were wind. However, in terms of capacity, about three-quarters were accounted for by wind and a fifth by solar.

The shift from a completely nationalised to at least partly privatised energy system created the window in which such CRE projects could emerge (Colombaiolli and Storti, 2022), but some key organisations were also influential The non-governmental organisation le Collectif pour l'énergie citoyenne was significant in lobbying for this facilitative framework, and Enercoop has been a key facilitator. Enercoop was founded in 2005 as a cooperative renewable energy supplier covering all technologies of photovoltaics, wind, hydro and biomass, and making its income from the sale of electricity (IRENA, 2021). In 2021 it supplied over 100,000 consumers – individuals, businesses and local authorities. It also plays a role in supporting CRE by buying energy from some 350 independent local energy producers. It was influential in overcoming early barriers to CRE, finding a solution to the need for a bank guarantee in order to benefit from the feed-in tariff or feed-in premium. Enercoop worked with the Belgian cooperative Ecopower, the ethical bank Triodos and the French bank Credit Coopératif to set up such a guarantee; in the event, this did not need to be activated. Now Enercoop can buy electricity directly from producers and CRE projects can sell electricity to either the main French energy company, EDF or Enercoop, with the benefit of the feed-in tariff or feed-in premium boosting profitability.

The CRE sector as a whole is highly heterogeneous. In a survey of 164 French energy communities, Dudka et al (2023) found four configurations:

- full citizen ownership (31 per cent), in which citizens were the sole participants in the project;
- shared citizen ownership (46 per cent), in which citizens were joined by public authorities and commercial actors;
- citizen crowdfunding (12 per cent), in which a crowdfunding platform enabled citizens to fund a project; and
- civic participation (12 per cent), in which public authorities acted on behalf of citizens and joined with commercial actors in the project.

Dudka et al argued that strong citizen engagement and a strong community logic dominated the French community energy landscape, while noting that the involvement of small and medium enterprises and local government have become more important over time. This has led to hybrid logics driving the CRE organisations.

Sebi and Vernay (2020) developed a separate typology of four different types of project which includes consideration of technology:

- citizen photovoltaic (PV) clusters, mainly accounted for by small rooftop projects;
- citizen-led wind farms, some wood-based plants and larger PV projects, which had a longer incubation period;
- projects with small production capacity but a strong emphasis on profitability, such as mini-hydro; and

- schemes what were co-developed with the public sector or private actors, notably biogas plans in collaboration with agri-businesses.

The first category dominates in terms of projects (63 per cent), but in terms of capacity it is the second and fourth categories that are most significant, with 55 per cent of capacity from the projects co-developed with public or private actors and 34 per cent from the larger citizen-led projects.

Some reported cases illustrate this diversity. The Occitania region was home to the first two wholly citizen-owned PV parks in France (Friends of the Earth Europe, 2020): 123 Soleil and le Watt Citoyen. These arose from cooperation between the regional authority and the Environment and Energy Management Agency for France, ADEME, which also led to the emergence of the ECLR network or Énergies Citoyennes Locales et Renouvelable in 2014. Since 2014 (as reported in Friends of the Earth Europe, 2020), 46 projects have been developed in the region involving 3,000 citizens and 40 communities. With the benefit of €800,000 of regional funding, some €2.6 million of local investment has resulted. The ECLR network was particularly important in sharing knowledge and providing a space for discussion and learning across the region.

Centrales Villageoises (nd) are local companies where shareholders are mainly citizens, local municipalities and local companies; the common model is adopted of a territorial scope, shared citizen governance, local economic benefits and a quality management approach. The concept was born in 2010, emerging from an EU-supported project and launched by five regional parks and AURA-EE (Auvergne Rhône-Alpes Énergie Environnement). Over 2010–14 there were eight pilot projects. But the model allows explicitly for replication, as has occurred across the AURA region and beyond. In 2018 a national association was set up to raise awareness, pool resources and build solidarity, reinforce professionalism and ensure high quality, and pursue innovative experiments, developing new legal and financial models and diversifying renewable energy and energy management projects. By 2021 there were over 5,000 shareholders with 35 PV plants in operation. Fifty-five territories were committed to the concept and some €9 million were invested,

In a study of New Aquitaine, Colombarolli and Storti (2022) pointed out how CRE organisations are involved not only in the energy service itself but also in other activities such as training and energy advice. They found that CRE organisations are generally flat in structure, with an emphasis on horizontal coordination and participatory decision making, but they can become more complex as organisations once they are embedded in a territorial structure, as when they become integrated with the actions of a local authority. It is the mix of physical, technological, institutional and community factors that determines the precise form of a CRE. Colombarolli and Storti stressed the variety of motivations that were involved in setting up individual projects, with initiatives arising from the grassroots and higher-tier organisations, and involving any or all of economic, social and environmental aims. The key feature of a CRE organisation is that it can combine general ecological interests with the mutual interests of participants but, broadly, Colombarolli and Storti saw communities of interest as more aligned with economic and individualistic motives, and communities of place with social motives. In the four cases that they studied, three main motives dominated: community engagement, producing jobs and local economic development, and promoting environmental awareness.

Another French case is the Forester–Citizen Heat joint project (Friends of the Earth Europe, 2020). This mobilises local savings to design, finance and operate wood-based heating systems in collaboration with local residents. In Lucinges, Haute Savoie a community heating network was co-financed with citizens and managed by the public authorities. Forty-five people originally invested. The project provides heating both in the centre of the village and through a 1 km network. As a result, 60 collective housing units, five individual houses, the school and its canteen, the town hall, the library, the community centre, two cultural centres, an organic beer brewery and one other commercial company received heating. The wood chips come from a nearby forest and the energy revenues are now largely kept within the village, a form of community wealth building. The support of the cooperative association Énergie Partagée was important; this association supports projects involving over 5,000 citizen investors in total.

Finally, OnCIMEè is a local project in Lorient, Brittany which arose from a partnership between Bretagne Énergies Citoyennes and the City of Lorient (Friends of the Earth Europe, 2020). It involves the rental of PV panels together with citizen engagement. Schools, administrative buildings and offices then self-consume the electricity generated from the PVs. The PVs belong to the project organiser but the municipality pays a sum of money to the organiser under a contract of about 15 years and allows them to install the PVs on the roofs of municipal buildings. The occupiers of the buildings are then able to self-consume the energy generated. As of 2019, there were over 100 shareholders and 400 rented PV panels.

Research has identified a number of key challenges that CRE in France has faced. Regardless of type, CRE projects depend heavily on their local public and on a supportive policy framework. Vernay and Sebi (2020) noted the problems of relying on volunteers, who may not be a stable resource and also may not be representative of the wider community. A shift to an employee model may be more resilient but can reduce the participatory dimension of such projects. The same authors also found that such projects remain vulnerable to policy change (Sebi and Vernay, 2020), echoing the finding of Rydin and Turcu (2019) that a large number of local energy projects in the UK came to an end because a particular policy expired or was replaced. Other barriers that Vernay and Sebi (2020) found include the difficulties of ensuring grid connection (a problem that can be solved only at the level of the electricity network as a whole), and the difficulties of cooperating with local authorities, particularly where the use of municipal rooftops is involved. Rydin et al (2015) similarly pointed to the complexity of some projects that combine use of public property rights with self-consumption alongside sale of electricity to the grid.

A key common theme is the importance of maintaining project viability. Vernay and Sebi (2020) noted the problem of getting loans to initiate projects, the risks involved in relying on government calls for tenders and the dependence on the feed-in tariffs. While self-consumption can seem the safest route to project viability, it limits the scope of projects. Hence it is relevant to look at the range of business models that the CRE sector deploys. Vernay et al (2023a) identified five models as operating in France:

- local integrated energy supply, usually initiated and led by a local authority;
- collective self-consumption, where a group of local building occupiers club together to arrange renewable energy for direct consumption, a model largely adopted by public bodies and business;
- neighbouring energy supply, where a new local renewable energy facility supplies local residents and businesses;
- citizen energy production, which is led by local residents coming together but is often facilitated by a local authority; and
- cooperative energy supply, where an existing cooperative engages in the energy market.

While each may prove feasible in specific circumstances, Vernay et al argued that none of these could produce the flexibility in the electricity system that is often stated as a goal of CRE. Furthermore, the other common goals – increasing renewable energy capacity, mobilising private capital to this end and empowering communities – are variably fulfilled by the different business models. This reinforces the point about the 'financial entanglements' that such local energy projects imply (Rydin et al, 2015).

Comparing France and the Netherlands, Vernay and Sebi (2020: 8) found that 'by competing solely against incumbents, the French ecosystem risks remaining a small niche that is unable to contribute to the transformation of the sector'. This is reinforced by the organisational identity of CRE organisations, which Vernay et al (2023b) found to have a great influence by acting as a filter and helping to process complexity. This had the consequence of impacting on the potential for scaling up, as some institutional logics and associated organisational identities were associated with specific localities and smaller-scale action.

A number of recommendations are made in the French research to overcome this situation (Vernay and Sebi, 2020; Colombarolli and Storti, 2022; Vernay et al, 2023a and 2023b). Efforts need to be made to overcome the collective action problem and achieve citizen engagement, ideally going beyond just those with strong ecological sensibilities. Social skills are important in maintaining projects alongside positive communications. More specifically, key actors who can foster diversity in the sector need to be supported, along with local capacity builders who can act as catalysts. Intermediaries are often vital in facilitating the adoption of business models which can be complicated to understand and operationalise, and local government can play a key role here. In addition to facilitating project mechanics, intermediaries can help build networks that foster and indeed constitute social capital. But a robust business model remains central. The availability of tried-and-tested models for the finances of CPE projects is necessary. This can involve the acceptance of hybrid structures, but also the availability of public sector resources, often at the regional scale, to support the economic viability of projects.

The role of planning in promoting community-based infrastructure

The foregoing discussion has explored the scope for community-based initiatives in relation to water, waste management and transport infrastructure, but it is clear that the greatest scope for expansion, particularly expansion that advances environmental goals, lies with the energy sector. However, examination of the role of community-based energy infrastructure makes it apparent that planning for such projects has to have regard to two aspects. First, as with many community-based projects, there needs to be attention to social capital within civil society and how that is fostered. This reinforces the lessons of earlier chapters. Second, planning for community-based infrastructure cannot happen without equivalent consideration of the wider energy infrastructure systems at regional and national scales. Partly this is about the scope for scaling up such community projects and partly about the way that they are integrated into wider systems through exports and imports of energy. This poses a challenge to planning, particularly local planning.

With regard to scaling up, Bauwens et al (2020) specifically looked at the potential with regard to community energy projects and argued that, while earlier research had emphasised internal tensions within hybrid organisations (hybrid across the private sector and civil society), they found the organisational mission statement to be vitally important. They saw this statement as imprinting the scaling strategy over time, partly because this shaped the ways in which social enterprises used market mechanisms to achieve their social goals. Organisational characteristics tended to be chosen in the early days of a project and the mission statement guided such organisational features alongside the available resources and available social technology. Thereafter, such features were difficult to change. Efficiencies were established for the given purpose, institutional forces generated path dependencies and the lack of a competitive environment removed one impetus for change. The main stakeholders engaged in a collective effort that contributed to imprinting from the outset onwards. The founders' own network resources and experience could be influential in shaping the initial mission statement, but so were the nature of the teams involved, market maturity for the specific energy sector, the policy regime and the culture of support for the non-profit sector.

Different mission statements went with different growth strategies and were based in different balances between customer and community orientation. Bauwens et al further distinguished between integrated hybrids – where commercial and social goals were advanced through a common set of activities because beneficiaries were also customers or the same staff members were responsible for both sets of goals – and differential hybrids – where the beneficiaries were distinct from the customers or the organisation ensured that different staff members performed different sets of interventions to social or commercial ends.

Looking at three Flemish examples, Bauwens et al (2020) saw three different scaling approaches. Ecopower, a mutual interest organisation with a greater orientation towards profit, exhibited strong organisational growth within a professionalised organisation structure with a history of success stories. It started quite early on looking for scaling-up opportunities, moving from wind turbines to solar energy, micro-hydro and biomass as forms of generation as well as a wood pellet factory to maintain the supply chain. It also developed relationships with other cooperatives. Bronsgroen was based on a 'small is beautiful' culture and focused instead on deepening and diversification of services offered to beneficiaries locally; its origins lay in the context of improving social housing estates. Beau Vert was a general interest company and had a green knowledge economy approach favouring organisational growth, dissemination of innovation and in-depth work with members. It had stepped back from competing for scarce wind turbine sites, however, favouring instead local ownership and local control. Rather than ask for additional capital from members, it concentrated on disseminating energy efficiency measures.

In the energy sector, as is the case with many other infrastructure sectors, scaling up is not just a matter of replicability or increasing the scale of operation. Connectivity remains very important. Self-sufficiency achieved project by project through self-consumption of energy produced is neither effective nor efficient, and thus proposals for individual community-owned energy projects need to be seen in the context of networks of distribution, both from producers and to consumers. Enabling community-based energy projects to connect to wider networks for sale of surplus energy (electricity, biomass, heat) and purchase to top up local supply in case of high demand requires attention to networks at the urban, regional and, ultimately, national scales. And where such connectivity is involved, the contractual arrangements for purchase and sale of energy are liable to become complex, implying the need for facilitating agents to understand and smooth processes arising from interconnectivity. Looking at the water sector, particularly in lower-income countries but making a more general argument, Spencer (2021) argued that small-scale services providers can fill in important gaps in larger infrastructure systems as cities grow, but this requires attention to how they operate in relation to each other.

Thus, planning systems need to consider community-based energy (including its potential to scale up over time) alongside broader infrastructure systems. Some countries (Turner 2018) have national plans for such infrastructure and for expanding, improving or replacing it, and this may speak to a leading role for central government in developing new infrastructure projects. Although, as Turner emphasises, there has been a shift towards a more responsive mode, with proposals coming from individual government agencies, private companies or combinations as in public-private partnerships. There is generally a concern with smooth regulation of such projects, resulting in strong central government policy direction in favour of such projects and/or light-touch, expedited or specialist regulation to cover all the details of the development of the projects. The question then becomes how to integrate community-based infrastructure projects. They may be actively or passively encouraged – say, through technical or financial support – but they are often not planned for, that is integrated within plans.

Moroni (2023) offers the possibility of developing an alternative perspective that actively includes community-scale infrastructure within wider plans. He starts from the argument that plans should focus specifically on infrastructure rather than also incorporate means to regulate all development. In doing so he defines infrastructure as involving streets, metro lines as well as social infrastructure such as public hospitals and, of course, energy infrastructure. He sees these infrastructure projects as involving action for a certain capacity within a certain time scale and at a certain location, supported by a budget. However, he also defines such infrastructure as led by the public sector and on public land. Regulation, through a variety of instruments, is then supposed to attend to all development projects on private land and/or initiated through non-state decision makers. Moroni's argument relies on the idea that infrastructure projects as he has defined them have a degree of closure and certainty that makes the drawing up of a plan possible. Everything else operates within a complex system that cannot be captured in a plan.

This puts community-based infrastructure in the 'private' and unplannable category, amenable to regulation only through various means. This ignores the possibilities of co-producing a plan that explicitly allows for community-based infrastructure to be planned alongside other infrastructure; other changes of land use and development projects for housing, commercial and industrial uses could then – according to Moroni's argument – occur within this infrastructural framework and be subject to regulatory instruments. There are sufficient similarities between small and large infrastructure and sufficient differences with development for different land uses to suggest this approach.

It would require plans for infrastructure at all scales, plans which would actively involve local communities in considering whether to propose a community-based scheme and then plan for the intended scale and location of such schemes in relation to other proposed infrastructure investment. Connectivity issues could be considered at an early stage, where the proposal was not for an off-grid and self-contained community system. This would overcome some of the problems highlighted by Walsh (2016) in analysing community wind energy projects in Ireland, where treating them as private projects led to considerable opposition at the regulatory stage. But this does involve both separating out infrastructure planning from the planning of other new development and finding ways to operate across scales so that community-based schemes can be included alongside the major infrastructure projects at a regional or national scale in a system of multilevel governance involving relevant stakeholders from all levels. This is an innovative but radical proposition, and is returned to in Chapter 10.

9

Urban commoning

Introduction

The previous chapters have considered a variety of initiatives, projects and organisations that offer an alternative to reliance on major inward investment and on large-scale capital as directed by market pressures. Most of these bear the term 'community' and suggest the importance of dynamics within civil society. However, the discussion of these has also emphasised their hybrid nature, that they are shaped by market as well as civil society dynamics. The borders between the private sector and the community sector are porous, and the most successful examples recognise that in how they are structured and operate. This applies to small localised firms also, which might otherwise be considered purely market actors.

Before drawing together the threads of this analysis and considering the institutional arrangements and policy frameworks that need to be put into place to foster such approaches, it is worthwhile considering the more radical options that come under the heading of urban commoning. Many writers within the post-growth paradigm strongly align themselves with commoning, as do Gibson-Graham (2006) themselves in their exposition of diverse economies. Commoning refers to the use of commons or assets held in common and describes a variety of practice worldwide, from the holdings of feudal peasants in Europe to the landownership of Indigenous peoples across many countries to the collective management of natural resources studied by Elinor Ostrom (1993; 2005; 2015) and her research teams. More recently, there has been a particular interest in urban communing, moving the focus from rural, agricultural and forested areas to instances of collective claims on and use of urban assets. This can range from squatting and the claiming of land as part of informal settlements to more organised forms of use, management and ownership of urban areas and buildings by a nominated group. There are strong links to Lefebvre's idea of the right to the city, as explored later in this chapter.

Such commoning has often been linked to new forms of urbanism, that is, new ways of living in urban areas. Foster (2020) offered a radical alternative reading of the right to the city in terms of what do-it-yourself (DIY) urbanism can potentially offer. DIY urbanism is understood in terms of citizen-led, temporary and small-scale interventions designed to reclaim and activate spaces for public use. 'DIY urbanism can serve as a site of prefigurative politics' and 'constitute an emerging form of networked cogovernance' (Foster, 2020: 311). But DIY urbanism is just one of many different concepts that are used to describe urban commoning. Authors have utilised a variety of concepts: everyday urbanism focuses on the quotidian activities of people, the associated use of urban space and how these activities are maintained; temporary urbanism looks at activities that do not persist in the city but aim to make use of overlooked and underused spaces; or interstitial urbanism or urban acupuncture, which identifies small, specific interventions in the urban fabric and urban society that nevertheless produce valuable results (Harris, 2015). Associated with this is the work on urban experimentation that emphasises specific projects with uncertain outcomes. This has also been put under the banner of reassemblage (Sendra, 2015).

Alawadi et al (2022) found the first use of everyday urbanism to date back to 1999, referencing Chase et al, 2008. The definition that they favoured is 'a process in which residents take incremental, small-scale planning and design into their own hands' (Alawadi et al, 2022: 2). It is typified by being people-generated and low budget. A key feature is the appropriation of space by people without the formal permission or approval of the state. Alawadi et al therefore argued that this enables change that meet residents' needs in terms of adaptability, interaction, a human scale and an environment that facilitates ordinary daily practices of local people. While the individual initiatives can seem very small scale, even insignificant, together they add up to making the city more attuned to local residents' everyday needs.

While Alawadi et al, like many everyday urbanism researchers, drew their examples and inspiration from lower-income, often informal, urban settings, the concept can also be used to identify underemphasised but locally important features of urban settings in higher-income countries with a dominance of urban formality. For example, garage sales, pop-up markets, community festivals, street fairs, art installations and picnicking on open spaces can all come under the everyday urbanism umbrella (Chase et al, 2008). Such activities are seen as inherently political and thus more aligned with the work of urban social movements than the other forms of community action covered earlier in this book. 'Everyday urbanism is one way urban residents exert some power over urban space in the face of globalisation and market capitalism' (Alawadi et al, 2022: 4).

Andres et al (2021) focused more on temporary urbanism and distinguished three different types. There is bottom-up temporary urbanism, which arises in unplanned and unregulated uses of spaces and practices. But they also identified top-down temporary urbanism, where the local state promotes interim uses such as gardening, playgrounds and other community spaces, as well as hybrid forms involving bricolage, creativity and experimentation. In her work with Kraftl (Andres and Kraftl, 2021), Andres situated temporary urbanism within the rhythms of everyday activity that Lefebvre identified. A careful focus on such rhythms shows how temporary urbanism can take quite different forms in different places and at different times: 'although temporariness is (evidently) a universal urban condition, diverse discursive and practical dynamics exist that direct urban temporariness along particular channels and shape space differently but significantly while impacting people's living environments' (Andres and Kraftl, 2021: 1239).

Thus, commoning fits within a broad and varied literature and associated set of propositions for urban change. However, these have at their heart a radical reclaiming of urban space, as exemplified by their links to the idea of the right to the city.

The right to the city

The emphasis on urban commoning has been closely related to Lefebvre's call for a right to the city (2009). While widely used as a slogan, this 'right' has a more specific meaning within Lefebvre's writing. Purcell (2014) made it clear that Lefebvre's vision is a revolutionary one based on his Marxism. However, Lefebvre's Marxism sought to move beyond both capitalism and the state, expecting to see the state 'wither away', to use the classic Marxist phrase. Lefebvre also saw politics not as resistance but, rather, as a continuous and positive struggle. So, the right to the city is, as Purcell (2014) put it, 'a cry that initiated a radical struggle to move *beyond* both the state and capitalism' (p 142). It is the declaration of an intention to struggle, of the commitment to become active and, if 'that struggle becomes strong enough, it will eventually overcome the capitalist city and the latter will be rendered obsolete' (Purcell and Tyman, 2015: 1135).

At the heart of this is the property relation. Capitalist cities are predicated upon private property relations and their use by capital. As such, people in urban agglomerations are alienated from urban space and the struggle involved in asserting the right to the city centrally concerns the appropriation of such urban space by inhabitants. As Purcell and Tyman (2015) stated: 'users must *reappropriate* the production of urban space and they must make it their own again' (p 1135). Hence the close connection to the idea of urban commoning, of taking land into common use by city residents. The right to the city implies 'an explicit repudiation of the right to private property' (Olsson and Besussi, 2023: 35). Thereby, Lefebvre saw the potential for the urban arena moving away from the city as an engine for capital accumulation and towards 'a space for encounter, connection, play, learning, difference, surprise, and novelty' (Purcell, 2014: 149). This becomes an example of *autogestion* (literally, self-management). The city is created by the production of space emerging from decentralised, bottom–up management (Olsson and Besussi, 2023). For Foster, *autogestion* 'would challenge neoliberal capitalism by placing urban decision making in the hands of inhabitants who operate under a noncapitalist logic and privilege collective needs over individual desires' (Foster, 2020: 312).

Purcell recognised that 'anyone who is involved in the day-to-day practice of urban politics might object to Lefebvre's right to the city, arguing that it is too radical, too impossibly utopian, to be of use' (Purcell, 2014: 150). Against this, he considered that there is potential within the struggle envisaged by Lefebvre: 'For Lefebvre the urban constitutes a revolution, but one that requires millions of everyday acts of resistance and creation' (p 151). The potential is realised by encouraging and enabling these million acts of resistance and creation: 'We must learn to perceive the fledgling urban, to call it forth, and to urge society forward toward its horizon' (p 151). This has much in common with Gibson-Graham's politics of becoming, as Foster (2020) explained. In this, postcapitalist possibilities are 'felt, imagined, and performed ... as playful and messy experiments' (Foster, 2020: 313). To quote Foster more fully: 'Building on cooperative experiences such as potlucks and community gardens, participants begin to acknowledge and perceive themselves as productive valuable economic subjects who can experience relations with other without relying on exploitative capitalist class processes' (Foster, 2020: 324). However, it remains questionable as to whether people actually wish to take on the tasks that such *autogestion* implies, particularly in the light of the many practical problems and challenges involved. The demands on the urban citizen or inhabitant are considerable, even if one excludes the conflicts with both representatives of capital and the state that may ensue along the way. After all, according to Purcell and Tyman (2015), Lefebvre saw the struggle as endless: 'It is perpetual. The revolution is continuous' (p 1134). In her study of Fort Worth, Texas, Foster admitted that many participants in the various collective endeavours favoured a market-led alternative (Foster, 2020). The next section highlights the problems and challenges, with a review of the experiences of urban commoning; the subsequent focus on community gardens and guerrilla gardening further reinforces this.

Experiences of urban commoning

Liverpool provides a well-researched example of starting from very localised commoning initiatives but attempting to put into effect the city-as-commons. It is a major English city of about half a million people, situated within a city region of some two and quarter million people in the north-west of the country. It has a long history as a port city and was centrally involved in the slave trade, linked through shipping lines to the plantations of North America and the West Indies and the cotton industries of India. It then developed as an industrial city with strong working-class political traditions. In the 20th century Liverpool suffered the effects of deindustrialisation and it has been the focus of repeated attempts at urban regeneration. Zielke et al (2021) argued that Liverpool has an unusually rich history of commoning. This cultural context combines with – at times – local government support for commoning.

The central site for commoning that has been researched is around the Granby area, a deprived inner-city neighbourhood (Thompson, 2017). In the 1960s, this was designated as the Granby Planning Action Area, over 1969–72 the Shelter Neighbourhood Action Project instigated a grassroots blueprint for regeneration, along the lines of community development projects elsewhere in the country. However, this had traction in only one small part of the Granby area. Elsewhere the policy of demolition, clearance and new housebuilding continued, it having been the preferred planning approach of the Labour City Council in the post-war period to 1973. This was combined with traffic-calming measures that had the effect of cutting the area off from other parts of the city, reducing 'eyes on the street' and allowing crime to flourish. By the 1980s, Granby was known as

Liverpool's ghetto, with astonishing jobless rates of 40 per cent among men and 90 per cent among Black teenagers.

The Liberal Democrat party gained control of the city council from 1988. They saw housing associations as the only realistic solution to the housing crisis and urban decay in the city. They divided the inner-city area into five zones and allocated a housing association to lead in each one. With the change in national government (Labour), this approach was then reframed by the Housing Market Renewal programme, which again brought demolition back onto the agenda, this time to restructure oversupply in housing markets in order to make new housebuilding by the private sector viable again. Liverpool's a deprived inner-city neighbourhood of Granby was part of the Housing Market Renewal pathfinder scheme. In this context, Granby Four Streets emerged as a campaign to save a small number of streets from demolition.

After the withdrawal of the pathfinder scheme in 2010, redevelopment did occur. Part of this was through a mix of Cooperative Development Society co-ops using the community land trust (CLT) model (see Chapter 6) and a mutual homeownership society, which leased the buildings from the CLT. The remainder was undertaken by two local housing associations. The result was a mix of tenures and occupiers. Thompson (2015) reported plans to acquire four corner buildings for community-owned enterprises, studios, cafes and shops. Significantly, the Granby Triangle also saw examples of commoning through guerrilla gardening, blurring the boundary between public and private space and reclaiming land for a community garden where the council-funded project Growing Granby provided an educational programme on ecology and gardening. The community garden was facilitated by a short-term lease from the housing association, Liverpool Mutual Homes. Another aspect of the activity on public space in the area was a monthly street market.

The CLT membership extended beyond the Granby Street neighbourhood into the wider Liverpool 8 area and therefore represented a wider, diverse community. Thompson (2015) reported some tensions within the wider membership and argued that '[t]rust is the magic ingredient holding the entire CLT endeavour together' (p 1036). It is clear that first, the failure of the market-led pathfinder scheme, and then the impact of austerity on the ensuing council strategy, opened up a space in which the CLT vision and the associated community gardening on public and private land was able to become established.

Thompson (2015) pointed out that relatively few local residents were involved. The Northern Alliance Housing Cooperative that was established in response comprised largely idealistic young professionals, designers and students. Perhaps the fact that the Granby Four Streets project won the Turner Prize (a major British art prize) in 2015 is indicative of this. It was also significant that the project relied on philanthropy. A private social finance company, HD Social Investments, backed by a wealthy philanthropist, provided financial support and also commissioned the design statement from fashionable architects Assemble. Thus, while community activism and the failure of the existing council strategy under austerity opened up the space for the commoning vision and allowed modest achievements, there remained issues about who was commoning and what resources were needed to enable the commoning.

Another Liverpool example, which Killick (2017) has researched, is the creation of the Small Cinema as a challenge to the dominant narrative of the arts as part of the creative city, fostered by a creative class. Killick argued that the 'discourse around the creative industries has proven to be little more than a veneer for business interests as the UK shifted from an industrial to a service-based economy' (p 4). The Small Cinema was positioned as an alternative to the current regeneration efforts centred on the capital-led redevelopment of the city centre. It was to be 'a model of de-financialised growth' (p 8). The Small Cinema was a project of the community interest company Re-Dock, established in 2015. This sought to promote cinematic arts at low cost for the local community. Tickets were a maximum of £4, no one was turned away for inability to pay and management was provided by local volunteers. The whole enterprise was supported by an 'established but informal' relationship between Re-Dock and their landlord, Creative Space Team Ltd. This enabled them to have free ground-floor space in a building on the basis that the cinema would act as a positive asset to the building and would also be available as a facility to the landlord and other tenants. Unfortunately, even this free grant of property rights of occupation proved insufficient, and the Small Cinema closed in 2017.

Taking the perspective of the whole city of Liverpool as a commons, Zielke et al (2021) saw the failure to establish a strong and sustained commoning effort as lying in the context and recent history of the urban area. While there is a heritage of working-class politics and of commoning, by the early 21st century this had been impacted by long-term economic decline, welfare cutbacks and regeneration professionals being repeatedly 'parachuted in' to present solutions. All of these have eroded the fragile traditions of commoning. Rather than the shared trust, solidarity and hope that commoning requires, Zielke et al found mistrust, exhaustion and competition between areas for scarce resources, all of which led to cynical resignation and acceptance of austerity neoliberalism.

Zielke et al's project sought to leverage university resources within a quintuple helix of university, local industry, local government, civil society and citizens in the Dingle area of Liverpool. Dingle had an unusually large number of social enterprises, charities, non-governmental organisations (NGOs), associations and clubs. The neighbourhood had been the recipient of significant European Union funding in the late 20th/early 21st centuries which produced some physical improvements and support for key community assets. However, rapid scaling up of the existing social economy had led to the size of organisations and the responsibilities of managers outstripping capabilities. Over time, the older generation, who had strong networks of connections within the local community, withdrew, and social capital declined. With growing resource scarcity and austerity politics, the community became ever more atomised.

Volunteers in commoning efforts reported being left tired, stressed, apathetic, burnt-out and angry by the shift of responsibility for the neighbourhood onto the community. Commoning requires constant work in listening and translation in order to build collaboration: 'Effective commoning has something to do with translating across that incommensurability and developing affective capabilities – and material conditions – within communities to do so' (Zielke et al, 2021: 10). In this context, the research team's attempts to promote multi-actor public–commons partnerships for co-design and co-production of local initiatives foundered. Commoning may, therefore, fail due to the absence of local traditions of cooperative organisation and mutual aid, or those traditions may be eroded by the pressures of austerity neoliberalism, which result in limited resources, high levels of precarity and fractured solidarities within communities. Zielke et al (2021) therefore called for efforts to treat the city as a common to be combined with Gibson-Graham's (2006) community economy, that is, deeper understanding of the diverse nature of the economy rather than remaining in oppositional mode.

Looking elsewhere, Bianchi (2022) examined two examples of urban commons in Barcelona, Spain: the squat in Puigcerdà and the community centre in Can Batlló. This city was also seen as fertile ground for commoning, as it has a history of both squatting and the cooperative movement. In addition, Spain saw a burgeoning of urban commons in response to the aftermath of the 2007/08 financial crisis, under the 15-M Movement. The focus of Bianchi's analysis was on whether these are resisting capitalism, being co-opted by the state in the support of capitalism or there is a possibility of the state being supportive and cooperating with the commoning movement. Bianchi's emphasis was on the contingent nature of the various strategies that the state adopts in relation to such commoning initiatives, rather than assuming a given approach in favour of supporting capitalism. Thus, the state's relationship with commoning was characterised by contradictions, compromises and incompleteness, characteristics which the commoning initiative could exploit if it was alert to them.

This analysis can be seen in the case of Can Batlló, a self-managed cultural space in a low–middle-income community in Barcelona's La Bordeta neighbourhood. In 2009, residents formed a coalition of groups and engaged in active demonstrations in support of Can Batlló (CB) as a neighbourhood platform. The centre-left administration of the city agreed to support this CB platform and leased one building on the 14-hectare site to the platform just before a liberal-conservative coalition took over in June 2011. The lease could be renewed annually. It became a self-managed cultural centre providing a meeting space, a cafe, an auditorium and a library. The city council did repairs to the building to render it structurally sound and, slowly, additional spaces on the site have become part of CB platform. This provided for a collaborative carpentry workshop, an urban vegetable garden, a collective brewery, a bicycle workshop, a collective printing service and a family space. The success of this platform led to the liberal-conservative coalition implementing policies to expand self-managed spaces in the city, including both the grant of temporary vacant spaces to citizen-based organisations and the transfer of the management of public facilities to such organisations. On the one hand, this can be seen as empowering community organisations. On the other, it also responsibilises them for delivering services which might be seen as the appropriate remit of the state. It is notable that the election of a leftist coalition to the city administration in 2015 did not remove support for self-governing initiatives. Certainly the longevity of the CB platform contrasts with the squatting case, where migrants were summarily evicted. As of 2019, the CB platform had their agreement modified to cover 30 years, with a further possible 20-year extension.

Other cases suggest caution about the impact that such commoning can have. Véron (2023) looked at community food spaces in Berlin, considering their potentially transformative impact. However, they found that they could also be exclusionary, supporting gentrification and neoliberalism more generally. 'Community food initiatives may simultaneously contribute to exclusionary dynamics and neoliberal subjectivities *and* emancipatory politics and transformative change' (Véron, 2023: 2). Foster (2020) studied the Six Points project in Fort Worth, Texas. Here, in 2012, the possibility of using vacant property for artist studios and student-run art galleries arose after market-led plans for redevelopment failed. This evolved into the Build a Better Block initiative, which instituted bike lanes in the area along with new street furniture, including seating and sidewalk vending opportunities. In 2014, the initiative expanded to include street murals and other public artworks, a temporary dog park and pet adoptions, various markets, a community garden and community performances. Many of these challenged official regulatory codes, but also city-led ideas for improving the streets and installing public art. Notably these activities did not occur on privately owned property but, rather, in public or abandoned spaces. However, Foster (2020) stated that 'these post-capitalist possibilities were fleeting and fragile' (p 325) and also that many participants continued to favour market-led development (p 316). As she concludes 'the case study raises difficult questions regarding the relationship between a politics of becoming and structural forms of power' (p 322), and further, 'the relationship between claiming a right to the city and development of postcapitalist futures is much more tenuous' (Foster, 2020: 325).

Finally, Daskalaki (2018) looked at two initiatives in Greece that arose in the aftermath of the financial crisis of 2008/09 and the ensuing austerity politics imposed on that country, partly by the European Union. One was Micropolis, a self-organised space associated with the occupation of part of the Aristotle University of Thessaloniki, where a variety of assemblies, workshop, films and festivals were organised. The other was Navarinou Park, an area squatted to prevent development as a multiplex carpark, where a variety of planned and spontaneous activities occurred, including artistic, political and social events; a community garden was also started. Daskalaki found evidence of social learning, socio-spatial solidarity and also the early stages of the formation of assemblages of resistance, but recognised that these were temporary and represented only a 'crack in dominant views about economic and monetary structures' (p 164). She used the concept of drasis – 'the unexpected unfolding of an event in a specific space and time' (p 155) – to indicate the prefigurative potential of these initiatives, but also by implication that they were not transformative in themselves.

These researched examples of experiences of urban commoning highlight just how tentative they are. A focus on urban gardening through guerrilla gardening and community gardens provides further clues as to how such commoning may generate real differences.

Focus on guerrilla gardening and community gardens across the world

Guerrilla gardening (although the term is often criticised for its macho and military connotations) generally refers to the use of someone else's land for cultivation, often illicitly and certainly without the landowner's consent. Examples are found worldwide, with informal practices of urban agriculture quite common in lower-income countries (Hardman et al, 2018). The question of whether this is illegal depends on the specific justice system involved and the attitude of the public authorities. Adams et al (2015) argued that in a British context guerrilla gardening rarely crosses the line into illegality, tending instead to be involved in contravening planning policies or civil law. But it still acts in opposition to the state to some extent. What often starts as guerrilla gardening can turn into the establishment and maintenance of community gardens, as the following cases show.

Appropriation of land for a community garden in Hellinikon, Athens, Greece is presented by Apostolopoulou and Kotsila (2022) as spatial *autogestion*, to use Lefebvre's term, and resistance to neoliberal urbanism. It occurred in the context of a broader social movement opposed to the privatisation and development of the former international airport in Athens. The authors point out that, while the aim was to challenge the production of increasingly neoliberalised urban space, 'neither urban commoning in general nor gardening in particular are de facto egalitarian and emancipatory' (p 297). In this case, asserting the 'public character' of the airport land was a stated goal alongside organic food production, genetic diversity and education. The garden was very active from 2011 to 2017, despite internal challenges of management, and became known internationally. However, it went into decline for two reasons. Internally, there were disagreements about political orientation and, externally, all governments, even the leftist SYRIZA government elected in 2015, treated the airport site as an asset and supported its development and the maximisation of its value as a development site. While this example of commoning arose in reaction to neoliberal development plans for a site, eventually it was unable to resist the logic of those plans.

A focus on community gardens suggests an attempt to establish a more settled basis for land-based activities than guerrilla gardening, recognising the need for certainty through property rights alongside the necessity of community activism. This form of urban commoning can evolve from earlier illicit gardening. For example, in Hong Kong, countryside gardens were built by the so-called 'morning walkers', groups who walked in the hills and mountains of the territory between 6 am and 9 am (Hung, 2017). They involved a mix of planting, artworks and facilities including hospitality spaces. While illegal, they were tolerated by the government provided that they did not give rise to administrative problems. However, when the country parks were designated, they became formalised. The existing gardens were required to be registered and official maps started to indicate their locations, alongside signage in the country parks. They were recognised, some were zoned as Morning Walker Gardens and some were enhanced through funding for facilities. A form of co-management emerged in which morning walker groups maintained the gardens and, in return, had some formal rights, including access.

Reviewing the literature on community gardens, Eizenberg (2012) finds three types of analysis. The first sees community gardens as spaces of contestation concerned with injustices and the impact of neoliberalism. The second takes a more Foucauldian perspective to consider them as controlled spaces producing citizen-subjects. The third is more critical of community gardens, seeing them as a space of neoliberalism giving rise to gentrification and producing financial gains under the guise of the environmental agenda through the improvements to the locality. Empirically, Eizenberg emphasised that community gardens are important carriers of culture, particularly for specific ethnic groups. Here, gardens can produce vegetables and herbs aligned to certain groups' cuisines. He identified casita gardens for the Latinx community, farm gardens for the African-American community and eclectic culture gardens oriented towards the white communities and often in gentrifying or gentrified areas. For some communities, the gardens can act as sites for the transfer of particular knowledge about horticulture, cuisine and cultural heritage more generally.

Purcell and Tyman's (2015) exploration of New York City community gardens emphasised the origins of many community gardens in commoning activity by the Green Guerrillas, bringing together groups that engaged in gardening for a mix of political and prosaic food-growing reasons. They pointed to how, in the late 1970s, the city authorities created the Green Thumb programme to regularise much of the illegal gardening activity. This established leases and released funds for some projects, although it also imposed some constraints on their activities. Purcell and Tyman reported that Green Thumb continued to administer over 250 community gardens, although often offering only short-term leases. By the early 1990s, Eizenberg (2012) found that there were up to 1,000 community gardens in New York. By the early 2000s this had fallen to 650, but 550 had preservation status. The New York mayor, Rudi Guiliani, had wanted to sell off 112 city-owned community gardens for development, leading to a public outcry. As a result, three schemes were set up. Under the first, some 400 gardens were preserved under the remit of the Parks and Recreation and Department. This meant that they could not be 'deparked' without a complicated process and the provision of equivalent compensatory land elsewhere. Clearly, this inhibited moves to urban development. The second scheme covered 67 gardens which were purchased by the non-profit organisation Trust for Public Land. Finally, the New York Restoration Project, another non-profit organisation, purchased 59 gardens to safeguard them. This shows the importance of public sector support for the urban commons and also the central role that landownership plays.

Pudup (2008) examined two community garden projects in the San Francisco Bay Area, US: the Garden Project and the Edible School Yard. In both cases the role of the projects in seeking to change the subjectivity of community members was noted. As such, Pudup aligned these initiatives with a neoliberal governmentality and specifically roll-out neoliberalism (Peck and Tickell, 2002). A long history of community gardens in the area was identified (Pudup, 2008), from the late 19th century through to the present. The purpose and focus changed over time and community gardens have had multiple motivations: reacting to neighbourhood blight and degradation of the urban environment, improving food security for the local community, particularly in poorer areas, and a form of collective empowerment that builds social capital and organisational capacity. However, the gardens have also operated in a context that emphasised the role of community gardens in promoting public health (and avoiding burdens on health services), providing a source of employment and training and reconnecting alienated city children with nature. The latter – the direct contact with nature – was seen as a way of transforming people, a form of self-actualisation that is personal and individual rather than social. Under this banner, community gardens have become a part of public policy. They are organised around communities defined in a variety of ways: communities of interest (in gardening), of identity (as with a religious affiliation or ethnic group) or those with a shared life experience (as being at school or incarcerated in a prison). Thus, the Garden Project worked with ex-offenders, while the Edible School Project aimed to 'grow people' as well as plants through its effect on students.

In a study of a neighbourhood greenway project in Strathcona, Vancouver, British Columbia, Blomley (2004) found that it was initiated by community groups but had funding and support from the city council. That said, its ongoing existence depended on maintenance by the community groups. The reason why the city council were interested was that they saw this community-based initiative on public land as part of a crime prevention effort, reducing public disorder associated with the drugs trade and sex work through environmental design measures. In order to make this work, it was an integral part of the project that communities would develop a proprietorial feeling towards this public space. The gardening activity was seen as an act of both taking over a public space and caring for it. Through this action, the space became defensible and monitored. Ownership was central: 'Formal city ownership is acknowledged, but layered by a collective entitlement' (Blomley, 2004: 631). The greenway belonged to the municipality, the public, the neighbourhood, the street and some of the residents specifically.

In Greece, Kapsali (2023) studied a self-organised park in Thessaloniki known as Svolou. This was created in 2014 from the effort of some ten people using the local library as a meeting place. Under this banner a Spring Dinner was organised, becoming an annual communal dining event. There have also been a Degrowth Picnic and a Circular Economy Festival, highlighting links to the environmental sustainability agenda. A pocket park of some 430 m^2 was created from 2017 on, owned by the municipality and the schools buildings agency. The mechanisms included learning assemblies and working groups, primarily to share and expand relevant knowledge within the community. These had both formal and informal aspects. There was institutional underpinning for the park through a formal agreement with the municipality, but the landscaping was co-designed. Kapsali also critiqued the initiative for being, to some extent, exclusionary. The local community was a relatively privileged one with good links to political actors and with a high representation of university staff and students. In addition, the completed park had a fence and a closable door, so that use was not freely available.

The initiative was not in conflict with the political or governmental authorities and did provide benefits at the local level. In particular, it created micro-spheres of socialities and solidarities. However, Kapsali saw it as having a limited impact in the context of austerity urbanism and, further, as being in danger of reproducing neoliberal rationalities of individual responsibility or self-responsibilisation (Raco, 2000). Grassroots urban initiatives, therefore, 'produce temporary self-organised spaces and experiment with innovative grassroots space-making but often remain entrapped at the local level without being able to develop broader contestations of an uneven urban development model' (Kapsali, 2023: unpaginated).

Many such cases come from liberal democracies, which creates a particular context for such commoning experiments. Zhu et al (2020) presented cases of self-claimed vegetable lots on public green space in urban China, specifically in Hangzhou. Such activities were clearly in contravention of the top-down heirarchical form of government in China. The state presented such gardening as 'uncivilised behaviour'. In one area, any poor family that was subsidised by the community state organisation would have their subsidies stopped if they appropriated land for vegetable growing. Discouraging self-gardening was a responsibility for local government officials, one that their performance was judged against. However, interestingly, local officials often turned a blind eye to self-gardening, only uprooting vegetables and destroying plots just before inspections by higher-tier governments. Many self-gardens survived by being effectively hidden, with almost half of non-gardeners in Zhu et al's survey not being aware of their existence. But those that were aware did sometimes object, partly on the basis that self-gardening contravened the official policy of joint ownership of all land, partly because of local inconvenience. Yet self-gardening in China persisted and has even grown. Many of the self-gardeners were rural migrants (often forced migrants) who saw their activities as a way of saving on food costs as well as passing the time; urban living was often described by these migrants as boring.

The idea of maintaining a sense of rurality through self-gardening was also present in Borcic et al's (2016) research on illegal gardening in Zagreb, which was in socialist Yugloslavia up to 1992 and is now in Croatia. They suggested that during the socialist era, appropriated common gardens were 'secluded, private pseudo-rural places in a semi-authoritarian, communal and (supposedly) urban and industrial society' (Borcic et al, 2016: 51). They contrasted this with the situation in Poland, where access to a garden was considered a worker's right and even a duty. However, in post-socialist times the fate of such gardening changed.

In contemporary times, attempts to appropriate land for gardening in Zagreb met with opposition from the city government, which ordered their destruction. As a result, citizens' action occurred in support of the gardening, forcing a city-wide policy on urban gardening and a new citizens' movement called Parkticipacija (Parkticipation). The result was the opening of the first official community garden in 2013, but also the almost complete takeover of this attempt at commoning by the city government. All such gardens became subject to a two-year contract with the city, which was personally signed off by the mayor. The process of applying for these contracts was strictly regulated, with set criteria for applicants and their prioritisation. Other Central and Eastern European examples are provided by Trendov (2018) and Djokic et al (2018).

Partly as a result of such empirical findings, there is a growing body of work which seeks to take a critical perspective on such commoning and to resist the normative claims often made for such activities. For example, Adams and Hardman (2014) looked at a case in an English Midlands city and suggested that the initiative was less 'resistant' or 'celebratory' than would fit with many pro-commoning narratives. The site was a strip of local authority-owned land alongside an inner ring road, near a public house and student accommodation. The gardening group operated very visibly in the daytime, wearing high-visibility jackets. They were seeking to beautify the area, an aim very much in line with city council policy. Many members enjoyed the gardening as a social activity and did not identify with the image of a group operating outside the mainstream. They did not necessarily see their gardening as transgressive, unless and until they were challenged by a police officer, local authority officer or member of the public, which happened only occasionally. A related paper (Adams et al, 2015) also pointed to the negative outcomes that can arise, such as negative amenities if management and cultivation are not maintained, and highlighted the limited consultation that can occur with local residents and the way that commoning practices can actually exclude local users of the spaces. And, not all appropriation of land necessarily presents itself as being in the local public interest. Kouros (2022) provided an interesting case study from Limassol, Cyprus, where public land was appropriated in a form of tactical gardening, which enrolled public land as an adjunct to private property ownership and thus excluded community members. This involved using sidewalks and other public areas for orchard trees, planters and small gardens, providing amenity landscaping, privacy, food and firewood. Sometimes these were used to demarcate territory in a form of micro-privatisation, although it could also be seen as leading to individuals managing these public lands instead of the local state.

The role of planning in urban commoning

At the heart of urban commoning is the appropriation of land for the activities of a specified group in the collective interest of that group and, sometimes, others who may engage with those activities. This puts local planning in a difficult position, as support of urban commoning may be seen as interference with private property regimes, encompassing property rights of both private actors (firms and people) and the state. Research shows numerous examples of the local state resisting or actively opposing such commoning efforts on this basis, quite apart from how it relates to their policies of urban development, regeneration and growth. Thus, the first role of planning in relation to commoning is the challenging one of acceptance of such appropriation of land and buildings. This can be easier where the land and buildings are vacant and abandoned (and a public interest case can be made for their productive occupation and use) or are part of the public estate and the appropriation can be tolerated by the local state.

That said, it is clear that in many cases the longevity of the commoning project depends on a form of property right being granted to the community group. Table 9.1 develops a four-fold typology along two axes. On one axis there is the extent to which the activity is oriented towards commercial or market-based dynamics or not; on the other axis is the extent to which formal land rights are involved or not.

This typology makes clear the overlaps with the various activities discussed in previous chapters. For example, the market-oriented activities supported by a formal land right cover the categories of small and medium businesses as well as cooperatives. Even social enterprise is an element of this, although other aspects would fit under the banner of sanctioned community welfare. Some temporary urbanism examples fit in here, as where a developer grants a temporary or meanwhile lease to a commercial activity for a part of the development site that does not fit into the development programme for some time. This might be a pop-up food enterprise or a beer garden, for example. But other forms of local enterprise may operate without such formal sanctioning of land occupation. Sites may simply be taken over on a short- or longer-term basis for selling goods and services. This is common in lower-income countries, but examples in other contexts would be pop-up shops on pavements and other available public spaces or the taking of land for cultivation of food for sale, or the occupation of an empty building or site for a ticketed party. Land appropriation for non-commercial purposes is, of course, at the heart of urban commoning, as this chapter has explored.

Table 9.1: Forms of community action

	Commercial activity	Non-commercial activity
Formal land rights	**Sanctioned community business** Market-oriented activities supported by a granted land right	**Sanctioned community welfare** Community-oriented activities supported by a granted land right
Land appropriation	**Guerrilla community enterprise** Appropriation of land in order to support market-oriented activities	**Guerrilla community welfare** Community occupation of land to fulfil community-oriented needs and demands

Where a formal land right is used to support activities for the local community's welfare, then some support is required from the landowner to grant the lease. This may be willingly given, say by a developer who is happy for a non-commercial meanwhile use to occur on their land. Or it may require the public sector to intervene to facilitate the granting of such a lease by the owner, perhaps using a public grant or tax incentive or even compulsory purchase powers. Or the public sector may donate its land to such community action. The essence here is that the activities occurring are not profitable in monetary terms and so there has to be some other basis for the grant of the land right, either a gifting relationship or public sector support. This can provide the basis of a community orchard or garden or a variety of other urban community activities, such as a community kitchen in a gifted building. Negotiating such property arrangements could be a role for local planning.

This involves recognising that state-supported urban commoning is likely to involve some form of property right and, further, that they are also likely to be as hybrid as many of the other initiatives discussed in preceding chapters. In their study of two French projects – the Grands Voisins in Paris aimed at increasing neighbourliness and the Transfert project in Nantes – Bragaglia and Rossignolo (2021) sought to examine whether these constituted a new form of 'tailor-made' urbanism or were increasingly subject to the profit logic of the market. The Grands Voisins project concerned a hospital that had been closed in 2012 and was proposed for an eco-district development in 2023. It was agreed with some NGOs that the site could be used for temporary purposes between 2015 and 2020. The result was a mix of uses, including housing for the homeless and refugees, low-rent office space for start-ups and local entrepreneurs and a new community space for social and creative activities. The governance was shared between three organisations: a housing association looked after the housing and two non-profit associations managed the business, hospitality and outdoor space between them. There was a strong event-driven logic which resulted in some 600,000 visitors per annum and brought the area into the realm of commercial social, hospitality and tourism business.

The Transfert project was part of the Îsle de Nantes regeneration scheme that started in the early 2000s, itself a response to the closure of shipyards in the city. The frame of the 'creative city' was used for the regeneration effort. Transfert Project operated on the site of a former slaughter house that had been demolished in 2015 leaving a 15-hectare vacant site. Situated within a larger area, it was intended as a free zone of art and culture. In 2017 one area was designated for a development of some 8 000 new houses to be completed by 2030. In 2018 the artistic association Pick Up Production signed an agreement for the temporary use of the vacant site, leading to regular spring–summer seasons of artistic and cultural activities. The first season attracted some 170,000 visitors. There was some limited space for the Roma community also.

Bragaglia and Rossignolo (2021) found that both projects encapsulated an intrinsic tension between being a contemporary panacea and acting as a Trojan horse for market logics, describing them as 'inextricably Janus-faced' (p 383). They saw temporary urbanism as beginning as a self-organising alternative to capitalism but increasingly, over two decades, being co-opted by city governments and becoming part of urban development strategies. Not only could those projects support development strategies deemed successful in market terms – by creating a lively and distinctive ambience that commercial development could internalise for monetary value – but it also fitted with the financial constraints of austerity that many local councils were facing. That said, the social benefits of such temporary urbanism initiatives were often overlooked in favour of maintaining the 'creative city' policy narrative (see Chapter 1).

Given the involvement of different actors, Bragaglia and Rossignolo (2021) emphasised the different foci and interests involved in such commoning initiatives. Thus, civil society actors were motivated by exercising creativity and social innovation, enabling participation, putting new ideas into practice, utilising available urban space, improving the sense of community and benefiting from free space or cheap rents. By contrast, the public sector actors were also concerned with encouraging creativity, social innovation and participation but saw this more in policy terms, so that they enabled partial solutions to urban issues by testing out new uses and reconverting empty space. This was done cheaply and managed to combine economic growth and liveability. Where private sector actors were involved they picked up on the testing of new uses of space, alongside preserving existing areas, attracting people to those areas and thereby increasing land values and creating new identities; illegal occupation of land was unacceptable. Here there is another key role for planning in negotiating between these different actors and their interests while maintaining the distinctive urban commoning features of a project.

Alawadi et al (2022) found through their research in Abu Dhabi that everyday urbanism is facilitated by a mix of formal planning by the state along with a range of bottom-up initiatives that are allowed to flourish. They also pointed out that there are downsides to such activities, particularly around public safety and potential social exclusion. Addressing these downsides provides a further rationale for supporting such everyday urbanism with some form of planning. Alawadi et al thus saw six roles for planning in relation to everyday urbanism:

- providing spaces for adaptation, growth and resident-led interventions;
- including public and private land;
- encouraging residents' creativity and spontaneity;
- providing flexible zoning and a policy framework to facilitate meaningful changes;
- respecting the process of incremental resident-led changes and their impacts; and
- understanding the nuances of residents' cultures before prescribing policies and design interventions.

Reviewing the case of Salford, England, Hardman et al (2018) found a city council happy to actively encourage informal use of open land and using a variety of marketing tools to reach guerrilla gardeners. They saw this as a way of regenerating the city and enabling urban agriculture to meet some food needs, particularly for more vulnerable households. Looking across the activities of Incredible Edible Salford, the (lone) Guerrilla Gardener and the Pendleton Guerrillas, they found a very diverse movement in terms of participants. However, the facilitating role of the local authority was clear. There was a nominated officer, and through his actions the Pendleton Guerrillas were initiated. Bureaucratic procedures such as planning permission and risk assessment were not enforced so as not to hinder the initiatives. Sites were identified by the local authority and others to act as meanwhile sites for gardening activity. In effect, while guerrilla gardening was sanctioned by the local authority, Hardman et al argued that this probably brought new participants into the movement but also excluded other, more radical, potential members who sought the thrill of oppositional politics. It does, however, also highlight that existing rigidly applied planning procedures might inhibit such commoning and that a light touch by a supportive local authority is most likely to expand the movement in an area.

In their study of 'interventionist agriculture' in Kingston, Ontario, Canada, Crane et al (2013) also argued that traditional forms of planning have to be loosened up to allow for the different character of urban commoning. This is described as: 'subversion, critique, playfulness, spontaneity, self-organisation, illegality and anonymity'. That said, Crane et al also pointed to the importance of active support by the local authority for such endeavours. In Kingston, they found the local authority to be playing an increasingly important role and, in particular, facilitating community gardens on city land – although there was no equivalent policy with regard to non-municipal or private land. The local authority, for example, helped with liability and insurance cover as well as access to water infrastructure.

But there is also a role for local planning in building local affect towards a locality, which Spijker and Parra (2018) identified as essential for the place-keeping that embeds commoning. They developed their argument through a comparative analysis of London, England and Groningen, Netherlands. Both city governments had programmes in favour of urban gardening. In Groningen there was an appointed green participation coordinator, who built projects in collaboration with community groups, often as a follow-up to guerrilla activity. Authorisation of the use was a key part of such project development. In London, facilitation and support fell to the relevant London boroughs (local authorities below the level of the Greater London Authority). These varied in their attitudes to commoning, some actively supporting, others less so. However, in most cases it was down to the community group to identify sites and initiate projects, with the municipality more in the background, often supporting only those cases which they saw as having a reasonable chance of success. Spijker and Parra noted that there were few cases of municipalities taking enforcement action against commoning.

This is, perhaps, not the form of planning envisaged by the Lefebvrian perspective on the right to the city. This, after all, was supposed to involve the decline and eventual disappearance the state, including state planning. Instead, Olsson and

Besussi (2023: 38) argue that the right to participation within planning processes can be understood as a right to planning 'conceptualized as the right to access and form the space-shaping social field of planning where a struggle for the right to the city in a Lefebvrian sense … takes place'. Here planning is a continuous and permanent challenge to and reorganisation of uneven power relations. It is the access to planning and the recognition afforded within planning that potentially transforms the role of planning. Interestingly, Olsson and Besussi also argue that this gives rise to new social identities as a new form of urban citizenship is enacted. This is a more radical reformulation of planning, but one that is dependent on an arguably utopian takeover of local planning by groups that are engaged in *autogestion* as part of urban commoning.

Perhaps it is more realistic to think about how local planning can be reformed to limit its ability to undermine urban commoning. This would involve working with the appropriation of land and buildings and/or supporting the regularisation of property rights to such land and buildings. It would include allowing activities which might otherwise contravene regulations but also working with groups to ensure that fundamental public health and safety concerns were addressed alongside possible exclusionary tendencies. Also relevant here would be the commitment to resist gentrification and redevelopment, for, as Kryzynski (2023) argues, this necessarily removes the physical basis for commoning efforts and often appropriates commoning for a pro-growth policy, leveraging such efforts as part of the creative city narrative. Instead, Kryzynski suggests the importance of remaining rooted in an area's collective history and being responsive to the needs and desires of the local population while prioritising accessibility and inclusive management, as well as solidarity towards other social justice efforts. It seems clear that without such support from formal organisations it is likely that the constant reproduction required to maintain such commoning projects, particularly those with a necessarily long lifespan such as horticultural projects, will be absent (Crane et al, 2013).

10

Planning without growth
as rebalancing a diverse economy

Introduction

This book has explored different ways in which the goods and services that people and firms need can be provided without buying into a pro-growth agenda that prioritises large-scale inward investment to an area and the growth-dependent planning agenda that is demanded to support this. It has looked at the way that a variety of small-scale organisations, both market oriented and community based, operate, analysing what contributes to their success and how planning, particularly local planning, can support them. This final chapter draws out the key insights across earlier chapters. These concern the essential hybridity of organisations, the importance of the local small business and social economy sectors within diverse economies, the centrality of social capital in a locality, the need to provide for secure forms of landownership, including common ownership, and the need to circulate knowledge of effective and viable business models within diverse economies.

The chapter then clarifies what a future rebalanced in terms of diverse economies would look like and assesses the social and environmental implications, highlighting further roles that a planning system could play. Throughout, the proposition for planning without growth has been pragmatic. It is suggested as an option for how planning could be effective without the promotion of growth – either economic growth or urban growth – in an area. It does not see this as a one-size-fits-all solution but, rather, as contributing to the toolkit that is available to planning authorities. The discussion at the end of this chapter makes it clear that planning also needs to pay close attention to social inclusion and equity and to promoting environmental goals through infrastructure planning and development management.

Insight 1: The essential hybridity of organisations engaged in providing goods and services

The diverse economies approach emphasises the variety of different ways in which goods and services can be provided and the diversity of organisations that can be involved, including market-oriented businesses, social enterprises and kinship or friendship networks. The case studies in the preceding chapters suggest that there is scope for expanding this diversity or, rather, rebalancing a diverse economy towards small local businesses and the social economy; but, to do so, the essentially hybrid nature of both such small businesses and social enterprises needs to be recognised.

159

This internal hybridity is the key to ensuring their longevity and, therefore, to widening the scope of organisations involved in providing goods and services. There are two dimensions to this.

First, all organisations require financial viability so as to be sustainable. Reliance on grants and subsidies from the public sector or philanthropic sources is likely to be unstable and places the responsibility for long-term success on actors outside the business or social enterprise, with attendant risks. This means that some form of market calculation is required by the organisational leaders to ensure viability. Small businesses need to make a degree of profit, whereby income exceeds costs, to repay investors or debtors and invest for the future. Most social enterprises engage in some market-oriented activity to bring in income, cross-subsidising their other activities. In the absence of growth in economic activity more generally, financial viability can be difficult to achieve. Most small businesses and social enterprises struggle with this, at least from time to time. But this does not lessen the importance of recognising the role of market demand in the viability of diverse economies' organisations.

The second dimension is the parallel recognition of the importance of civil society and its constituent social capital to both small businesses and social enterprises. Research, starting from the work of Robert Putnam (1993), has noted that locally embedded small and medium businesses (SMEs) depend to some extent on local social capital. Strengthening the links and common norms that constitute that local social capital can make those local businesses more viable and successful, with consequent benefits for the local population also. Social enterprises are more centrally dependent on social capital to provide for their core functions of providing goods and services, given the involvement of volunteer labour of various kinds. Indeed, the extent of their dependence often renders them rather vulnerable, due to the challenges of maintaining social capital (see later, Insight 3) and hence the need to balance activities arising from the contribution of social capital with more market-oriented ones.

Taken together, small firms and social enterprises are reliant on both the monetised market and the social capital of civil society. Hybridity and the ability to recognise and capitalise upon it are essential for the survival of these organisations. But there is a further implication for how we theorise and understand economic processes, particularly at the more local scale. While conventional economic analysis may have strengths in understanding markets in aggregate and macro flows of finance, it struggles to provide the fine-grained understanding at the level required for local economic development. Once smaller organisations, such as local firms and social enterprises, are the focus of attention, the scale of markets and supply chains shrinks, and then the non-hybrid assumptions of conventional economics become less applicable. Attention needs to be paid to both markets and civil societies to foster local well-being, and to the surplus that is generated, which is also hybrid, needs to be captured in a combination of monetary appreciation or profits, social capital and other non-monetary assets.

More generally, this insight is quite challenging for conventional economics, with its focus on the monetary, the central role of capital and an acceptance of market valuations as an indicator of significance. Neo-classical economics, Marxist economics and modern macro-economics all fail to appreciate the importance of the essential hybridity of many organisations involved in the provision of goods and services. Instead, they all throw the emphasis onto movements of large capital, and the key boundary is between the state – with its monetary and fiscal policies and potential offer of subsidies – and market-oriented enterprises. Such large enterprises remain constructed as uniquely economic, even where they are highly dependent on the state for support. Rejecting notions of hybridity ensures that this construction continues to have purchase in public and policy discourses.

It is also challenging for many anarchist-inspired perspectives, which offer the prospect of a society that is separated from the influence of market-based actors, that is, firms. They may see the solution in the expansion of the public sector or civil society. Recognising that community-based organisations also have a relationship to the market is often resisted. Instead, there is a desire to change society in a more wholesale manner, often associated with fundamental shifts in social values and political alignments. This is clearly more idealistic than pragmatic in approach. Critical thought needs these deep challenges to how we view the world, but it can be argued that action at the scale of planning systems needs more emphasis on what can be achieved in the short to medium term.

Accepting inherent hybridity as a feature of our society involves focusing on the interconnections between actors within government organisations, those active in market-oriented dynamics and those embedded in local civil societies. Fostering those interrelationships will help to rebalance diverse economies by spreading the variety of ways that goods and services are provided, and this in turn will offer a future that is not entirely growth dependent. The following insights offer some pragmatic suggestions for achieving this.

Insight 2: The need to foster the local business community and social economy

People and firms need goods and services, and they need employment. While the provision of goods and services and the nature of employment do not need to be market oriented, a reliance entirely on non-monetised forms of exchange of goods, services and labour severely constrains their availability. It would also be a significant move away from the way that societies are currently organised. Earlier chapters have shown that the social economy can deliver in a variety of ways, but there remains a need to reach a certain level of aggregate demand or conventional economic activity in order to meet current expectations of consumption within society. Thus, ensuring livelihoods and quality of life means fostering all aspects of diverse economies, both the conventional market-oriented business sector and the social economy. However, this need not mean buying into the growth-led political agenda. Chapters 4 and 5 have shown how small local businesses and cooperatives can thrive and form a significant part of the local economy. Indeed, it should not be forgotten that both these sectors already account for considerable employment and value added. SMEs dominate in terms of number of firms and also employment (Henriques and Catarino 2016; Fatima et al, 2021; Herce et al, 2024). Social enterprises in Europe account for about 10 per cent of business organisations and 6 per cent of employment and, given the difficulties in accounting for social enterprises and the variety of ways these are defined, such figures are likely to be an underestimate.

This does mean a policy approach that is oriented to developing the existing diverse economies of an area rather than solely concentrating on attracting inward investment for new, larger business ventures. It highlights the importance of local economic development for endogenous sectors and of developing a solid knowledge base about these sectors, and it involves attention to economic organisations not purely on the basis of their market value or addition to gross value added. Care needs to be taken with the way that financialisation may be implicated in such local business activity. Sources of finance for local businesses that take a financialised form can lead to pressures on those businesses arising from trade, often speculative trade at a distance in the financialised assets. These pressures can divert attention from creating a financially sustainable business providing goods and services. For these reasons, the community wealth-building approach has explored the value of creating local and regional banks that not only know the local economic landscape well but are also focused on developing strong businesses rather than trading in financialised assets (see later for further discussion of community wealth building).

It should be emphasised that a focus on fostering local businesses, whether smaller firms or cooperatives, does not mean local autarky. Such businesses may well have long supply chains in and out of the firm, connecting them to suppliers and consumers near and far. Some will be addressing local needs, including the under-valued economy highlighted by foundational economy commentators; but others will be connected to global marketplaces and may be part of the provision of higher-value products and services at a distance. The discussion of Mondragon cooperatives in Chapter 5 suggests that this can dilute some of the core principles by which cooperatives operate, but this is not inevitable; it can be addressed through the nature of the contracts within the supply chains (see also later). The overall point is that it is possible to maintain a focus on and support for the local diverse economies while accepting the value of engaging with a network of economic actors at a broader scale.

For this, the information base for local planning needs to be reoriented to support the needs of small local businesses and social enterprises. This requires a different form of knowledge of local communities, less focused on development land, development pressures and market prices for buildings and more on the extent, form and needs of the organisations providing local goods, services and employment and the resources of the local civil society. The typologies of the foundational economy provide a useful starting point for how the provisioning of goods and services can be reimagined and there is plentiful work on understanding how local civil societies can be described and local social capital measured (for example, Healey, 2022; Lin and Erickson, 2008). However, such information needs to be deeply contextualised, drawing out the key features of the locality and rooted in the needs of local organisations.

Planning systems also have a specific role in drawing up local plans and the implementation of planning regulation. Both can be used to protect land and built-environment assets of importance to local communities from market-led development. But, further, they can be used to facilitate alternative landownership and business models, as where land is allocated and ring-fenced for occupation and development by community organisations, small firms and social enterprises. Positive policies for development of community-based infrastructure or by local community land trusts (CLTs) could be included, for example. There is also the possibility of linking up such plans with stronger connections to a local sense of identity, place and heritage. Here, place-making is not about branding and attracting inward investment but, rather, about liveability for existing residents and supporting the local foundational economy.

An example of this is provided by Thompson's (2023) account of how community wealth building was adopted in Plymouth, which he characterises as a municipal–cooperative enterprise model. This involved support of the city's cooperative movement by actively engaging in public–commons partnerships and also supporting community enterprises more broadly through a state-endowed charitable trust. It leveraged the history of the area in terms of cooperatives dating back to the mid-19th century. The challenge that was specifically posed to the council was the decline of the Royal Navy dockyards and linked maritime industries. This left dockside districts in need of some form of regeneration. Encouraging diverse economies was found to be the way forward with a CLT building housing, a makers' hub, energy social enterprises alongside considerable training and awareness efforts and funding through dedicated streams, from local authority-supported crowdfunding to an investment fund. Thompson summarises the Plymouth experience as: 'Plymouth's dual model of "letting a thousand flowers bloom" ... has produced an efflorescence of diverse innovation in cooperative development.'

How much could be expected from such a shift in local planning approaches? Sonnino and Griggs-Trevarthen (2013) looked at five community food enterprises in Oxfordshire, including a farmers' market, a community market, a community garden and a bakery. They saw social entrepreneurs as having the capacity to empower local communities through collective mobilisation of local resources. They did, however, emphasise the need for a development strategy at the regional scale to capture the gains of individual and potentially isolated initiatives. This is particularly the case if social entrepreneurship is to be used to make significant moves towards an alternative future. Such futures are indeterminate; they could involve an alternative to capitalism, they could supplement capitalism without impacting on capitalist enterprise, or they could vary between competing with market provision and operating in parallel. Sonnino and Griggs-Trevarthen concluded that the very local embeddedness of social enterprises can constrain the extent to which they can be scaled up, but they do see potential for the spread of the social economy through the transfer of knowledge and replication of local initiatives in new locations. This is scaling out rather than scaling up, and focusing on the number of initiatives rather than their size. It seeks to capture the power of the small but many. Local planning can play a role here through providing the kinds of support discussed in preceding chapters.

For Turnbull (2023), social enterprises could be a kind of 'space within the system to effect change' (p 2) by prefiguring alternatives in the way that Gibson-Graham (2006) envisage. Their work is, therefore, situated within everyday, implicit or quiet activisms. Murtagh and Boland (2019) were more equivocal and raise the need for local policy and politics to keep a close eye on how such organisations operate. They point out that social enterprises can be co-opted and behave in regressive ways, but they could also contribute to 'alternative neighbourhood economies, local circuits of wealth distribution and more stable community organisations' (p 7). Along the way, they need to 'manage what is socially legitimate as well as financially viable' (p 20). This issue is discussed further later in the chapter, highlighting both that local planning systems can provide arenas where ethical debate on these issues can occur, but also the need for safeguards against inequitable outcomes.

Insight 3: The central importance of social capital to diverse economies

The discussion so far has highlighted the central importance of social capital both to the small business sector and the social economy. It is integral to the operation of diverse economies, especially if one considers numbers of organisations and employment rather than value generated, that is, a people-based metric rather than a market-oriented financial one. Social capital is a measure of the connections between people or organisations, the number and strengths of such connections and the shared norms, particularly norms concerning mutuality, reciprocity and trust. As such, it can take a variety of forms.

Bonding social capital connects homogeneous actors strongly, with common norms often taking centre stage (Rydin and Holman, 2004). It can describe the cosy community of a small village or the frightening camaraderie of a mafia-style organisation. And it necessarily involves boundaries, so that strong bonding social capital connects those inside the community or network but also excludes others. The norms can be reassuring and positive in their outcomes but can also result in naming and shaming and insidious social control. This means that it is not enough to have bonding social capital present, but it needs to be bonding social capital with positive outcomes for the actors or organisations being considered. This has implications for the kinds of safeguards that, again, need to be put in place to ensure inclusion and prevent discrimination.

Two other forms of social capital are bridging and linking (Rydin and Holman, 2004). Bridging social capital links heterogeneous actors and is often relatively weak. It plays an important role from time to time, despite this weakness. Linking social capital is defined as acting across tiers or scale, from the neighbourhood to the locality, the region and the country. It can be an important way of forging alliances within the multiscalar governmental sector, and this can support the winning of grants and contracts from public anchor organisations operating at scale. But it is also of importance in connecting businesses operating in different locations and at different scales. There is also the concept of bracing social capital, which was coined more specifically to describe the kind of multi-actor networks that are effective in building policy and implementing it (Rydin and Holman, 2004). Central to bracing social capital is a combination of bonding and bridging social capital to minimise the transaction costs of flows across the network.

There are number of features of how social capital works that are worth bearing in mind. Firstly, the linkages and norms of different kinds of social capital imply an opportunity for building connections and activating resources along those connections. But they do not guarantee this. There has to be agency involved in activating the networks that constitute social capital. Often there is a key individual or set of individuals who are in a central location within social capital networks, are skilled at managing those networks in order to release and activate resources and are strongly motivated towards collective action across the network. The idea of bracing social capital suggests that there is a network form – known as the hub and spoke model – that is particularly effective when such network managers exercise their agency. It places the network manager at a location within the network with high connectivity and, from this location or hub, resources such as information can spread readily across the network.

Furthermore, while it is difficult and time-consuming to build social capital, it can be quite readily destroyed. This was apparent in many of the accounts of social enterprises in the preceding chapters. It is dependent on the individuals who activate social capital through local networks, and these individuals may move away, not be able to continue in this role or choose not to. There is a history to the creation of social capital that enables its functioning. So, a policy that seeks to promote livelihoods and well-being without recourse to the pro-growth agenda will need to consider carefully where mature and emergent social capital currently exists within a locality and how to foster and maintain it. Work by Tomaney et al (2023) has highlighted how social infrastructure such as libraries, community centres, sports clubs and religious institutions can play a central role in building and reproducing social capital. These are also features of the local built environment, and therefore planning potentially has a significant role in protecting them and, thereby, providing the physical basis for social capital.

It should be noted that while social capital is often conflated with the idea of community, they are not identical. The concept of community, as discussed in Chapter 7, is heavily normative in its prevailing usage and focuses largely on residents. The way that social capital has been discussed here covers linkages and norms within and between both business and residential communities. It is also a much more precise concept than community, with an emphasis on how certain links and norms are activated in specific circumstances by particular actors. The number of members of a social capital network are more limited than the total local population, which is often subsumed within the idea of an inclusive local community. This has benefits, as it offers more precise levers for local policy actors to use when trying to create, maintain and ensure the longevity of local social capital. It does, however, have implications for inclusion and equity as already mentioned and as discussed further later.

Many of the means for building, maintaining and fostering social capital necessarily fall to national policy. In relation to planning systems, ideally, the planning of the built environment should be recognised as materialising and embedding social capital (Hanna et al, 2009), and this should be a prioritised goal, over the generation of development value and achieving increments in land value or facilitating large-scale market-led development and investment. But, given the fragility of social capital, there is also a need for policies, programmes and funds to support local social capital in specific areas. In effect, this calls for a policy of community development, something that has long been absent in England, although there is plentiful experience with community development programmes in many other countries (Bamber et al, 2010).

This implies a national policy framework that goes beyond conventional ideas of what local planning is about. Here, planning is not just about managing new development and shaping urban growth. Rather, it is about creating a liveable place where goods, employment and services are provided to local people, leveraging local resources of social capital and enterprise with the support of local and national governments. The provision of social infrastructure by the local state can be an important support for social capital, but also further investments of all kinds by local firms, social enterprises and community groups. This implies also bringing community development, local economic development and planning into a closer dialogue with each other.

Given the points raised earlier about the potentially 'dark' side to social capital, this also suggests the need for frameworks to act as safeguards regarding inclusion and discrimination and reinforces the importance of ethical discussions within local planning arenas. This is highlighted by reports of extreme right-wing groups in Germany under the Reichsbürger movement seeking to increase rural landownership in order to build community-based organisations that espouse and further their extremist values (Connolly, 2023). The role of national policy is to establish a normative framework for how such locally based initiatives are allowed to operate. A commitment to community-based initiatives in goods and service provision should not be too 'rose tinted', otherwise it will fail to recognise the dangers that may be inherent in empowering the grassroots.

Insight 4: The way that landownership provides essential security

A concrete means of support for local social capital that has been repeatedly highlighted in preceding chapters is the provision of land and associated premises.

A place to be is essential for small firms and social enterprises and is a core requirement for the activities of CLTs and community-based infrastructure projects. It also enables social infrastructure. But the security and long-term viability of these projects and initiatives requires much more than just a location. It is clear that holding a property right has a number of advantages. It provides the security that underpins the longevity of a project or initiative, the ability to plan into the longer term and the potential to leverage ownership of a property right for finance. Most simply, it means the absence of a payment to someone else who would otherwise own the premises and site. Sometimes the ownership of a property right is integral to the business model, as with CLTs and community infrastructure.

In discussing property rights, it is relevant to recognise the variety of such rights that exist. In particular, a distinction can be made between individual and common property rights. Individual rights are held by a person or an organisation. They can be essential for a business or a social enterprise to operate. Common property rights can take a variety of legal forms but involve a collective group of actors owning a site or building together. Collective ownership of this kind involves mutual recognition of the rights of all members of the group and a means for resolving conflicts when they arise, a means that all members of the group agree to. While many within the post-growth movement hail the benefits of common property ownership, the preceding chapters have shown that a range of property rights may be relevant to projects and initiatives that seek to delink from the drive for growth. Much depends on the specific context, including the nature of the group and the purpose of the project or initiative, as well as national features such as the legal framework.

That said, issues around landownership typically invoke some of the more fundamental power structures in a society. Shifting these can be difficult. In much of the UK, there have been strong trends towards privatisation of land previously held within the public estate, alongside the growing involvement of financial institutions in landownership and the promotion of financialised means of owning land. In this context, transferring property rights into the ownership of organisations that wish to promote projects and initiatives outside a pro-growth agenda can be difficult. For example, the localism agenda (Holman and Rydin, 2012) promoted in England in the 2010s included the right to bid for a building that was designated a community asset, potentially preventing its sale on the open market to an outside bidder. However, the price of the building was still set by the market and there were no public funds set aside for community purchase. The right to bid only gave the local community some time to try to raise the purchase price.

However, it is possible to establish a national programme of support for community-based organisations to buy property rights to land and buildings. The Scottish Government is an exemplar here, having given communities the right to buy certain land and offering a fund to support the purchase and also the ongoing management of that property. This is detailed in Chapter 7. History is relevant here, with much land being owned by feudal landlords or their successors in title who are often absentee owners; there is also the tradition of crofting or small-scale agricultural landholdings. The Scottish populace's negative experience of this history prompted the establishment of programmes to support community ownership of land, but it also provides a model that other countries could learn from. One example of this is the work of the Liverpool City Region Land Commission, which provides a wide-ranging analysis and set of recommendations for putting diverse landownership at the core of policies for the region (Liverpool City Region Land Commission, 2021).

Small businesses, if not taking the form of social enterprises, are often assumed to be able to cope on the open market in the pursuit of a location for their activities. Furthermore, such businesses typically rent, rather than owning a long-term property right in their buildings and sites. This raises the importance of another policy initiative, often undertaken by local government: the provision of affordable workspaces for small local businesses. This was discussed in Chapter 4. Location and affordability are the key considerations here. Direct local government provision is most likely to ensure both these characteristics meet the needs of small local businesses. Indeed, Ferm (2016) warned against relying on a growth-dependent planning logic to provide affordable premises for smaller businesses. She found that if such premises are incorporated to new development, they often resulted in higher-value small firms outbidding local firms, contributing to economic gentrification.

Recognising the importance of landownership and the need to adopt a range of common landownership rights that might be needed by community groups and social enterprises are important steps forward, but there is also a need for the provision of funds for acquisition and management support. The exemplar of Scotland has been mentioned, although the attitude to community ownership is closely linked to the specific landownership history there (Shucksmith, 2010; Mackenzie, 2013). A considerable shift is involved here in terms of seeing land policy as central to national government policy frameworks and, further, making land policy about more than just public and private landownership. Forms of common ownership need to be recognised within a land policy that aims to devolve significant landownership to community groups and social enterprises.

Insight 5: The need to attend to contractual relationships and business models

The preceding chapters have repeatedly indicated the need to consider the contractual relationships and business models that are involved in the various projects and initiatives. This goes back to the need for viability if long-term survival is to be ensured. Viability results from the business model that is adopted and the way that contracts determine the flow of funds into and out of the organisation, and that can include specific grants. This means that the relationships across market and civil society actors are mediated by contracts and business models, and these determine if the relationships are sustainable. The details matter. Small shifts alter the flow of resources between actors, with consequences for the financial sustainability of the activity.

The difficulty is that the detailed nature of these contracts and business models will be tailored to the specific circumstances of each project or initiative. But this does not mean the constant reinvention of the wheel. There is scope for project to learn from project, initiative from initiative, provided that allowance is made for the way that circumstances may differ and the adjustments that may be needed. This is about the transfer of ideas and knowledge and implies a role for a key knowledge-transfer actor, probably from within the public sector. A good example of this is the way that learning about the so-called Preston Model is circulating. While the originators of this set of ideas declare it not to be a transferable model, they have been instrumental (along with others) in circulating the key ideas and developing a discussion on how they might be applied in a variety of locations. This centrally involves considering business models and contracts.

The Preston Model or, more generally, the community wealth-building approach, has at its heart the argument that local firms and social enterprises can be helped by utilising local procurement and building local supply chains (McInroy, 2018; Manley and Whyman, 2021). In particular, it involves a policy of supporting local firms and cooperatives through the procurement of local anchor institutions. These are larger, immobile organisations that are grounded in the locality. These can include the local authority itself, hospitals and major educational institutions, but potentially private bodies also; whatever sector they are in, community wealth building requires a commitment to supporting the local economy and expressing this through procurement policies and practices, that is, 'buying local'.

The key focus here is the support of local firms and development of local supply chains, with the implication that this will also provide new markets and customers for smaller firms in the locality. In relation to local urban development, where local planning might be thought to have some direct influence, this would mean more emphasis on using local developers and construction firms, particularly by the anchor institutions such as the local authority and other public or quasi-public institutions. It also means that developers – large and small – should be using local procurement policies for their own supply chains.

There is also the possibility of looking more widely at the sources of finance that enable investment in providing goods and services. The potential role of a regional bank has already been mentioned, where loans are based both on detailed local knowledge and on a degree of local commitment. But there are a wide range of alternative finance sources that could be explored, including community finance (Hicks, 2020a), crowdfunding (Gasparro and Monk, 2020) and a variety of financial self-help groups (Lehmann and Smets, 2020). In a sense, planning cannot avoid engaging with these details of the working of diverse economies if it is to be able to plan without recourse to the growth dynamics of inward investment and market-led urban development.

Indeed, the circulation of knowledge about business models and contractual arrangements, alongside alternative forms of landownership, is something that is best undertaken at the local level to ensure that the knowledge is appropriately tailored to local circumstances. This could extend to training in skills for entrepreneurship and management, including management of land and buildings. Small firms and social enterprises find this challenging and it can limit the viability of their activities. This could well be married with enhanced efforts for local procurement, given that local authorities are key anchor institutions. Again, this is stretching the role of planning beyond the promotion, management and regulation of new urban development, and yet, it can be a deeply meaningful way to change localities to the benefit of their local communities.

Looking ahead to a rebalanced diverse economy

If these insights are built upon and result in policy action at national and local scales, what might we see in terms of a future economy and society? And how would it relate to the debates about growth and planning outlined at the start of this book?

The hope is that certain elements within diverse economies would be thickened by such an approach, rebalancing the economy or society as a whole, through scaling out rather than scaling up. There would be greater emphasis on and strength of the SME sector, the social economy and that part of provisioning that is grounded in civil society. This means that people would be provided with more goods and services locally, although these firms and (to a lesser extent, probably) social economy organisations would also be supplying to others outside the locality. This would boost their viability. Local government policy and support may encourage stronger local supply chains, perhaps integrating SMEs and social enterprises to a greater extent. But there are also likely to be supply chains stretching across distance, linking local firms and social enterprises with remote suppliers also.

These firms and social enterprises could widen the range of goods and services on offer in the locality and are likely to contribute to the foundational economy, specifically the overlooked economy. They would be a more visible physical presence within that locality, particularly if the local authority enabled, offered and protected premises that provided appropriate and affordable accommodation. In addition, they would be supported by measures that sought to strengthen social capital, and one of the most visible ways would be through provision of social infrastructure within the locality.

It is important to remember that this expansion of underappreciated aspects of diverse economies would not necessarily result in the decline of the existing formal market sectors of the economy. They would still have a role to play in delivering goods and services. Seeking to delink from the pursuit of growth does not mean that existing economic activity will necessarily be lessened. Even a degrowth approach has to acknowledge the relevance of this sector; it cannot be replaced entirely by SMEs, the social economy and civil society. Relevant for a planning perspective, this means that private sector-driven urban development would also continue to some extent. It may be balanced to a greater extent by CLTs and community-based development and public provision of commercial spaces, but there will remain a role for private sector developers in changing the built environment. This raises questions about the social and environmental consequences of this continuance of existing private sector modes of provisioning and urban development.

Past experience has shown the potential for gentrification and social inequality arising from market-led private sector development, and financialisation seems to have exacerbated this by putting a premium on higher-value projects, whether residential or commercial, and displacing – directly or indirectly – lower-value land uses, including housing, commercial or industrial. Even allowing for state support of alternatives and the prospects of opposition from within civil society, this is likely to continue. Furthermore, the pressures towards financialisation and globalisation are also likely to remain. National policy could seek to push back on these trends, but there is also scope to do so within the planning system. This would mean delinking planning policies from narratives of mass inward investment, attracting global capital and following a world-city path, and would involve a shift in planning discourses away from current visions of preferred economic development and towards alternative diverse economies and foundational economy narratives (Rydin 2022).

This is likely to be most challenging in areas where it looks like there would be benefits from the globalised, financialised, inward investment route. Undoubtedly, there will be social groups that can afford and would appreciate the urban environment that this route offers, and others that might aspire to it. But the costs also need to be borne in mind and are likely to become increasingly apparent. The most obvious of these is the impact on housing and the rapid escalation in housing costs in areas that are subject to these growth pressures. Here, there are opportunities for affordable housing to be unlocked by CLTs and other community-based housing, going alongside public housing and regulation of private rented housing. Here, a rebalanced economy could prove both effective and politically attractive. It should be remembered that there remains a tax base even within a rebalanced economy, arising from market-based income, and thus a role for the public sector can be sustained.

Then there is a need to take account of the environmental imperative. While some of post-growth initiatives and projects discussed in earlier chapters did have explicitly environmental goals – notably the community-based infrastructure projects in the domain of renewable energy – many did not. Furthermore, the activities of the projects will continue to have an environmental impact. It is the product of the scale of economic activity and resource efficiency (resource use per unit of economic activity) that creates environmental impacts. Many small, local firms and social enterprises lack the capacity to invest in resource efficiencies or new modes of producing and distributing goods and services so as to reduce environmental burdens. Problems of scarce time as well as personnel and management capacity compound the limited knowledge that is found within many such small organisations, whether market-oriented businesses or not (Cagno and Trianni 2013; Henriques and Catarina, 2016; Fresner et al, 2017).

Research on SMEs in China found that informational barriers were the core barrier (Kostka et al, 2013), and Pickard and O'Dywer (2023) found that smaller organisations often have a lack of knowledge about environmental issues and of how to tackle them. However, Palm and Backman (2020) found that facilitating the creation of situated local knowledge in collaboration with the small firms, and putting the emphasis on developing new practices through experimentation, was the way around this (see also Backman, 2018). There will be a need to provide specific, tailored support to the small business and social economy sectors in retooling for carbon reductions and resource efficiencies, taking into account the challenges they face.

Beyond such knowledge circulation and co-creation, there will remain a need to regulate for environmental protection, and planning systems, in particular, will have to continue to regulate for green urban development and to encourage greater urban retrofit and preserve embodied carbon within existing built-environment assets. Planning systems could also explore the possibilities of fostering a circular economy approach locally or regionally. As discussed in Chapter 2, these policy approaches may not completely delink economic activity and environmental impact, but, in the context of other measures and initiatives, they can make a contribution towards environmental sustainability. A rebalanced economy would also require ongoing and even strengthened environmental regulation both within the small business and social enterprise sectors and also in relation to the continuation of other forms of economic activity. There remains a need for existing and evolving patterns of providing goods and services to go through a transition to much greater resource efficiency, particularly around energy. This means ensuring energy efficiency across a great number of sectors: large firms, smaller firms, the social economy and civil society.

However, resource efficiency is also centrally affected by the infrastructure that sets the context for behaviour and decision making in a wide range of organisations. Therefore, energy efficiency, resource efficiency and low carbon possibilities need to determine investment in infrastructure so as to encourage a low-carbon, resource-efficient transition. Community-based options and demand management and efficiencies at the level of the firm, social enterprise and household are unlikely to achieve the resource efficiencies and carbon reductions that the literature reviewed in Chapter 2 indicates are necessary so as to remain within sustainability bounds. Thus, there is every indication that wider technological change and investment in infrastructure is required.

The nature of this infrastructural change is a matter of debate. There is a tendency to favour mega-projects to deliver infrastructure at scale; the public sector seems to find it structurally easier to deal with a limited number of large companies in infrastructure planning, just as they favour the larger developers in growth-dependent planning. But experience of failures on such projects arising from the inability to handle a variety of risks at least poses the question of whether there are no other alternatives. At issue here is the possibility of infrastructures operating at a variety of scales and including community-based options. Figure 10.1 illustrates

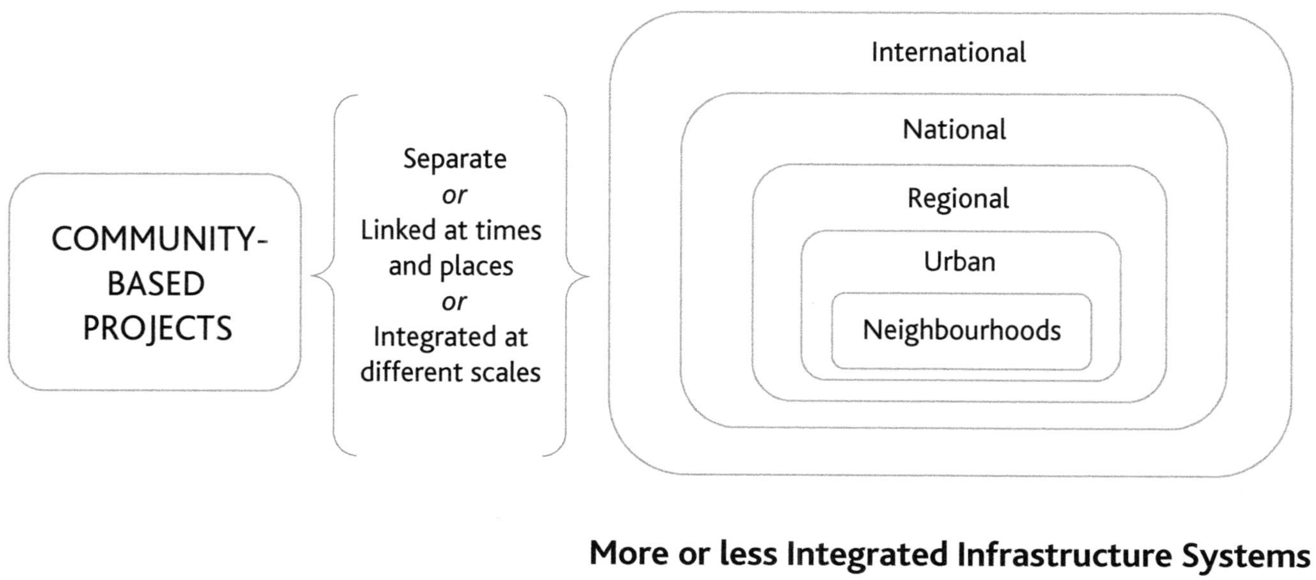

Figure 10.1: Community-based infrastructure and wider system

this, suggesting that community-based infrastructure could in some cases be entirely separate of other systems, could link periodically or in specific places or could be actively integrated.

Thus, a community energy project could be intermittently connected to a private wire or a broader electric grid, selling surplus electricity through, say, a feed-in tariff and also buying it when needed. A local water collection and treatment facility may remove the need for connection to a wider water supply network completely, or it may be just that community-managed sustainable urban drainage systems reduce the burden of drainage on the water network. Local waste facilities can turn some waste streams into the basis for profitable enterprises, while other waste streams remain the responsibility of public and private waste-management organisations. Community bike schemes could be available at public transport hubs and could even be integrated into private sector bike-share schemes. The options are many. The key principles that such schemes need to follow are: the ability to implement infrastructure improvements and to do so within a reasonable timescale (unlike many mega-projects); to incorporate capacities for repair and maintenance to ensure their operability into the future; and to have finance schemes which enable investment and do not disadvantage any social groups by the financial model adopted. Rather than aiming for comprehensive, integrated systems that are planned *de novo*, this approach puts the emphasis on accommodating a degree of incremental change and prioritising deliverability, flexibility and resilience over time.

In this scenario, infrastructure investment needs to be driven by its use value and its environmental impact, not primarily by financial return. Again, this throws a negative light on the way that financialisation has impacted on infrastructure sectors (Chapter 8) and suggests a return to infrastructure being planned and partly delivered by the public sector. This raises questions of financing through means other than growth-predicated taxation and/or the global investment market. As Leyshon (2024) points out, this can be problematic in small and open economies. However, there are innovative means of raising finance that fall into the category of sticky or patient capital, and rebalancing public budgets also may release funds for what will, in the longer term, turn out to be cost effective (Jackson et al, 2024). Planning systems can be important here in developing strategies for and implementing collectives of infrastructure projects – across energy, water, waste and transport – that will pragmatically deliver a green technology transition with such financing.

This all presupposes a national political context and associated policy frameworks genuinely sympathetic to the kinds of post-growth pathways discussed in this book, not one that seeks to subvert post-growth to another agenda. There is plentiful literature about the dangers of such pathways being used to cloak or sweeten austerity. The UK provides a salutary history lesson here with the experiences of the localism agenda under the Conservative–Liberal Democrat Coalition government that was elected in 2010. In some ways, this picked up on the communitarian thread of the New Labour government of 1997–2010, influenced by the work of Etzioni (1968) that saw community and individuals' role within communities as central to the way that society worked and, by implication, something that public policy should support. The Coalition government put this in a different context, seeking to align it with their pro-growth and pro-market ideology (Tait and Inch, 2016).

It also operated in the context of stringent public spending cuts. The incoming Coalition government of 2010 introduced the most substantial public spending cuts of the post-war period (Clayton et al, 2016). The spending review of October 2010 set £81 billion of savings to 2014/15, while a further £10 million of cuts to the welfare budget were announced in 2012, alongside a clear indication that reductions would continue until 2018. This was partly a response to the fiscal crisis engendered by the 2008/09 global financial turmoil and partly in line with Conservative party ideology. In this context, the localism agenda was used to shift responsibility for local services to communities wherever possible. The Localism Act of 2011 covered a wide variety of policy reforms (Bentley and Pugalis, 2013), but among these was the right of a community to challenge existing local service providers with a view to taking over the service, as well as the right to buy a designated community asset.

The result of this context for expanding community management and ownership of assets under localism was the creation of 'austerity localism' in which the state readily withdrew from services provision and encouraged the local community to take these on board. This was less community empowerment than the responsibilisation of communities to fulfil functions that had been seen as part of the public sector and even the welfare state (Raco, 2000; Hastings et al, 2015). Clayton et al (2016) saw the result of expanding localism in conditions of austerity as the severance of relationships and trust with public authorities, 'creating forms of disconnect between those in power and those who feel on the receiving end of damaging decisions' (p 737). There are numerous examples of this within the research literature (Moore and McKee, 2014).

Those in favour of community-based approaches need, therefore, to be cautious about the demands made on communities and to recognise the ongoing importance of a national agenda that will be genuinely supportive. As the foregoing discussion has indicated, there will be a need for governmental support at local and national levels for diverse economies to become rebalanced and for the full potential of small, localised firms, social enterprises and civil society to deliver well-being and environmental sustainability within localities without recourse to growth narratives.

Concluding words

This book has shown how the diverse economies approach, incorporating the insights of the foundational economy framework, can offer a different perspective on planning and growth. Such a diverse economies approach differs from the literature on green growth and the circular economy, which takes a conventional view of the economy as the domain of monetised and market-based activities. But it also differs from the analysis developed within much of degrowth and post-growth literature that seeks to posit an alternative to the capitalist, market-based society, which leads to an emphasis on activities that are seen as being beyond the market and rooted in civil society. The argument of this book is that this is a chimera. It suggests a separation between market-based activity and community-based activities which cannot exist in current societies except as small pockets of self-sufficiency. Furthermore, it ignores the extent to which current market-based activities rely on the social capital generated within civil society and the extent to which community-based activities engage with monetised exchanges through the market.

It is clear that the kinds of approach discussed in this book under the heading of pragmatic post-growth planning are a more detailed way of delivering 'good growth' with a strong commitment to meeting the needs of local communities and, in particular, less affluent groups through protecting and enhancing the overlooked and undervalued aspects of the market economy and through rendering diverse economies more visible and robust. However, compared to the literature discussed in Chapter 2, this is a more bottom-up, community-based approach rather than relying on top-down management through indicator systems and monitoring. It also provides a more detailed version of what good growth would look like, fleshing out in detail what diverse economies can be.

The assessment of this post-growth approach against the parameters of green growth is more problematic, as indicated earlier. In general, the social and economic benefits to local communities, firms or specific groups tend to be emphasised above the environmental benefits of doing economic activity in a different way. Technology shift would occur largely through the amalgamation of various community infrastructure initiatives, but the scale of this can be questioned, as Chapter 8 covered. Some initiatives, such as urban gardens, make a significant contribution in social terms and may help at the margins with food poverty, but they have a limited environmental impact. The need for larger-scale infrastructural change has been addressed and reliance on strong environmental regulatory standards, say in the case of CLT developments, has also been mentioned. One can only conclude that post-growth planning will make a contribution to environmental sustainability, but the scale of that cannot be assured. But the critiques of green growth also highlight that the scale of growth may outstrip any resource efficiencies, to the point where its contribution to environmental sustainability may also be questioned. It seems that environmental sustainability will require supported development of diverse economies, renewed infrastructure systems that will significantly reduce carbon and resource dependence and tight regulation to enhance related efficiencies.

Finally, one comes to the degrowth literature. While drawing inspiration from many of the grassroots initiatives and projects highlighted in the degrowth literature, it is fair to conclude that the post-growth approach outlined in this book may be in conflict with degrowth perspectives (Bärnthaler, 2024; Savini,

2024). The discussion is premised on the importance of economic activity – understood within a diverse economies framework – to deliver goods, services, employment and surpluses. This fits somewhat uncomfortably with the idea of reducing the level of economic activity, at least in higher-income societies, that degrowth proposes. There is a closer fit with the common underlying critique of financialisation and how it is shaping the global economy, and this supports the call for an economic policy focused more on productive economic activity as well as the overlooked and foundational parts of the economy.

The analysis here looks at the problems from a pragmatic point of view, considering what seem to be the limits of political acceptability and the need to take action and achieve impacts within a short timescale. This might seem a less-than-radical perspective, and indeed it is. However, the hope is that an expansion of the small-scale productive economy, the overlooked economy, the foundational economy and the social economy could deliver a significant change in the life chances and experiences of many communities. It provides an agenda for planning that goes beyond siphoning off part of the development value that has been enabled by pro-growth planning. At least it opens up alternative pathways for debate, and thus new hopes for the future.

References

Adams, D. and Hardman, G. (2014) 'Observing Guerrillas in the Wild: Reinterpreting practices of urban guerrilla gardening', *Urban Studies* 51(6): 1103–1119.

Adams, D., Hardman, M. and Larkham, P. (2015) 'Exploring Guerrilla Gardening: Gauging public views on the grassroots activity', *Local Environment* 20(10): 1231–1246.

Adams, D., Disberry, A. and Hutchison, N. (2017) 'Still Vacant after All These Years: Evaluating the efficiency of property-led urban regeneration', *Local Economy* 32(6): 505–524.

Aernouts, N. (2020) 'Designing Commons: Exploring interplays between commons, space and spatial design', *Urban Design International* 25: 63–76.

Aernouts, N. and Ryckewaert, M. (2018) 'Beyond Housing: On the role of commoning in the establishment of a Community Land Trust project', *International Journal of Housing Policy* 18(4): 503–521.

Alawadi, K., Hashem, S. and Maghelal, P. (2022) 'Perspectives on Everyday Urbanism: Evidence from an Abu Dhabi neighborhood', *Journal of Planning Education and Research*, available online at: https://doi-org.libproxy.ucl.ac.uk/10.1177/0739456X221097.

Andres, L. and Kraftl, P. (2021) 'New Directions in the Theorisation of Temporary Urbanisms: Adaptability, activation and trajectory', *Progress in Human Geography* 45(5): 1237–1253.

Andres, L., Bakareb, H., Brysonc, J., Khaembad, W., Melgaçoe, L. and Mwanikif, G. (2021) 'Planning, Temporary Urbanism and Citizen-led Alternative-substitute Place-making in the Global South', *Regional Studies* 55(1): 29–39.

Apostolopoulou, E. and Kotsila, P. (2022) 'Community Gardening in Hellinikon as a Resistance Struggle against Neoliberal Urbanism: Spatial autogestion and the right to the city in post-crisis Athens, Greece', *Urban Geography* 43(2): 293–319.

Artinger, F. M., Gigerenzer, G, and Jacobs, P. (2022) 'Satisficing: Integrating two traditions', *Journal of Economic Literature* 60(2): 598–635.

Backman, F. (2018) 'Local Knowledge Creation with the Use of Industrial Energy Efficiency Networks (IEENs): A Swedish case study', *Energy Research and Social Science* 42: 147–154.

Ball, M., Shepherd, E. and Wyatt, P. (2022) 'The Relationship between Residential Development Land Prices and House Prices', *Town Planning Review* 93(4): 401–421.

Bamber, J., Owens, S., Schonfeld, H. Ghate, D. and Fullerton, D. (2010) 'Effective Community Development Programmes: A review of the international evidence base', Dublin: The Centre for Effective Services.

Baranova, P., Paterson, F. and Gallotta, B. (2020) 'Configuration of Enterprise Support towards the Clean Growth Challenge: A place-based perspective', *Local Economy* 35(4): 363–383.

Bärnthaler, R. (2024) 'Problematising Degrowth Strategising: On the role of compromise, material interests, and coercion', *Ecological Economics*, available online at: https://doi.org/10.1016/j.ecolecon.2024.108255.

Barry, J. (2019) 'Planning in and for a Post-growth and Post-carbon Economy', in S. Davoudi, R. Cowell, I. White and H. Blanco (eds) *The Routledge Companion to Environmental Planning*, Abingdon, Oxon: Routledge, pp 120–129.

Basáñez, L. (2019) 'The Synergy between Employment Policies and Cooperatives with Regard to New Forms of Work: An overview based on Spanish constitutional law', *Boletín de la Asociación Internacional de Derecho Cooperativo* 54: 55–73.

Bassett, E. M. (2007) 'The Persistence of the Commons: Economic theory and community decision-making on land tenure in Voi, Kenya', *Center for African Studies, African Studies Quarterly*, 9(3).

Bastida, M., Garcia, A., Pinto, L. and Blanco, A. (2022) 'Motivational Drivers to Choose Worker Cooperatives as an Entrepreneurial Alternative: Evidence from Spain', *Small Business Economics* 58: 1609–1626.

Bauwens, T. (2021) 'Are the Circular Economy and Economic Growth Compatible? A case for post-growth circularity', *Resources, Conservation and Recycling* 175: 1–3.

Bauwens, T., Huybrechts, B. and Dufays, F. (2020) 'Understanding the Diverse Scaling Strategies of Social Enterprises as Hybrid Organizations: The case of renewable energy cooperatives', *Organization and Environment* 33(2): 195–219.

Bengtsson, B. (1992) 'Not the Middle Way but Both Ways: Cooperative housing in Sweden', *Scandinavian Housing and Planning Research* 9(sup2): 87–104.

Bentley, G. and Pugalis, L. (2013) 'New Directions in Economic Development: Localist policy discourses and the Localism Act', *Local Economy* 28(3): 257–274.

Berglund, L. (2020) 'The Shrinking City as a Growth Machine: Detroit's reinvention of growth through triage, foundation work and talent attraction', *International Journal of Urban and Regional Research* 44(2): 219–247.

Bernt, M. (2009) 'Partnerships for Demolition: The governance of urban renewal in East Germany's shrinking cities', *International Journal of Urban and Regional Research* 33(3): 754–769.

Besser, T. (2009) 'Changes in Small Town Social Capital and Civic Engagement', *Journal of Rural Studies* 25: 185–193.

Beswick, J. and Penny, J. (2018) 'Demolishing the Present to Sell off the Future? The emergence of "financialized municipal entrepreneurialism" in London', *International Journal of Urban and Regional Research* 42(4): 612–632.

Bianchi, I. (2022) 'The Local State's Repertoires of Governance Strategies for the Urban Commons: Nuancing current perspectives', *EPC Politics and Space* 40(8): 1784–1800.

Biczkowski, M. (2020) 'LEADER as a Mechanism of Neo-endogenous Development of Rural Areas: The case of Poland', *Miscellanea Geographica* 24(4): 232–244.

Blomley, N. (2004) 'Un-real Estate: Proprietary space and public gardening', *Antipode* 36(4): 614–641.

Bloom, P. and Chatterji, A. (2009) 'Scaling Social Entrepreneurial Impact', *California Management Review* 51(3): 114–133.

Blundel, R. and Lyon, F. (2015) 'Towards a "Long View": Historical perspectives on the scaling and replication of social ventures', *Journal of Social Entrepreneurship* 6(1): 80–102.

Bock, B. (2016) 'Rural Marginalisation and the Role of Social Innovation: A turn towards nexogenous development and rural reconnection', *Sociologia Ruralis* 56: 552–573.

Boland, P. (2014) 'The Relationship between Spatial Planning and Economic Competitiveness: The "path to economic nirvana" or a "dangerous obsession"?' *Environment and Planning A* 46: 770–787.

Borcic, L., Cvitanovic, M. and Lukic, A. (2016) 'Cultivating Alternative Spaces – Zagreb's Community Gardens in Transition: From socialist to post-socialist perspective', *Geoforum* 77: 51–60.

Bosworth, G., Annibal, I., Carroll, T., Price, L., Sellick, J. and Shepherd, J. (2015) 'Empowering Local Action through Neo-Endogenous Development: The Case of LEADER in England', *Sociologica Ruralis* 56(3): 427–449.

Bradshaw, T. (2008) 'The Post-Place Community: Contributions to the debate about the definition of community', *Community Development* 39(1): 5–16.

Bragaglia, F. and Rossignolo, C. (2021) 'Temporary Urbanism as a New Policy Strategy: A contemporary panacea or a Trojan horse?', *International Planning Studies* 26(4): 370–386.

Bragaglia, F., Caldarice, O. and Rivolin, U. (2023) 'Outside-in: Co-production and the spatial planning systems in Italy and England', *Planning Theory*, available online at https://doi.org/10.1177/14730952231203516.

Brent, J. with Dorney, P., Teddy, P., Pierce, M. and Brent, C. (2009) *Searching for Community: Representation, power and action on an urban estate*, Bristol: Bristol University Press/Policy Press.

Bresnihan, V. (1990) 'A Community Success Story: Connemara West', *Irish Jesuits Studies* 79(313): 63–68.

Bresnihan, P. and Hesse, A. (2020) 'State and Community Enterprise: Negotiating water management in rural Ireland', in J.K. Gibson-Graham and K. Dombroski (eds) *The Handbook of Diverse Economies*, Northampton, Northants: Edward Elgar Publishing, pp 90–97.

Bretos, I., Errasti, A. and Marcuello, C. (2019) 'Multinational Expansion of Worker Cooperatives and their Employment Practices: Markets, institutions and politics in Mondragon', *ILR Review* 72(3): 580–605.

Brummer, V. (2018) 'Community Energy – Benefits and Barriers: A comparative review of community energy in the UK, Germany and the USA, the benefits it provides for society and the barriers it faces', *Renewable and Sustainable Energy Reviews* 94: 187–196.

Bryden, J. and Scott, I. (1990) 'The Celtic Fringe: State-sponsored versus indigensous local development initiatives in Scotland and Ireland', in W. Stöhr (ed) *Global Challenge and Local Response*, London: Mansell Publishing, pp 90–132.

Buch-Hansen, H. and Koch, M. (2019) 'Degrowth through Income and Wealth Caps?', *Ecological Economics* 160(160): 264–271.

Buciuni, G., Canello, G. and Gereffi, J. (2022) 'Microfoundations of Global Value Chain Research: Big decisions by small firms', *EPA Economy and Space* 54(6): 1086–1111.

Bunce, S. (2016) 'Pursuing Urban Commons: Politics and alliances in community land trust activism in East London', *Antipode* 48(1): 134–150.

Bunce, S. and Aslam, C. (2016) 'Land Trusts and the Protection and Stewardship of Land in Canada: Exploring non-governmental land trust practices and the role of urban community land trusts', *Canadian Journal of Urban Research* 25(2): 23–34.

Cagno, E. and Trianni, A. (2013) 'Exploring Drivers for Energy Effiiency within Small- and Medium-sized Enterprises: First evidences from Italian manufacturing enterprises', *Applied Energy* 104: 276–285.

Cahen, C., Lilli, E. and Saegert, S. (2022) 'Ethical Action in the Age of Austerity: Cases of care in two community land trusts', *Housing Studies* 37(3): 393–413.

Centrales Villageoises Association (nd) available at: https://www.centralesvilla geoises.fr

Chan, F., Griffiths, J., Higgitt, D., Xu, S., Zhu, S., Tang, Y.-T., Xu, Y. and Thorne, C. (2018) '"Sponge City" in China: A breakthrough of planning and flood risk management in the urban context', *Land Use Policy* 76: 772–778.

Chase, L., Crawford, M. and Kaliski, J. (eds) (2008) *Everyday Urbanism*, New York, NY: Monacelli Press.

Chaves-Avila, R. and Gallego-Bono, J. (2020) 'Transformative Policies for the Social and Solidarity Economy: The new generation of public policies fostering the social economy in order to achieve sustainable development goals: the European and Spanish cases', *Sustainability* 12(10): 4059.

Chaves-Avila, R. and Savall-Morera, T. (2019) 'The Social Economy in a Context of Austerity Policies: The tension between political discourse and implemented policies in Spain', *ISTR Voluntas* 30: 487–498.

Cheshire, P., Hilber, C. and Koster, H. (2018) 'Empty Homes, Longer Commutes: The unintended consequences of more restrictive local planning', *Journal of Public Economics* 158: 126–151.

Clayton, J. Donovan, C. and Merchant, J. (2016) 'Distancing and Limited Resourcefulness: Third sector service provision under austerity localism in the north east of England', *Urban Studies* 53(4): 723–740.

Colombarolli, C. and Storti, L. (2022) 'Dissecting Communities of Renewable Energy: A comparative investigation in New Aquitaine (France)', *Review of Social Economy*, available at: https://doi.org/10.1080/00346764.2022.2096916.

Connolly, K. (2023) 'Far-right Extremists Stage Rural Land Grab across Germany', *The Guardian*, 27 December.

Conte, V. and Anselmi, G. (2022) 'When Large-scale Regeneration Becomes an Engine of Urban Growth: How new power coalitions are shaping Milan's governance', *EPA Economy and Space* 54(6): 1184–1199.

Cooke, P. and Morgan, K. (1998) *The Associational Economy: Firms, regions and innovation*, Oxford: Oxford University Press.

Corvellec, H., Stowell, A. and Johansson, N. (2022) 'Critiques of the Circular Economy', *Journal of Industrial Ecology* 26(2): 421–432.

Coutard, O. (2008) 'Placing Splintering Urbanism: Introduction', *Geoforum* 39: 1815–1820.

Coyle, D. (2011) *The Economics of Enough: How to run the economy as if the future matters*, Princeton, NJ: Princeton University Press.

Crabtree, L. (2014a) 'Community Land Trusts: Embracing the relationality of property', in J.K. Gibson-Graham and K. Dombroski (eds) *The Handbook of Diverse Economies*, Northampton: Edward Elgar Publishing, pp 292–299.

Crabtree, L. (2014b) 'Community Land Trusts and Indigenous Housing in Australia: Exploring difference-based policy and appropriate housing', *Housing Studies* 29(6): 743–759.

Crane, A., Viswanathan, L. and Whitelaw, G. (2013) 'Sustainability through Intervention: A case study of guerrilla gardening in Kingston, Ontario', *Local Environment* 18(1): 71–90.

Creamer, E., Eadson, W., van Veelen, B., Pinker, A., Tingey, M., Braunholtz-Speight, T., Markantoni, M., Foden, M. and Lacey-Barnacle, M. (2018) 'Community Energy: Entanglements of community, state, and private sector', *Geography Compass* 12: 1–16.

Creamer, E., Allen, S. and Haggett, C. (2019) '"Incomers" Leading "Community-led" Sustainability Initiatives: A contradiction in terms?', *EPC Politics and Space* 37(5): 946–964.

Currie, M., Pinker, A. and Copus, A. (2019) 'Strengthening Communities on the Isle of Lewis in the Western Isles, United Kingdom', *RELOCAL Case Study Report*, available online at: https://relocal.eu.

Curry, N. (2022) 'The Rural Social Economy, Community Food Hubs and the Market', *Local Economy* 36(7–8): 569–588.

Daly, H. (1992) *Steady-state Economics* 2nd edn, London: Earthscan Publications.

Daskalaki, M. (2018) 'Alternative Organizing in Times of Crisis: Resistance assemblages and socio-spatial solidarity', *European Urban and Regional Studies* 25(2): 155–170.

De Saille, S. and Medvecky, F. (2020) *Responsibility Beyond Growth: A case for responsible stagnation*, Bristol: Bristol University Press.

DeFilippis, J. (2004) *Unmaking Goliath: Community control in the face of global capital*, New York, NY: Routledge.

DeFilippis, J., Stromberg, B. and Williams, O. (2018) 'W(h)ither the "Community" in Community Land Trusts?', *Journal of Urban Affairs* 40(6): 755–769.

DeFilippis, J., Williams, O., Martin, D. and Esfahani, A. (2019) 'On the Transformative Potential of Community Land Trusts in the United States', *Antipode* 51(3): 795–817.

Defourny, J. and Nyssens, M. (2013) 'Social Innovation, Social Economy and Social Enterprise: What can the European debate tell us?' in F. Moulaert, D. MacCallum, A. Mehmood and A. Hamdouch (eds) *International Handbook on Social Innovation: Collective action, social learning and transdisciplinary research*, Cheltenham, Glos: Edward Elgar, pp 40–52.

Department of Communities and Local Government (2007) *Making Assets Work: The Quirk Review of community ownership and management of public assets*, London: Department of Communities and Local Government.

Di Domenico, M., Hough, H. and Tracey, P. (2010) 'Social Bricolage: Theorising social value creation in social enterprises', *Entrepreneurship, Theory and Practice* 34(4): 681–703.

Dietz, R. and O'Neill, D. 2013 *Enough Is Enough: Building a sustainable economy in a world of finite resources*, London: Earthscan.

Dillon, D. and Fanning, B. (2015) 'Tottenham after the Riots: The chimera of community and the property-led regeneration of "Broken Britain"', *Critical Social Policy* 35(2): 188–206.

Diprose, G. (2016) 'Negotiating Interdependence and Anxiety in Community Economies', *Environment and Planning A* 48(7): 1411–1427.

Djokic, V., Trajkovic, J., Furundzik, D., Krstic, V. and Stojiljkovic, D. (2018) 'Urban Garden as Lived Space: Informal gardening practices and dwelling culture in socialist and post-socialist Belgrade', *Urban Forestry and Urban Greening* 30: 247–259.

Doherty, B., Haugh, H. and Lyon, F. (2014) 'Social Enterprises as Hybrid Organizations: A review and research agenda', *International Journal of Management Reviews* 16: 417–436.

Dubb, S. (2016) 'Community Wealth Building Forms: What they are and how to use them at the local level', *Academy of Management Perspectives* 30(2): 141–152.

Dudka, A., Moratal, N. and Bauwens, T. (2023) 'A Typology of Community-based Energy Citizenship: An analysis of the ownership structure and institutional logics of 164 energy communities in France', *Energy Policy* 178: 113588.

Dufays, F., O'Shea, N., Huybrechts, B. and Nelson, T. (2020) 'Resisting Colonization: Worker cooperatives' conceptualization and behaviour in a Habermasian perspective', *Work, Employment and Society* 34(6): 965–984.

Durham County Council (2016) *Shildon Masterplan Update*, Durham: Durham County Council.

Durham County Council (2018) *Shildon Regeneration Framework 2013*, Durham: Durham County Council.

Durham County Council (2020) *County Durham Plan*, Durham: Durham County Council.

Earley, A. (2023) 'Achieving Urban Regeneration without Gentrification? Community enterprises and community assets in the UK', *Journal of Urban Affairs*, available online at: https://doi.org/10.1080/07352166.2023.2229459.

Eisenschitz, A. and Gough, J. (1993) *The Politics of Local Economic Policy: The problems and possibilities of local initiative*, Basingstoke: Macmillan Press.

Eizenberg, E. (2012) 'Actually Existing Commons: Three moments of space of community gardens in New York City', *Antipode* 44(3): 764–782.

Ellen Macarthur Foundation (nd) available online at: https://www.ellenmacarthur foundation.org.

Elster, J. (1989) 'From Here to There; Or, if cooperative ownership is so desirable, why are there so few cooperatives?' *Social Philosophy and Policy* 6: 93–111.

Emery, M. and Flora, C. (2006) 'Spiraling-Up: Mapping community transformation with community capitals framework', *Community Development* 37(1): 19–35.

Engelsman, U., Rowe, M. and Southern, A. (2018) 'Community Land Trusts, Affordable Housing and Community Organising in Low-income Neighbourhoods', *International Journal of Housing Policy* 18(1): 103–123.

Esteves, R., Mitchener, K., El-Ganainy, A., and Eichengreen, B. (2021) *In Defense of Public Debt*, New York, NY: Oxford University Press.

Etzioni, A. (1968) *The Active Society: A theory of societal political processes*, London: Collier-Macmillan; New York: The Free Press.

European Commission (nd) *EU Social Economy Gateway*, available online at: https://social-economy-gateway.ec.europa.eu/index_en.

European Union (2019, amended 2023) Renewable Energy Directive 209/28/EC, amended EU/2023/2413. Brussels: CEC.

Evans, S. (2009) *Community and Ageing: Maintaining quality of life in housing with care settings*, Bristol: Bristol University Press/Policy Press.

Fairbairn, B. (nd) 'The Meaning of Rochdale: The Rochdale Pioneers and the co-operative principles', University of Saskatchewan Centre for the Study of Cooperatives Occasional Paper Series, available online at: http://ageconsearch.umn.edu.

Fairbairn, B. (1994) 'History from the Ecological Perspective: Gaia Theory and the problem of cooperatives in turn-of-the-century Germany', *The American Historical Review* 99(4): 1203–1239.

Fasenfest, D., Ciancanelli, P. and Reese, L. (1997) 'Value, Exchange and the Social Economy: Framework and paradigm shift in urban policy', *International Journal of Urban and Regional Research* 21(1): 7–22.

Fatima, Z., Oksman, V. and Lahdelma, R. (2021) 'Enabling Small Medium Enterprises (SMEs) to Become Leaders in Energy Efficiency Using a Continuous Maturity Matrix', *Sustainability*, available online at: https://doi.org/10.3390/su131810108.

Fell, T. and Mattsson, J. (2021) 'The Role of Public-Private Partnerships in Housing as a Potential Contributor to Sustainable Cities and Communities: A systematic review', *Sustainability* 13: 7783.

Ferm, J. (2014) 'Delivering Affordable Workspace: Perspectives of developers and workspace providers in London', *Progress in Planning* 93: 1–49.

Ferm, J. (2016) 'Preventing the Displacement of Small Businesses through Commercial Gentrification: Are affordable workspace policies the solution?' *Planning Practice and Research* 31(4): 402–419.

Ferm, J. and Jones, E. (2016) 'Mixed-use "Regeneration" of Employment Land in the Postindustrial City: Challenges and realities in London', *European Planning Studies* 24(10): 1913–1936.

Ferm, J. and Raco, M. (2020) 'Viability Planning, Value Capture and the Geographies of Market-Led Planning Reform in England', *Planning Theory and Practice* 21(2): 218–235.

Ferm, J., Panayotopoulos-Tsiros, D. and Griffiths, S. (2021) 'Planning Urban Manufacturing, Industrial Building Typologies, and Built Environments: Lessons from inner London', *Urban Planning* 6(3): 350–367.

Ferrer, J., García-Cortijo, M.-C., Valero, J.-S., Pinilla, V. and Serrano, R. (2023) 'Cooperatives and Sustainability Drivers in the Spanish Wine Sector: What differences do we find with investor owner firms?', *Annals of Public and Cooperative Economics*, available online at: https://doi-org.libproxy.ucl.ac.uk/10.1111/apce.12432.

Findlay-King, L., Nichols, G., Forbes, D. and Macfadyen, G. (2018) 'Localism and the Big Society: The asset transfer of leisure centres and libraries – fighting closures or empowering communities?' *Leisure Studies* 37(2): 158–170.

Fiorentina, S. (2018) 'Re-making Urban Economic Geography: Start-ups, entrepreneurial support and the Makers Movement: a critical assessment of policy mobility in Rome', *Geoforum* 93: 116–119.

Fiorentina, S. (2019a) 'Different Typologies of "Co-working Spaces" and the Contemporary Dynamics of Local Economic Development in Rome', *European Planning Studies* 27(9): 1768–1790.

Fiorentina, S. (2019b) 'The Maker Faire of Rome as a Window of Observation on the New Perspectives for Local Economic Development and the New Urban Entrepreneurial Ecosystems', *Local Economy* 34(4): 364–381.

Fiorentina, S. (2023) 'Public-led Shared Workspaces and the Intangible Factors of Urban Regeneration in UK coastal towns', *Urban, Planning and Transport Research* 11(1), available online at: https://doi.org/10.1080/21650020.2023.2260853.

Fischer, A. and McKee, A. (2017) 'A Question of Capacities? Community resilience and empowerment between assets, abilities and relationships', *Journal of Rural studies* 54: 187–197.

Fisher, J. and Nading, A. (2021) 'The End of the Cooperative Model (as we knew it): Commoning and co-becoming in two Nicaraguan cooperatives', *EPE Nature and Space* 4(4): 1232–1254.

Fisker, J., Johansen, P. and Thuesen, A. (2022) 'Micropolitical Practices of Multispatial Metagovernance in Rural Denmark', *EPC Politics and Space* 40(4): 970–986.

Fonte, M. and Cucco, I. (2017) 'Cooperatives and Alternative Food Networks in Italy: The long road towards a social economy in agriculture', *Journal of Rural Studies* 53: 291–302.

Foster, N. (2020) 'Rethinking the Right to the City: DIY urbanism and postcapitalist possibilities', *Rethinking Marxism* 32(2): 310–329.

Foundational Economy Collective (2018) *Foundational Economy: The infrastructure of everyday life*, Manchester: Manchester University Press.

Fraser, N. (1995) 'Recognition or Redistribution? A critical reading of Iris Young's *Justice and the Politics of Difference*', *The Journal of Political Philosophy* 3(2): 166–180.

Fratini, C., Georg, S. and Jørgensen, M. (2019) 'Exploring Circular Economy Imaginaries in European Cities: A research agenda for the governance of urban sustainability transitions', *Journal of Cleaner Production* 228: 974–989.

Fresner, J., Morea, F., Krenn, C., Uson, J. and Tomasi, F. (2017) 'Energy Efficiency in Small and Medium Enterprises: Lessons learned from 280 energy audits across Europe', *Journal of Cleaner Production* 142: 1650–1660.

Friends of the Earth Europe, REScoop.eu and Energy Cities (2020) *Community Energy: A practical guide to reclaiming power*, available online at: https://www.rescoop.eu/toolbox/community-energy-a-practical-guide-to-reclaiming-power.

Froud, J., Haslam, C., Johal, S. and Williams, K. (2020) '(How) Does Productivity Matter in the Foundational Economy?' *Local Economy* 35(4): 316–336.

Galway County Council (nd) *Census 2011 Results for Galway County, Population Results,* Social Inclusion Unit, Galway, Ireland: Galway County Council.

Galway County Council (2015) *Galway County Development Plan,* Galway, Ireland: Galway County Council.

Ganapati, S. (2010) 'Enabling Housing Cooperatives: Policy lessons from Sweden, India and the United States', *International Journal of Urban and Regional Research* 34(2): 365–380.

Garcia, E., Vale, B. and Vale, R. (2021) *Collapsing Gracefully: Making a built environment that is fit for the future,* Cham, Switzerland: Springer.

Gasparro, K. and Monk, A. (2020) 'Demystifying "Localness" of Infrastructure Assets: Crowdfunders as local intermediaries for global investors', *EPA Economy and Space* 52(5): 878–897.

Geissdoerfer, M., Savaget, P., Bocken, N. and Hultink, E. (2017) 'The Circular Economy: A new sustainability paradigm?' *Journal of Cleaner Production* 143: 757–768.

Geissdoerfer, M., Morioka, S., De Carvalho, M. and Evans, S. (2018) 'Business Models and Supply Chains for the Circular Economy', *Journal of Cleaner Production* 190: 712–721.

Gibson-Graham, J.K. (2006) *The End of Capitalism (As We Knew It): A feminist critique of political economy,* Minneapolis, MN: University of Minnesota Press.

Gieling, J., Haartsen, T., Vermeij, L. and Strijker, D. (2019) 'Out of love for the village? How general and selective forms of attachment to the village explain volunteering in Dutch community life', *Journal of Rural Studies* 71: 181–188.

Gkartzios, M., and Norris, M. (2011) '"If You Build It, They Will Come": Governing property-led rural regeneration in Ireland', *Land Use Policy* 28(3): 486–494.

Gkartzios, M. and Scott, M. (2013) 'Attitudes to Housing and Planning Policy in Rural Localities: Disparities between long-term and mobile rural populations in Ireland', *Land Use Policy* 31: 347–357.

Glover, L. (2017) *Community-owned Transport,* Abingdon, Oxon: Routledge.

Goodwin-Hawkins, B., Oedl-Wieser, T., Ovaska, U. and Morse, A. (2022) 'Rural Service Hubs and Socially Innovative Rural–Urban Linkages: A conceptual framework for nexogenous development', *Local Economy* 36(7–8): 551–568.

Gordon, M. (2002) 'The Contribution of the Community Cooperatives of the Highlands and Islands of Scotland to the Development of the Social Economy', *Journal of Rural Cooperation* 30(2): 95–117.

Gouldson, A. and Murphy, J. (2000) 'Environmental Policy and Industrial Innovation: Integrating environment and economy through ecological modernisation', *Geoforum* 31(1): 33–44.

Graham, S. and Marvin, S. (2001) *Splintering Urbanism: Networked infrastructures, technological mobilities and the urban condition*, Abingdon, Oxon: Routledge.

Grant, J. (ed.) (2018) *Seeking Talent for Creative Cities: The social dynamics of innovation*, Toronto: University of Toronto Press.

Green, J. (2016) 'Community Development and Social Development: Informing concepts of place and intentional social change in a globalizing world', *Research on Social Work Practice* 26(6): 605–608.

Ha, H., Won Lee, I. and Feiock, R. (2016) 'Organizational Network Activities for Local Economic Development', *Economic Development Quarterly* 30(1): 15–31.

Haberl, H., Weidenhofer, D., Virág, D., Kalt, J.G., Plank, B., Brockway, P., Fishman, T., Hausknost, D., Krausmann, F., Leon-Gruchalski, B., Mayer, A., Pichler, M., Schaffartzik, A., Sousa, T., Streeck, J. and Creutzig, F. (2020) 'A Systematic Review of the Evidence on Decoupling of GDP, Resource Use and GHG Emissions, Part II: Synthesizing the insights', *Environmental Research Letters*, available online at: https://doi.org/10.1088/1748-9326/ab842a.

Habermas, J. (1987) *The Theory of Communicative Action*, translated by Thomas McCarthy, 2, Lifeworld and System, Cambridge: Polity.

Hackett, K., Saegertb, S., Dozierb, D. and Marinovab, M. (2019) 'Community Land Trusts: Releasing possible selves through stable affordable housing', *Housing Studies* 34(1): 24–48.

Hall, S. (2011) 'High Street Adaptations: Ethnicity, independent retail practices, and localism in London's urban margins', *Environment and Planning A* 43(11): 2571–2588.

Hanna, K., Dale, A. and Ling, C. (2009) 'Social Capital and Quality of Place: Reflections on growth and change in a small town', *Local Environment* 14(1): 31–44.

Hardman, M., Chipungu, L., Magidimisha, H. and Larkham, P. (2018) 'Guerrilla Gardening and Green Activism: Rethinking the informal urban growing movement', *Landscape and Planning* 170: 6–14.

Harris, E. (2015) 'Navigating Pop-up Geographies: Urban space-times of flexibility, interstitiality and immersion', *Geography Compass* 9(11): 592–603.

Harvey, D. (1989) 'From Managerialism to Entrepreneurialism: The transformation in urban governance in late capitalism', *Geografiska Annaler Series B* 71(1): 3–17.

Haskel, J. and Westlake, S. (2018) *Capitalism without Capital*, Oxford: Princeton University Press.

Hastings, A., Bailey, N., Gannon, M., Besemer, K. and Bramley, G. (2015) 'Coping with the Cuts? The management of the worst financial settlement in living memory', *Local Government Studies* 41: 601–621.

Healey, P. (2022) *Caring for Place: Community development in rural England*, New York, NY: Routledge.

Henriques, J. and Catarino, J. (2016) 'Motivating towards Energy Efficiency in Small and Medium Enterprises', *Journal of Cleaner Production* 139: 42–50.

Herce, C., Martini, C., Toro, C., Biele, E. and Salvio, M. (2024) 'Energy Efficiency Policies for Small and Medium-sized Enterprises: A review', *Sustainability*, available online at: https://doi.org/10.3990/su16031023.

Hicks, J. (2020a) 'Community Finance: Marshalling investments for community-owned renewable energy enterprises', in J.K. Gibson-Graham and K. Dombroski (eds) *The Handbook of Diverse Economies*, Northampton, Northants: Edward Elgar Publishing, pp 370–378.

Hicks, J. (2020b) 'Community Enterprise: Diverse designs for community-owned energy infrastructure', in J.K. Gibson-Graham and K. Dombroski (eds) *The Handbook of Diverse Economies*, Northampton, Northants: Edward Elgar Publishing, pp 56–64.

Hicks, J. and Ison, N. (2018) 'An Exploration of the Boundaries of "Community" in Community Renewable Energy Projects: Navigating between motivations and context', *Energy Policy* 113: 523–534.

Highlands and Islands Enterprise (nd) *Highland and Islands Area Profiles 2010*, Highlands and Islands Enterprise.

Hobson, J., Lynch, K., Roberts, H. and Payne, B. (2019) 'Community Ownership of Local Assets: Conditions for sustainable success', *Journal of Rural Studies* 65: 116–125.

Holman, N. and Rydin, Y. (2012) 'What Can Social Capital Tell Us about Planning under Localism' *Local Government Studies* 22(3): 496–517.

Hopkins, L. and Knapp, G.-J. (2018) 'Autonomous Planning: Using plans as signals', *Planning Theory* 17(2): 274–295.

Hubacek, K., Chen, X., Feng, K., Wiedmann, T. and Shan, Y. (2021) 'Evidence of Decoupling Consumption-based CO_2 Emissions from Economic Growth', *Advanced in Applied Energy*, available online at: https://doi.org/10.1016/j.adapen.2021.100074.

Hung, H. (2017) 'Formation of New Property Rights on Government Land through Informal Co-management: Case studies on countryside guerilla gardening', *Land Use Policy* 63: 381–393.

Huron, A. (2018) *Carving Out the Commons: Tenant organizing and housing cooperatives in Washington, D.C.*, Minneapolis, MN: University of Minnesota Press.

Ibourk, A. and El Aynaoui, K. (2023) 'Agricultural Cooperatives' Sustainability and the Relevance of Start-up Support Programs: Evidence from cooperatives' level in Morocco', *Sustainability* 15: 3460.

IRENA (Coalition for Action) (2021) *Community Energy Toolkit: Best practices for broadening the ownership of renewables*, Abu Dhabi: International Renewable Energy Agency.

Jacobs, J. (1961) *The Death and Life of Great American Cities*, New York, NY: Random House.

Jackson, T. (2009) *Prosperity without Growth: Economics for a finite planet,* London: Earthscan.

Jackson, T. (2021) *Post Growth: The limits to capitalism,* Cambridge: Polity Press.

Jackson, T. (2024) 'Confronting the Dilemma of Growth: A response to Warlenius (2023)', *Ecological Economics,* available online at: https://doi.org/10.1016/j.ecolecon.2023.108089.

Jackson, T. and Victor, P. (2015) 'Does Credit Create a "Growth Imperative"? A quasi-stationary economy with interest-bearing debt', *Ecological Economics* 120: 32–48.

Jackson, T. and Victor, P. (2018) 'Confronting Inequality in a Post-growth World: Basic income, factor substitution and the future of work', CUSP Working Paper No. 11, available online at: www.cusp.ac.uk.

Jackson, T. and Victor, P. (2020) 'The Transition to a Sustainable Prosperity: A stock-flow-consistent ecological macroeconomic model for Canada', *Ecological Economics* 177: 1–14.

Johannisson, B. (2007) 'Enacting Local Economic Development: Theoretical and methodological challenges', *Journal of Enterprising Communities: People and Places in the Global Economy* 1(1): 7–26.

Kamizaki, K. and Rankin, K. (2020) 'Planning the Social Economy: The spatial politics of community economic development in Toronto', in C. Berndt, J. Peck and N. Rantisi (eds) *Market/Place: Exploring spaces of exchange,* Newcastle-upon-Tyne: Agenda Publishing, pp 213–232.

Kapsali, M. (2023) 'Grassroots Temporary Urbanism as a Challenge to the City of Austerity? Lessons from a self-organised park in Thessaloniki, Greece', *The Geographical Journal,* available online at: https://doi-org.libproxy.ucl.ac.uk/10.1111/geoj.12519.

Keblowski, W., Lambert, D. and Bassens, D. (2020) 'Circular Economy and the City: An urban political economy agenda', *Culture and Organization* 26(2): 142–158.

Kerry County Council (2021) *Kerry County Development Plan,* Kerry, Ireland: Kerry County Council.

Killick, A. (2017) 'Building a Small Cinema: Resisting neoliberal colonization in Liverpool', *Architecture MPS* 12(1): 3.

Kim, A. and Eisnelohr, A. (2022) 'Community Land Trusts for Sustainably Affordable Rental Housing Redevelopment', *Cityscape* 24(1): 233–256.

Koirala, B., Koliou, E., Friege, J. and Hakvoort, R. (2018) 'Energetic Communities for Community Energy: A review of key issues and trends shaping integrated community energy systems', *Renewable and Sustainable Energy Reviews* 56: 722–744.

Kostka, G., Moslener, U. and Andreas, J. (2013) 'Barriers to Increasing Energy Efficiency: Evidence from small- and medium-sized enterprises in China', *Journal of Cleaner Production* 57: 59–68.

Kosunen, H., Atkova, I. and Hirvonen-Kantola, S. (2020) 'Co-evolutionary Urban Planning of a Finnish City for its Low Growth Neighbourhoods', *Planning Theory and Practice* 21(4): 552–569.

Kouros, T. (2022) 'Reaping the Fruits of Informal Urbanism: An ethnography of tactical gardening in Limassol, Cyprus', *Built Environment* 48(2): 188–205.

Krähmer, K. (2021) 'Are Green Cities Sustainable? A degrowth critique of sustainable urban development in Copenhagen', *European Planning Studies* 29(7): 1272–1289.

Kruger, R., DeFilippis, J., Williams, O., Esfahani, A., Martin, D. and Pierce, J. (2020) 'The Production of Community in Community Land Trusts', *City and Community* 19(3): 638–655.

Krugman, P. (2008) *The Return of Depression Economics and the Crisis of 2008,* London: Penguin.

Kruzynski, A. (2023) 'Commoning Property in the City: The ongoing work of making and remaking', in J.K. Gibson-Graham and K. Dombroski (eds) *The Handbook of Diverse Economies,* Northampton, Northants: Edward Elgar Publishing, pp 283–291.

Lang, M. and Marsden, T. (2018) 'Rethinking Growth: Towards the well-being economy', *Local Economy* 33(5): 496–514.

Layard, A. (2019) 'Planning by Numbers: Affordable housing and viability in England', in M. Raco and F. Savini (eds) *Planning and Knowledge: How new forms of technocracy are shaping contemporary cities,* Bristol: Policy Press, pp 213–224.

Lavoratori, K. and Castellanni, D. (2021) 'Too Close for Comfort? Micro-geography of agglomeration economies in the United Kingdom', *Journal of Regional Science,* available at: https://doi.org/10.1111/jors.12531.

Lefebvre, H. (2009) *La Droit à la ville* (3rd edition) Paris: Anthropologie/ Economica/Anthropos

Lehmann, J.-M. and Smets, P. (2020) 'An Innovative Resilience Approach: Financial self-help groups in contemporary financial landscapes in the Netherlands', *EPA Economy and Space* 52(5): 898–915.

Lewis, L. (2022) '"Degrowth": Marxism is back for the modern age', *Financial Times,* 7 November: 24.

Leyshon, A. (2024) 'An Abundance of Caution for a "Stagnation Nation"? Financial services policy development in post-growth Britain', *EPA: Economy and Space,* available online at: https://doi.org/10.1177/0308518X241258872.

Lin, N. and Erickson, B. (2008) *Social Capita: An international research program,* Oxford, New York: Oxford University Press.

Liverpool City Region Land Commission (2021) *Our Land: Final report,* London: CLES.

Lloyd, G. and Black, S. (1993) 'Highlands and Islands Enterprise: Strategies for economic and social development', *Local Economy* 8(1): 69–81.

Lloyd, M.G. and Shucksmith, D.M. (1985) 'Economic development and land policies in the highlands and islands of Scotland', *Land Use Policy* 2(2): 114–125.

Lønning, D. (2018) 'The Power of Human Agency: Successful community development strategies in Norway's rural northern margins', *Community Development Journal* 53(3): 518–536.

Lowe, J. and Thaden, E. (2016) 'Deepening Stewardship: Resident engagement in community land trusts', *Urban Geography* 37(4): 611–628.

Lowe, N. and Vinodrai, T. (2020) 'The Maker–Manufacturing Nexus as a Place-connecting Strategy: Implications for regions left behind', *Economic Geography* 96(4): 315–335.

Luckin, D. and Sharp, L. (2004) 'Remaking Local Governance through Community Participation? The case of the UK community waste sector', *Urban Studies* 41(8): 1485–1505.

Lusagga Kironde, J. and Yhdego, M. (1997) 'The Governance of Waste Management in Urban Tanzania: Towards a community based approach', *Resources, Conservation and Recycling* 21: 213–226.

Lynch, N. (2022) 'Unbuilding the City: Deconstruction and the circular economy in Vancouver', *EPA Economy and Space* 54(8): 1586–1603.

Maasakkers, M. (2016) *The Creation of Markets for Ecosystem Services in the United States: The challenge of trading places*, London: Anthem Press.

Mackenzie, A.F.D. (2013) *Places of Possibility: Property, nature and community land ownership*, Chichester, West Sussex: Wiley-Blackwell.

Manley, J. and Whyman, P. (eds) (2021) *The Preston Model and Community Wealth Building: Creating a socio-economic democracy for the future*, Abingdon, Oxon: Routledge.

Marango, S., Bosworth, G. and Curry, N. (2020) 'Applying Neo-endogenous Development Theory to Delivering Sustainable Local Nature Conservation', *Sociologia Ruralis* 61(1): 116–140.

Martin, R. and Sunley, P. (2003) 'Deconstructing Clusters: Chaotic concept or policy panacea?', *Journal of Economic Geography* 3(1): 5–35.

Matson, J. and Theyer, J. (2013) 'The Role of Food Hubs in Food Supply Chains', *Journal of Agriculture, Food Systems, and Community Development* 3(4): 1–5.

Mazzucato, M. (2018) *The Value of Everything: Making and taking in the global economy*, London: Penguin Books.

McCullogh, K. (2018) 'Resolving the "Highland Problem": The Highlands and Islands of Scotland and the European Union', *Local Economy* 33(4): 421–437.

McInroy, N. (2018) 'Wealth for All: Building new local economies', *Local Economy* 33(6): 678–687.

McIntosh, A. (2001) *Soil and Soul: People versus corporate power*, London: Aurum.

Meadows, D., Meadows, D., Randers, J. and Behrens III, W. (1974) *The Limits to Growth: A report for the Club of Rome's project on the predicament of mankind*, London: Pan.

Meadows, D., Randers, J., and Meadows, D. (2005) *The Limits to Growth: The 30-year update*, London: Earthscan.

Meehan, J. (2014) 'Reinventing Real Estate: The community land trust as a social invention in affordable housing', *Journal of Applied Social Science* 8(2): 113–133.

Meijer, M. and Syssner, J. (2017) 'Getting Ahead in Depopulating Areas: How linking social capital is used for informal planning practices in Sweden and The Netherlands', *Journal of Rural Studies* 55: 59–70.

Mens, J., van Bueren, E., Vrijhoef, R. and Heurkens, E. (2021) 'A Typology of Social Entrepreneurs in Bottom-up Urban Development', *Cities* 110: 103066.

Merrell, I., Rowe, F., Cowie, P. and Gkartzios, M. (2020) '"Honey Pot" Rural Enterprise Hubs as Micro-clusters: Exploring their role in creativity-led rural development', *Local Economy* 36(7–8): 589–605.

Midheme, K. and Moulaert, F. (2013) 'Pushing Back the Frontiers of Property: Community land trusts and low-income housing in urban Kenya', *Land Use Policy* 35: 73–84.

Monk, S., Pearce, B. J. and Whitehead, C. M. E. (1996) 'Land-use planning, land supply and house prices', *Environment and Planning A* 28(3): 495–511.

Moore, T. (2021) 'Planning for Place: Place attachment and the founding of rural community land trusts', *Journal of Rural Studies* 83: 21–29.

Moore, T. and McKee, K. (2014) 'The Ownership of Assets by Place-Based Community Organisations: Political rationales, geographies of social impact and future research agendas', *Social Policy and Society* 13(4): 521–533.

Moroni, S. (2023) 'Distinguishing "Planning" from the "Plan": Institutional and professional implications of taking urban complexity seriously', *European Planning Studies* 31(11): 2327–2341.

Motoyama, Y. (2020) 'Beyond Formal Policies: Informal functions of mayor's offices to promote entrepreneurship', *Local Economy* 35(2): 155–164.

Muellbauer, J. (2022) 'Growth-friendly Reforms for the UK's Broken Planning System', *Financial Times*, 7 November: 25.

Mundaca, L., Busch, H. and Schwer, S. (2018) '"Successful" Low-carbon Energy Transitions at the Community Level? An energy justice perspective', *Applied Energy* 218: 292303.

Muringani, J., Fitjar, J. and Rodriguez-Pose, A. (2012) 'Social Capital and Economic Growth in the Regions of Europe', *EPA Economy and Space* 53(6): 1412–1434.

Murtagh, B. (2015) 'Community Asset Transfer in Northern Ireland', *Policy and Politics* 43(2): 221–237.

Murtagh, B. (2019) *Social Economics and the Solidarity City*, New York, NY: Routledge.

Murtagh, B. and Boland, P. (2019) 'Community Asset Transfer and Strategies of Local Accumulation', *Social and Cultural Geography* 20(1): 4–23.

Nadin, V. and Stead, D. (2013) 'Opening up the Compendium: An evaluation of international comparative planning research methodologies', *European Planning Studies* 21(10): 1542–1561.

Newing, A., Clarke, G., Taylor, M., González, S., Buckner, L. and Wilkinson, R. (2023) 'The Role of Traditional Retail Markets in Addressing Urban Food Deserts', *The International Review of Retail, Distribution and Consumer Research*, available online at: https://doi.org/10.1080/09593969.2023.2198251.

Norris, M. and Gkartzios, M. (2011) 'Twenty Years of Property-led Urban Regeneration in Ireland: Outputs, impacts, implications', *Public Money and Management* 31(4): 257–264.

Norris, M., Gkartzios, M., and Coates, D. (2014) 'Property-led Urban, Town and Rural Regeneration in Ireland: Positive and perverse outcomes in different ppatial and socio-economic contexts', *European Planning Studies* 22(9): 1841–1861.

North, P. (2020) 'Independent and Small Businesses: Diversity among the 99 per cent of business', in J.K. Gibson-Graham and K. Dombroski (eds) *The Handbook of Diverse Economies*, Northampton, Northants: Edward Elgar Publishing, pp 98–105.

Ó Cinnéide, M. and Keane, M. (1990) 'Applying Strategic Planning to Local Economic Development: The case of the Connemara Gaeltacht, Ireland', *The Town Planning Review* 61(4): 475–486.

Olsson, L. and Besussi, E. (2023) 'Lefebvre's Right to the City and a Radical Urban Citizenship: Struggles around power in urban planning', in M. Gunder, K. Grange and T. Winkler (eds) *Handbook on Planning and Power*, Cheltenham, Glos: Edward Elgar, pp 26–41.

Ortiz-Miranda, D., Moreno-Pérez, O. and Moragues-Faus, A. (2010) 'Innovative Strategies of Agricultural Cooperatives in the Framework of the New Rural Development Paradigms: The case of the Region of Valencia (Spain)', *Environment and Planning A* 42: 661–677.

Ostrom, E. (1993) 'Design Principles in Long-enduring Irrigation Institutions', *Water Resources Research* 29(7): 1907–1912.

Ostrom, E. (2005) *Understanding Institutional Diversity,* Princeton: Princeton University Press.

Ostrom, E. (2007) 'Challenges and Growth: The development of the interdisciplinary field of institutional analysis', *Journal of Institutional Economics* 3(3): 239–264.

Ostrom, E. (2015) *Governing the Commons: the evolution of institutions for collective action,* Cambridge: Cambridge University Press.

Palm, J. and Backman, F. (2020) 'Energy Efficiency in SMEs: Overcoming the communication barrier', *Energy Efficiency* 13: 809–821.

Parkinson, C. and Howarth, C. (2008) 'The Language of Social Entrepreneurs', *Entrepreneurship and Regional Development* 20: 285–309.

Partelow, S. and Manlosa, A. (2023) 'Commoning the Governance: A review of literature and the integration of power', *Sustainability Science* 18: 265–283.

Pascoe-Deslacriers, R. (2020) 'Putting Employers to Work in Economic Development in the Atlantic Provinces of Canada', *Local Economy* 35(2): 165–175.

Pearce D., Pearce, C. and Palmer C. (eds) (2002) *Valuing the Environment in Developing Countries: Case studies,* Cheltenham, Glos: Edward Elgar.

Peck, J. and Tickell, A. (2002) 'Neoliberalizing Space', *Antipode* 34(3): 380–404.

Penny, J. (2021) 'Revenue Generating Machines: London's local housing companies and the emergence local state rentierism', *Antipode* 54(2): 545–566.

Phillips, D. (1993) *Looking Backward: A critical appraisal of communitarian thought,* Princeton, NJ: Princeton University Press.

Pickard, J. and O'Dwyer, M. (2023) 'Most Small Companies Clueless on Net Zero Implications', *Financial Times*, 10 August.

Pike, A. and Tomaney, J. (1999) 'The Limits to Localization in Declining Industrial Regions? Trans-national corporations and economic development in Sedgefield Borough', *European Planning Studies* 7(4): 407–428.

Pike, A., Rodriquez-Pose, A. and Tomaney, J. (2006) *Local and Regional Development,* Abingdon, Oxon: Routledge.

Pike, A., Béal, V., Cauchi-Duval, N., Franklin, R., Kinossian, N., Land, T., Leibert, T., MacKinnon, D., Rousseau, M., Royer, J., Servillo, L., Tomaney, J. and Velthui, S. (2024) '"Left Behind Places": A geographical etymology', *Regional Studies* 58(6): 1167–1179.

Piketty, T. (2022) *A Brief History of Equality*, Cambridge, MA: Harvard University Press.

Pilling, D. (2018) *The Growth Delusion: The wealth and well-being of nations*, London: Bloomsbury.

Porter, M. (2000) 'Locations, Clusters and Company Strategy', in G. Clark, M. Feldman and M. Gertler (eds) *Oxford Handbook of Economic Geography*, pp. 253–274.

Preluca, A., Hakelius, K. and Mark-Herbert, C. (2022) 'Sustainability of Worker Co-Operatives', *Sustainability* 14: 11542.

Price, L., Deville, J. and Ashmore, F. (2022) 'A Guide to Developing a Rural Digital Hub', *Local Economy* 36(7–8): 683–694.

Pudup, M. (2008) 'It Takes a Garden: Cultivating citizen-subjects in organized garden projects', *Geoforum* 39: 1228–1240.

Purcell, M. (2014) 'Possible Worlds: Henri Lefebvre and the Right to the City', *Journal of Urban Affairs* 36(1): 141–154.

Purcell, M. and Tyman, S. (2015) 'Cultivating Food as a Right to the City', *Local Environment* 20(10): 1132–1147.

Purcell, T. and Ward, C. (2023) 'The Political Economy of Land Value Capture in the UK: Rent and viability in Salford's new municipalist turn', *EPA Economy and Space* 55(6): 1600–1617.

Putnam, R. with Leonardi, R. and Nanetti, R. (1993) *Making Democracy Work: Civic traditions in modern Italy*, Princeton, NJ: Princeton University Press.

Raco, M. (2000) 'Governmentality and Rights and Responsibilities in Urban Policy', *Environment and Planning A* 32(12): 2187–2204.

Raco, M. and Brill, F. (2022) *London,* Newcastle upon Tyne: Agenda Publishing.

Raco, M. and Moreira de Souza, T. (2018) 'Urban Development, Small Business Communities and the Entreprenuerialisation of English Local Government', *Town Planning Review* 89(2): 145–165.

Raco, M. and Tunney, E. (2010) 'Visibilities and Invisibilities in Urban Development: Small business communities and the London Olympics 2012', *Urban Studies* 47(10): 2069–2091.

Radtke, J. and Ohlhorst, D. (2021) 'Community Energy in Germany: Bowling alone in elite clubs?' *Utilities Policy* 72: 101269.

Raworth, K. (2017) *Doughnut Economics: Seven ways to think like a 21st-century economist*, London: Random House.

Ray, C. (2000) 'The EU LEADER Programme: Rural development laboratory', *Sociologia Ruralis* 40(2): 163–171.

Reade, E. (1987) *British Town and Country Planning,* Milton Keynes: Open University Press, pp 6–10.

Richter, B. and Hanf, J. (2021) 'Sustainability as "Value of Cooperatives": Can (wine) cooperatives use sustainability as a driver for a brand concept?' *Sustainability* 13: 12344.

Roberts, P., Collis, C. and Noon, D. (1990*a*) 'Regional Alternatives to Economic Decline in Britain's Industrial Heartland: Industrial restructuring and local economic intervention in the West Midlands conurbation', in W. Stöhr (ed) *Global Challenge and Local Response*, London: Mansell Publishing, pp 135–162.

Roberts, P., Collis. C. and Noon, D. (1990*b*) 'Local Economic Development in England and Wales: successful adaptation of old industrial areas in Sedgefield, Nottingham and Swansea', in W. B. Stöhr (ed) *Global Challenge and Local Response*, London: Mansell Publishing, pp 135–162.

Romero, R. and Harris, D. (2014) 'Who Speaks for (and Feeds) the Community? Competing definitions of "community" in the Austin, TX, urban farm debate', *City and Community* 18(4): 1162–1180.

Rosado, L. and Kalmykova, Y. (2019) 'Combining Industrial Symbiosis with Sustainable Supply Chain Management for the Development of Urban Communities', *Engineering Management Review* 47(2): 103–114.

Rothschild, J. (2009) 'Workers' Cooperatives and Social Enterprise: A forgotten route to social equity and democracy', *American Behavioral Scientist* 53(7): 1023–1041.

Russell, B., Beel, D., Rees Jones, I. and Jones, M. (2022) 'Placing the Foundational Economy: An emerging discourse for post-neoliberal economic development', *EPA Economy and Space* 54(6): 1069–1085.

Rydin, Y. (2013) *The Future of Planning: Beyond growth dependence*, Bristol: Policy Press.

Rydin, Y. (2019) 'Planning for Sustainability: Lessons from studying neighbourhood shopping areas', *Planning Research and Practice* 34(5): 522–536.

Rydin, Y. (2021) 'Artefacts in Dialogue: Regulatory planning and the search for legitimacy', in Y. Rydin, R. Beauregard, M. Cremaschi and L. Lieto (eds) *Regulation and Planning: Practice, institutions, materiality*, London: Routledge, pp 97–109.

Rydin, Y. (2022) 'Planning beyond the Backwash of a Growth Node: Old and new thinking in Cambridgeshire, England and Skåne, Sweden', in F. Savini, K. van Schonfeld and A. Ferreira (eds) *Post-growth Planning: Foundations for an urbanisation beyond the market economy*, Abingdon, Oxon: Routledge, pp 129–142.

Rydin, Y. (2023) 'Discovering the Diverse Economy of a "Left-behind" Town', *Planning, Practice and Research* 38(4): 504–519.

Rydin, Y. and Holman, N. (2004) 'Re-evaluating the Concept of Social Capital in Achieving Sustainable Development', *Local Environment* 9(2): 117–134.

Rydin, Y. and Turcu, C. (2019) 'Revisiting Urban Energy Initiatives in the UK: Declining local capacity in a shifting policy context', *Energy Policy* 129: 653–660.

Rydin, Y., Guy, S., Goodier, C., Chmutina, K. and Devine-Wright, P. (2015) 'The Financial Entanglements of Local Energy Projects', *Geoforum* 59: 1–11.

Rydin, Y., Holman, N. and Wolff, E. (2003) 'Editorial: Local sustainability indicators special issue', *Local Environment* 8(6): 581–590.

Saito, K. (2023) *Marx in the Anthropocene: Towards the idea of degrowth communism*, Cambridge: Cambridge University Press.

Saracu, A. and Trif, N. (2019) 'Community-led Local Development (CLLD): A tool for implementing regional development policies', *Annals of 'Dunarea de Jos' University of Galati Fascicle I. Economics and Applied Informatics* 25(3): 163–168.

Savini, F. (2021) 'Towards an Urban Degrowth: Habitability, finity and polycentric autonomism', *EPA Economy and Space* 53(5): 1076–1079.

Savini, F. (2024) 'Strategic Planning for Degrowth: what, who, how', *Planning Theory*, available online at: https://doi.org/10.1177/14730952241258693.

Schindler, S. (2016) 'Detroit after Bankruptcy: A case of degrowth machine politics', *Urban Studies* 53(4): 818–836.

Schneider, F., Kallis, G. and Martínez-Alier, J. (2010) 'Crisis or Opportunity? Economic degrowth for social equity and ecological sustainability', *Journal of Cleaner Production* 18(6): 511–518.

Schor, J. and Fitzmaurice, C. (2015) 'Collaborating and Connecting: The emergence of the sharing economy', in L. Reisch and J. Thøgersen (eds) *Handbook of Research on Sustainable Consumption*, Cheltenham, Glos: Edward Elgar Publishing, pp 410–425.

Shucksmith, M. (2010) 'Disintegrated Rural Development? Neo-endogenous rural development, planning and place-shaping in diffused power contexts', *Sociologia Ruralis* 50(1): 1–14.

Shucksmith, M., Brooks, E. and Madanipour, A. (2021) 'LEADER and Spatial Justice', *Sociologia Ruralis* 61(2): 322–343.

Sebi, C. and Vernay, A.-L. (2020) 'Community Renewable Energy in France: The state of development and the way forward', *Energy Policy* 147: 111874.

Sendra, P. (2015) 'Rethinking Urban Public Space', *City* 19(6): 820–836.

Seyfang, G., Park, J. and Smith, A. (2013) 'A Thousand Flowers Blooming? An examination of community energy in the UK', *Energy Policy* 61: 977–989.

Sharma, R. (2022) 'Economists See Recession Coming, So Maybe It's Not', *Financial Times*, 7 November: 25.

Sheikh, F. and Bhaduri, S. (2020) 'Grassroots Innovations in the Informal Economy: Insights from value theory', *Oxford Development Studies* 48(1): 85–99.

Simmonds, J., von Hase, A., Quétier, F., Brownlie, S., Maron, M., Possingham, H., Souquet, M., zu Ermgassen, S., ten Kate, K., Costa, H. and Sonter, L. (2022) 'Aligning Ecological Compensation Policies with the Post-2020 Global Biodiversity Framework to Achieve Real Net Gain in Biodiversity', *Conservation Science and Practice* 4(3): 12634.

Skerratt, S. (2013) 'Enhancing the Analysis of Rural Community Resilience: Evidence from community land ownership', *Journal of Rural Studies* 31: 36–46.

Skerratt, S. and Hall, C. (2011a) 'Management of Community-owned Facilities Post-acquisition: Brokerage for shared learning', *Local Economy* 26(8): 663–678.

Skerratt, S. and Hall, C. (2011b) 'Community Ownership of Physical Assets: Challenges, complexities and implications', *Local Economy* 26(3): 170–181.

Smith, A. and Stirling, A. (2018) 'Innovation, Sustainability and Democracy: An analysis of grassroots contributions', *Journal of Self-Governance and Management Economics* 6(1): 64–97.

Spencer, J. (2021) 'Small and big infrastructure: a community-planning theory of increments and interoperability', *Journal of Economic Policy Reform* 24(2): 151–169.

Spijker, S. and Parra, C. (2018) 'Knitting Green Spaces with the Threads of Social Innovation in Groningen and London', *Journal of Environmental Planning and Management* 61(5–6): 1011–1032.

Sonnino, R. and Griggs-Trevarthen, C. (2013) 'A Resilient Social Economy? Insights from the community food sector in the UK', *Entrepreneurship and Regional Development* 25(3–4): 272–292.

Sørvoll, J. and Bengtsson, B. (2018) 'The Pyrrhic Victory of Civil Society Housing? Co-operative housing in Sweden and Norway', *International Journal of Housing Policy* 18(1): 124–142.

Sperling, K. (2017) 'How Does a Pioneer Community Energy Project Succeed in Practice? The case of the Samsø renewable energy island', *Renewable and Sustainable Energy Reviews* 71: 884–897.

Spicer, J. and Casper-Futterman, E. (2020) 'Conceptualizing U.S. Community Economic Development: Evidence from New York City', *Journal of Planning Education and Research* 43(4): 940–957.

Standing, G. (2011) *The Precariat: the new dangerous class*. London: Bloomsbury.

Stehlin, J. and Payne, W. (2022) 'Mesoscale Infrastructures and Uneven Development: Bicycle sharing systems in the United States as "already splintered" urbanism', *Annals of the American Association of Geographers* 112(4): 1065–1083.

Stöhr, W. (ed) (1990) *Global Challenge and Local Response*, London: Mansell Publishing.

Swedish Institute (1983) *Fact Sheets on Sweden: The cooperative movement in Sweden*, available online at: https://digital.lib.usu.edu/digital/collection/coops/id/23551/.

Tait, M. and Inch, A. (2016) 'Putting Localism in Place: Conservative images of the good community and the contradictions of planning reform in England', *Planning Practice and Research* 31(2): 174–194.

Thompson, M. (2015) 'Between Boundaries: From commoning and guerrilla gardening to community land trust development in Liverpool', *Antipode* 47(4): 1021–1042.

Thompson, M. (2017) 'Life in a Zoo', *City* 21: 2.

Thompson, M. (2020) 'From Co-Ops to Community Land Trusts: Tracing the historical evolution and policy mobilities of collaborative housing movements', *Housing, Theory and Society* 37(1): 82–100.

Thompson, M. (2023) 'Whatever Happened to Municipal Radicalism?' *Transactions of the Institute of British Geographers* 48: 603–618.

Tierney, J., Weller, S., Barnes, T. and Beer, A. (2024) 'Left-behind Neighbourhoods in Old Industrial Regions', *Regional Studies* 58(6): 1192–1206.

Tilsted, J., Bjørn, Majeau-Bettez, G. and Lund, J. (2021) 'Accounting Matters: Revisiting claims of decoupling and genuine green growth in Noredic countries', *Ecological Economics*, available online at: https://doi.org/10.1016/j.ecolecon.2021.107101.

Tomaney, J., Blackman, M., Natarajan, L., Panayotopoulos-Tsiros, D., Sutcliffe-Braithwaite, F. and Taylor, M. (2023) *Social Infrastructure and Left Behind Places*, Abingdon, Oxon: Taylor & Francis for the Regional Studies Association.

Trendov, N. (2018) 'Comparative Study on the Motivations that Drive Urban Community Gardens in Central Eastern Europe', *Annals of Agrarian Science* 16: 85–89.

Tunesi, S., Baroni, S. and Boarini, S. (2016) 'Waste Flow Analysis and Life Cycle Assessment of Integrated Waste Management Systems as Planning Pools: Application to optimise the system of the City of Bologna', *Waste Management and Research* 34(9): 933–946.

Turnbull, N. (2023) 'Austerity's Afterlives? The case of community asset transfer in the UK', *The Geographical Journal*, available online at: https://doi.org/10.1111/geoj.12513.

Turner, C. (2018) 'The governance of polycentric national infrastructure systems: Evidence from the UK National Infrastructure Plan', *Environment and Planning. C, Politics and Space* 36(3): 513–529.

United Nations (nd*a*) *Human Development Index*, available online at: https://hdr.undp.org/data-center/human-development-index#/indicies/HDI.

United Nations (nd*b*) *Sustainable Development Goals*, available online at: https://sdgs.un.org/goals.

United Nations (nd*c*) *SDG Localization*, available online at: https://www.undp.org/governance/sdg-localization.

Urbano, D., Toledano, N. and Soriano, D. (2010) 'Analyzing Social Entrepreneurship from an Institutional Perspective: Evidence from Spain', *Journal of Social Entrepreneurship* 1(1): 54–69.

Van Holm, E. (2017) 'Makerspaces and Local Economic Development', *Economic Development Quarterly* 31(2): 164–173.

Van Veelen, B. (2018) 'Negotiating Energy Democracy in Practice: Governance processes in community energy projects', *Environmental Politics* 27(4): 644–665.

Vaughan, L. (2015) *Suburban Urbanities: Suburbs and the life of the high street*, London: UCL Press.

Vernay, A.-L. and Sebi, C. (2020) 'Energy Communities and their Ecosystems: A comparison of France and the Netherlands', *Technological Forecasting and Social Change* 158: 120123.

Vernay, A.-L., Sebi, C. and Arroyo, F. (2023a) 'Energy Community Business Models and their Impact on the Energy Transition: Lessons learnt from France', *Energy Policy* 175: 113473.

Vernay, A.-L., Olsthoorn, M., Sebi, C. and Gauthier, C. (2023b) 'The Identity Trap of Community Renewable Energy in France', *Energy Policy* 177: 113562.

Véron, O. (2023) '"We're Just an Ambulance at the Bottom of the Cliff": Strategies and (a)politics of change in Berlin's community food spaces', *EPA Economy and Space* 55(7): 1670–1689.

Veronesi, M., Algoed, L. and Torrales, M. (2022) 'Community-led Development and Collective Land Tenure for Environmental Justice: The case of the Caño Martín Peña community land trust, Puerto Rico', *International Journal of Urban Sustainable Development* 14(1): 388–397.

Vestbro, D. and Horelli, L. (2012) 'Design for Gender Equality: The history of cohousing ideas and realities', *Built Environment* 38(3): 315–335.

Vogel, J. and Hickell, J. (2023) 'Is Green Growth Happening? An empirical analysis of achieved versus Paris-compliant CO_2–GDP decoupling in high-income countries', *The Lancet: Planetary Health* 7: 759–769.

Vogel, J., Lind, H. and Lundqvist, P. (2016) 'Who is Governing the Commons: Studying Swedish housing cooperatives', *Housing, Theory and Society* 33(4): 424–444.

Waite, D. and Roy, G. (2022) 'The Promises and Pitfalls of Operationalising Inclusive Growth', *Regional Studies* 56(11): 1989–2000.

Walker, G. (2008) 'What are the Barriers and Incentives for Community-owned Means of Energy Production and Use?' *Energy Policy* 36(12): 4401–4405.

Walsh, B. (2016) 'Community: A powerful label? Connecting wind energy to rural Ireland', *Community Development Journal* 53(2): 228–245.

Ward, N. et al. (2005) *Universities, the Knowledge Economy and Neo-Endogenous Rural Development*, Centre for Rural Economy Paper No. 1. CRE, University of Newcastle, available online at: https://www.ncl.ac.uk/media/wwwnclacuk/centreforruraleconomy/files/discussion-paper-01.pdf.

Webster, A., Kuznetsova, O., Ross, C., Berranger, C., Booth, M., Eseonu, T. and Golan, Y. (2021) 'Local Regeneration and Community Wealth Building: Place making: co-operatives as agents of change', *Journal of Place Management and Development* 14(4): 446–461.

Whitelaw, S. and Hill, C. (2013) 'Achieving Sustainable Social Enterprises for Older People: Evidence from a European project', *Social Enterprise Journal* 9(3): 269–292.

Wiechmann, T. and Pallagst, K. (2012) 'Urban Shrinkage in Germany and the USA: A comparison of transformation patterns and local strategies', *International Journal of Urban and Regional Research* 36(2): 261–280.

Wijayantia, D. and Suryania, S. (2015) 'Waste Bank as Community-based Environmental Governance: A lesson learned from Surabaya', *Procedia – Social and Behavioral Sciences* 184: 171–179.

Williams, J. (2020) 'The Role of Spatial Planning in Transitioning to Circular Urban Development', *Urban Geography* 41(6): 915–919.

Williams, J. (2021) *Circular Cities: A revolution in urban sustainability*, Abingdon, Oxon: Routledge.

Williams, O. (2018) 'Community Control as a Relationship between a Place-based Population and Institution: The case of a community land trust', *Local Economy* 33(5): 459–476.

World Commission on Environment and Development (WCED) (1987) *Our Common Future*, Oxford: Oxford University Press.

Xue, J. (2022). 'A Critical Realist Theory of Ideology: Promoting planning as a vanguard of societal transformation', *Planning Theory* 21(2): 109–131.

Zhang, F. and Wu, F. (2022) 'Financialised urban development: Chinese and (South-)East Asian observations', *Land Use Policy*, available online at: https://doi.org/10.1016/j.landusepol.2021.105813.

Zhu, J., He, B.-J., Tang, W. and Thompson, S. (2020) 'Community Blemish or New Dawn for the Public Realm? Governance challenges for self-claimed gardens in urban China', *Cities* 102: 1–11.

Zielke, J., Hepburn, P., Thompson, M. and Southern, A. (2021) 'Urban Commoning under Adverse Conditions: Lessons from a failed transdisciplinary project', *Frontiers in Sustainable Cities* 3, available online at: https://doi.org/10.3389/frsc.2021.727331.

Zukin, S. (2010) *Naked City: The death and life of authentic urban places*, Oxford, Oxon: Oxford University Press.

Zukin, S., Kasinitz, P. and Chen, X. (2016) *Global Cities, Local Streets: Everyday diversity from New York to Shanghai*, Abingdon, Oxon: Routledge.

Index

S